11.05

CHURCHES IN CONTESTATION

CHURCHES IN CONTESTATION

Asian Christian Social Protest

Parig Digan

ORBIS BOOKS
Maryknoll, New York 10545

The Catholic Foreign Mission Society of America (Maryknoll) recruits and trains people for overseas missionary service. Through Orbis Books Maryknoll aims to foster the international dialogue that is essential to mission. The books published, however, reflect the opinions of their authors and are not meant to represent the official position of the society.

Copyright © 1984 by Parig Digan
Published by Orbis Books, Maryknoll, NY 10545
Manufactured in the United States of America

Manuscript editor: Mary J. Heffron

Library of Congress Cataloging in Publication Data

Digan, Parig.
  Churches in contestation.

  Bibliography: p.
  1. Christianity—Asia.   2. Sociology, Christian—Asia.
I. Title.
BR1065.D53   1984   261.8'095   83-19338
ISBN 0-88344-102-0 (pbk.)

CONTENTS

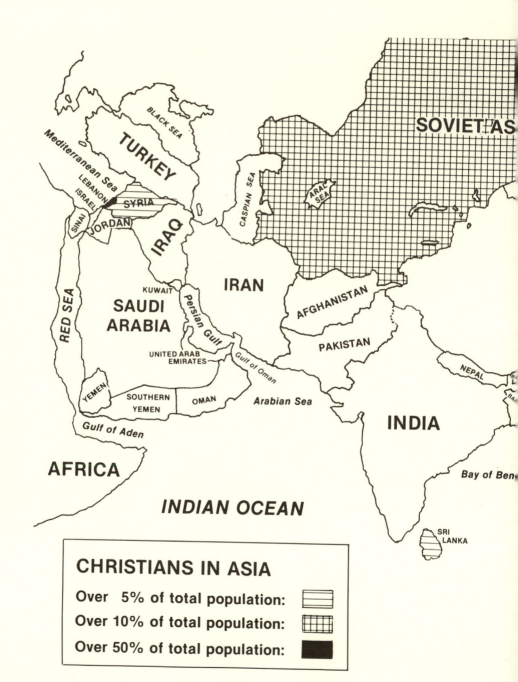

CHRISTIANS IN ASIA

Over 5% of total population:

Over 10% of total population:

Over 50% of total population:

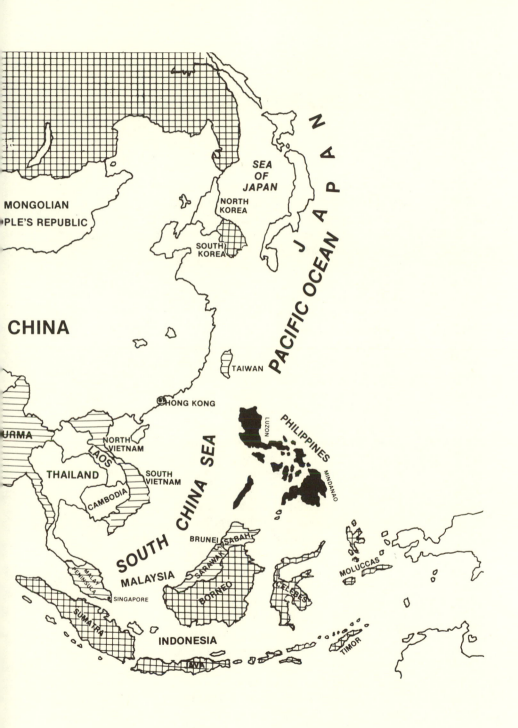

ABBREVIATIONS

ACFOD	Asian Cultural Forum on Development
ACPO	Asian Committee for People's Organization
AEC	Asia Ecumenical Center (CCA)
ASC-AMOR	Asian Service Center Asian Meeting of Religious Women
AMRS	Association of Major Religious Superiors
ASEAN	Association of Southeast Asian Nations
BAA	Bureau of (Jesuit) Asian Affairs
BIRA	Bishops' Institute for Religious Affairs (FABC)
BISA	Bishops' Institute on Social Action
BMA	Bangsa Moro Army
CBCI	Catholic Bishops' Conference of India
CBCP	Catholic Bishops' Conference of the Philippines
CCA	Christian Conference of Asia
CELAM	Consejo Episcopal Latinoamericano
CNL	Christians for National Liberation
CPP	Communist Party of the Philippines
EATWOT	Ecumenical Association of Third World Theologians
FABC	Federation of Asian Bishops' Conferences
IMCS	International Movement of Catholic Students
MNLF	Moro National Liberation Front
NASSA	National Secretariat of Social Action
NCCI	National Christian Council of India
NDF	National Democratic Front
NPA	New People's Army
OHD	Office for Human Development
PISA	Priests' Institute for Social Action
PPT	Permanent Peoples' Tribunal
SCM	Student Christian Movement
SELA	Socio-Economic Life in Asia (Jesuit)
SODEPAX	Society, Development, and Peace (Vatican & WCC)
URM	Urban Rural Mission
WCC	World Council of Churches
WCRP	World Conference on Religion and Peace
WSCF	World Student Christian Federation
YCW	Young Christian Workers

INTRODUCTION: THE PROBLEM

It is our resolve, first of all, to be more truly "the Church of the poor."
. . . We will not tie our hands by compromising entanglements with the
rich and powerful in our respective countries [Message of the First Asian
Bishops' Conference].[1]

The major thrust . . . in the next few years should be in building up
power for the powerless so that they can remedy the imbalance of power
and work for a more just and humane society [Report from the Sixth
Assembly of the CCA].[2]

When theology is liberated from its present class, race, and sex preju-
dices, it can place itself at the service of the people and become a power-
ful motivating force for the mobilization of believers in Jesus to partici-
pate in Asia's ongoing struggle for self-identity and human dignity [Final
Statement of the First Asian Theologians' Conference].[3]

The above pronouncements have a number of things in common. They
were all made in the 1970s—the first in 1970, the second in 1977, the third in
1979. They were all made by Asian Christians undertaking to speak for
Asia-wide constituencies of Christians: in the first case, by an assembly of
Roman Catholic bishops representing some 50 million Asian Catholics; in
the second case, by an assembly of non-Roman Christian leaders representing another 35 million Asian and Australasian Christians; in the third case,
by one of the few Asia-wide Christian groups (a group of theologians) attempting to transcend both national and confessional boundaries. They
each moved—along quite separate lines—in a direction quite novel at the
time for Asian Christians of any kind, so novel that it would have been
impossible to predict ten years earlier that such an orientation would ever be
proclaimed with any credibility in the name of such widely-ranging constituencies.

What was happening here could be considered a historical novelty on
several counts. It was an absolute novelty that church movements of this
kind anywhere should so boldly profess to switch sides—from that of the
powerful to that of the powerless in state and society. It was a relative nov-

1

elty that church movements of this kind should take so distinctly transnational a form.[4] It was a local novelty that this should have happened in Asia.

Let us come to grips first with this absolute novelty. It is the highly hy-
pothetical novelty of a "post-Constantinian" church.

One of the historical legacies of the past century is a widely accepted contention that Christian churches have an ingrained bias toward social conservatism, so that they serve essentially as legitimators and perpetuators of
currently dominant social forces and groups. The most militant proponents
of this thesis have been the Marxists; but apart from the Marxists there has
been a secular humanist tradition that regards the same thesis as historically
well-founded.

Does the record bear these critics out? It seems clear that they have an
arguable case at least in regard to a certain historical phase of Christianity.
It seems also that they could plausibly argue that this phase has extended
over most of the history of Christianity and up to the present time.

Recently it has become common to bracket the phase in question under
the heading of "the Constantinian era." This is understood as the era since
the transition in the fourth century A.D.—transition from a time when the
Church was an outcast or at least an outsider to a time when it was "established" as one of the pillars of society. This way of thinking implies that
ecclesiastical social conservatism may indeed be inseparably linked with a
situation in which the Church has a stake in the social status quo. But it also
implies that such a situation is not the only one for the Church to be in, and
that it may prove to have been quite exceptional when looked back on from
a point in the more distant future.

The rise of this new perspective on church history results from a double
reaction of some Christians to the role in which they have seen the Church
cast. On the one hand, they concede that the charge of social conservatism
has validity for much, perhaps even for most, of the record of the Church in
the world so far. On the other hand, they have undertaken to show not only
in words but also in deeds that this church bias toward social conservatism
is not so ingrained as to be impossible to change. A new emphasis in social
teaching, providing motivation for change, has been articulated during this
past century by globally representative spokespersons of the main Christian
traditions. A new and relatively large-scale effort to match deeds to words
has followed more slowly but has gathered momentum, especially in the
past decade, and especially in one continent, Latin America.

In another continent, Asia, things have been different. Yet there is an
Asian dimension in the history of the attempt to move the Christian
churches away from being forces for social conservatism and toward becoming forces for social change. It is that dimension this study undertakes
to investigate.

The field is large inasmuch as Asia holds more than half the human race
and much of the world's contemporary ferment. At the same time it is small
inasmuch as the Christian presence in Asia is only a small part (5 percent) of

the Asian scene, and only a small part (10 percent) of the Christian presence in the world.

In other words, the subject deserves a degree of attention it runs some risk of not getting. Some parts of the story are relatively well documented and written about; others have hardly been brought to the attention of a wider public than the people directly concerned in them. Not much has been done to bring the pieces of the picture together, and still less to fit the Asian picture into a larger global one.

Until recently it has been premature to attempt an appraisal of the situation. Now, however, enough has happened, especially in one decade, the 1970s, to make it both useful and desirable to put together the outlines of what is already a matter of record, and to provide tentative indications of prevailing trends in this area of history as another decade is under way.

Many major questions underlie this study.

What *ought* to be the role of the Church in society, given the historical ideals of the Church on the one hand and the realities of society on the other?

Among the ideologically conflicting answers to that question, from the conservative evangelical to the political radical, which has more right on its side?

How much distance is there between the ideal and real role of the Church in history in general, in the contemporary world in particular, and in Asia most particularly? Is the distance too great to be bridged convincingly? Is it perhaps the real moral of the story that the Church would do better to repair its strained relations with the powers that be in society and renounce any social pretensions altogether?

Or, on the contrary, is there evidence enough in the teaching of the past century and the practice of the past generation to show that social concern is bound up inseparably with the self-understanding of the Church, and that the Church is capable of mediating concern for social *change* as effectively as it once mediated concern for social stability?

These questions go far beyond the scope of this inquiry, although any findings it may bring together will have some bearing on them. The intention in this inquiry—to see what historical generalizations are possible on the basis of the Asian experience so far—leaves the larger questions open so as not to predetermine the shape of any conclusions and not to limit in advance their usefulness to readers with differing value systems.

It will not be necessary to ask *if* there has been any protest among Christians in Asia against the social, economic, or political status quo. In any group of a hundred million people or so, there is bound to be some. Our question is more specific: has Christian protest been quantitatively and qualitatively *significant*?

To be quantitatively significant, this protest would have to involve a proportion of the Christian faithful large enough not to be entirely neutralized by intensified conservatism elsewhere among the flock. To be qualitatively significant, it would have to involve a representative selection of the faithful: those involved would need to have a claim to speak not only for themselves but in some degree for the Church itself as community and as institution.

There can be no hard and fast rule as to what constitutes fulfillment of these conditions. A trend must at least have been set that shows signs of enduring—a trend not likely soon to be counteracted to the extent that it might as well have never happened.

What we want to find out, then, is whether there was evidence by the early 1980s of an enduring trend of Christian protest in Asia against the social status quo there. (We shall be taking *social* in its widest sense to cover everything not merely individual. We shall also be taking *protest* in its widest sense to cover every tendency to privilege change over the status quo.) We must first know what *has* been the status quo in Asia, and what about it could provide strong provocation for Christian protest. This will require some attempt to summarize the general historical background, the Christian historical background, and the Asian historical background, of the developments of the 1970s.

There are different levels on which changes in Christian attitudes to the social status quo can be monitored.

First, there is the level of individual attitudes among Christians themselves. Here there are rich mines of raw data, and some lodes of organized data, but little data controlled to measure changes in the same population over any period of time.

Next, there is the level of recorded reflection among Christians, especially Christians who undertake to express the Christian conscience as thinkers or publicists. The data here are more manageable, but also more controvertible. There is no sure way of knowing how representative such data might be.

Third, there is the level of formal statements of position by individuals or groups with definable mandates to speak for different segments of the Christian community. Here we have the most easily controllable data, as well as the most accessible, in that much of it is already gathered in documentary collections at both the global and the Asian levels.

Finally, there is the level of action relevant to change in the social status quo. This is the crucial test, whether by Christian or by Marxist criteria. It is a test that can be applied with relative clarity in the case of corporate Christian action, and with more ambiguity in the case of action by Christians having no mandate to act for more than themselves. It is in any case a test whose findings can be no more than provisional with regard to events that are very close in time. Historians writing in the year 2000 will be much wiser about these findings, not only because they will know what happened in the final decades of the century, but also because they will have a fuller historical perspective on what happened in the decades before it.

No one of these levels of monitoring Christian attitudes will be left entirely out of account in this inquiry. The main focus, however, as indicated by our title, *"Churches* in contestation,'' will be on the *corporate* kind of statements and actions in the direction of change.

It will quickly appear that there has been a potentially epoch-making change in the kind of statements to which responsible Christian bodies in Asia are prepared to commit themselves in relation to the issue of social stability versus social change. What will remain to be seen is whether this change is actually epoch-making. While there has been significant change in the actions as well as the words of the institutional churches, it is not so clear whether the distance between the two has been narrowed or increased. Temporarily at least, it might be the case that church promises have gotten further than ever ahead of church performance.

There are peculiar difficulties in analyzing the data coming from Asia in the past quarter century.

During that period free inquiry has been the exception rather than the rule. The aftermath of World War II left Asia divided into armed camps, with information strictly controlled in communist countries from the beginning, and with situations of similar control existing or developing in the others. At one time in the mid-1970s (during the Emergency in India), a free press ceased to be accessible (even to the elite) among 95 percent of the Asian population.

Even where restrictions were not imposed, or after they were lifted, they remained in the background as an inhibiting proximate possibility almost everywhere outside Japan. Even publications originating in areas free from direct restrictions (as in Hong Kong)—to the extent that they depended on circulation in other countries of Asia—have not been completely uninhibited in their reporting. At the same time, publications that profess to speak for the grassroots usually exist in conditions that make it hard to judge their reliability or even their precise historical context.

In short, investigators of such burning questions as the real or the ideal role of the Church in relation to the Asian status quo must live with a situation of polarization where words are weapons and the inviolability of truth is the first casualty in the war of words. They must live with the fact that they can never stand entirely outside the struggle, even if they feel they ought to.

For all that, some understanding surely remains possible. It must be attempted, if only because not to attempt it would be to accept the one thing that nobody accepts. For in a war of words the one thing that nobody accepts is that it makes no difference which side wins.

Given the ambiguities of history, however, it had better be attempted without any illusion that any one side identifiable now is likely to be looked back on later as having been either entirely right or entirely wrong, or as having been either entirely vindicated or entirely discredited by events.

1

THE GLOBAL BACKGROUND

The General Global Background

Social protest would have a long history if it included everything that could go under that name. Karl Marx set the trend in that respect when he wrote in 1848, in the famous words of *The Communist Manifesto*, "The history of all hitherto existing society is the history of class struggles." Many others, including many who would balk at that formula and its implications, would have no difficulty in recognizing the likelihood of a certain amount of resentment and resistance whenever and wherever there exists an unequal distribution of the good things of this world.

The trouble is that history has always been written by society's victors, not by its victims. Those who had something to protest about had scarcely been heard from in history until a more or less coherent movement of peasant or proletarian revolution began to give them a voice during the nineteenth and twentieth centuries. In a world that professes to believe in the uplifting of the oppressed, whether on the basis of Western or Eastern ideologies, there can be little doubt that far more oppression has gone on in history and prehistory than has ever come to light. The slave wars and peasant insurrections that have forced their way into the chronicles of existing societies can be no more than the tip of an iceberg of discontent.[1]

The past two centuries have created a fundamentally new situation in terms of bringing the concerns of the "toiling masses" to light. It has been during this period that, thanks most immediately to the movement called Marxism, it has ceased to be possible for the agendas of the powerful to leave little or no place for the working men and women of the world.

Some of the remoter historical sources of this development lie back much farther than two centuries, being derived from the Judaeo-Christian tradition itself. Yet it took something more than historical Christianity, something more even than the revolutionary Christianity of the Reformation, to

6

give social concern the salience it has had in all public discourse in the wake of the modern social revolutions in England, America, France, Japan, Russia, Germany, China, and elsewhere.[2] We shall have to return to the historical paradox implied in this. What concerns us for the moment is to spell out in some detail what has been involved in the widespread modern calling into question of hitherto prevailing notions of social order.

The prevailing notions of social order that have been called in question may for our purpose be reduced to one: the notion that there is something sacrosanct about the social status quo by virtue of its mere existence and without regard to its inequality or injustice.

How society came to be divided into "haves" and "have-nots" can be explained as a falling away from an original idyllic situation or ideal. As far as that idea goes, there is no essential difference between the first of the written Hebrew prophets, Amos, and the first of the prophets of Communism, Marx.

But the division can also be explained (especially when it has existed so long that it seems part of the nature of things) as having the sanction of whatever power is seen as guiding the affairs of humanity. That explanation naturally has commended itself to most of those who in history have had control of the explaining—that is, the "haves." The form of the ideological justification varies according to the culture; but the essential message generally corresponds to that embodied in a Victorian nursery rhyme:

> The rich man in his castle, the poor man at his gate—
> God made them high and lowly, and ordered their estate.

Such an assumption as this could escape close scrutiny in a static, rural, preindustrial society, in which ultimate reality itself tended to be seen in static terms, whether it was called God or Fate or Dharma or Cosmic Harmony. By the same token, once the first Western societies had entered the current of modern change, it could no longer be so easy for anyone to get away with a pattern of acting that already appeared as a confidence game to Rousseau in the eighteenth century. As Rousseau saw it, that pattern consisted of drawing a line around a piece of land; of declaring, "That's mine"; and of "finding people simple enough to believe it."[3]

To get accustomed to living in a changing world is to cease to be "simple enough to believe" that any supposedly fixed past or present is an adequate standard to set for the future. The mere fact of change, by showing that the way things have been is not necessarily the way things will be, strikes the first blow at the assumption that things are necessarily the way they ought to be.

Since part of the change has consisted in the spread of information beyond the control of the people who had most interest in keeping things the way they had been, a point was bound to be reached when the dispossessed would be led to believe just the opposite of what they had been told before.

They would be led to believe that, even in the forcible overthrow of the entire existing order, they had nothing to lose and a world to win.[4]

Not all the have-nots were led all the way in that belief; and not all of those who wholly committed themselves to it found their commitment vindicated. As is well known, no question is more fiercely disputed today than the question of whether the balance sheet of the first century and a third of Marxism is positive or negative.

What is *not* in question is that the terms of the debate on social order changed during that period along with the changes in society. Today the debate is no longer between advocates and opponents of change; it is between advocates of more change and advocates of less, or between advocates of revolutionary and advocates of evolutionary change. Insofar as the change in question is change in the direction of reducing blatant inequalities, the debate is not about the need for change, but only about its proper pace.

In short, we are now in a world in which both the fact of and the need for some kind of social change are taken for granted.

It is a world in which the claims of the people to power are no longer in dispute, while the reality of the people's power is more disputed than ever.[5]

It is a world more than half of whose population has recently passed from colonial domination to national rule, while the economic dependency of most of the human race has only been thrown into sharper relief.[6]

It is a world whose inequalities are so notorious that new intercontinental interest blocs ("Group of Ten," "Group of 77") have been formed on the basis of them, while a plan for a New International Economic Order was endorsed without objection by the United Nations in 1974.[7]

It is a world in which these inequalities have come to be denounced not only by the spokespersons of the poor majority and by the world-minded on both sides, but even by the spokesperson of the United Nations body most representative of the rich minority—the World Bank.[8]

It is a world, in fine, in which the fact and the need of change are taken for granted, as is the global interdependence of structural relationships and of the mechanisms by which these influence each other.

There is still room, of course, for fundamental differences in the moral and ideological assessment of these mechanisms. They can be seen either as being still capable of serving the general interest, or as being beyond redemption.

In the eyes of that part of that world which is more acted upon than acting, these mechanisms appear as irredeemably conservative and exploitative. In a Marxist analysis, they appear as ultimately self-destructive.

On the other hand, for those people who are at the administering rather than at the receiving end of these mechanisms, it is easier to accept the more reassuring view implicit in World Bank reports: that, while the rich have admittedly grown "on the back of the poor," the best hope of the poor still lies "at the tail of the rich."[9] Even in that view there is a more sophisticated recognition than has hitherto been forthcoming from capitalist quarters: that, in this newly interdependent world, new concessions in terms of global structural change are now demanded by the interests of both North and South.[10]

It is in the setting of such a world that we must now see what has been happening within the Christian churches on the one hand, and within the Asian countries on the other.

The Global Christian Background

Is there a case for the division of Christian history into a pre-Constantinian, a Constantinian, and a post-Constantinian phase? Is there a basis for the assumption implicit in such a division—the assumption that the Constantinian norm is not necessarily the permanent one?

As an unsympathetic outsider might put it, Can the leopard change its spots? As a loyal churchperson might put it, Can the Church, consistently with its mission, make distinctions in bestowing its blessing on the powers that be? As a sociologist might put it, Is there any exception to the rule by which large institutions, such as churches, tend to favor the status quo in society precisely in the measure that the institutions are rooted there?

Humanly speaking, it would be difficult to demonstrate any long-term and large-scale exception to this sociological rule. If self-preservation is the first law of individuals, it is still more the first law of collectivities and of the protective incrustations they develop. Whether we think in terms of the Marxist diagnosis of religions as "the opium of the people," or in terms of Max Weber's theory about "the routinization of charisma," we are reminded that it is the lot of religion to be "human, all too human," and that it can never wholly escape this lot as long as religion really enters into human life.

In any case, large-scale phenomena require large-scale explanations, in which generalization must necessarily range far beyond all the facts that can be collected in any one head. If scholars were divided about the balance sheet of Christianity in the days of Celsus and Porphyry only a century or two after Christ, it need not surprise us that they have continued to be divided in the days of Voltaire, Marx, Nietzsche, and Freud.

No end to the argument is ever really in sight, least of all in regard to the question of whether or not there is anything in Christianity that actually transcends history. To this day it can happen that the second thoughts of a "believer" can proclaim "the misery of Christianity" and launch "a plea for a humanity without God," at the very moment the second thoughts of an "unbeliever" proclaim that "God is not yet dead."[11] Given the mere size of the phenomenon called Christianity, while it lasts there is always bound to be this mixture of the most contradictory reactions to it. There will always be some who are disillusioned with it, even among those brought up to regard it as eternal truth; and there will always be some who are newly fascinated with it, even among those brought up to regard its pretensions as definitively discredited.

We must limit our question to make it more manageable. An exception to the normal patterns of history or sociology is not, after all, the first thing we need to look for in order to establish that Christianity, after some sixteen centuries during which it was generally a force for social stability rather than for social change, may now be showing a capacity to play a different social role. It need not be the first thing to be looked for even by those who believe in divine providence, and who are satisfied that the purposes of providence would be best served today by a post-Constantinian Church, in the sense above indicated. For there is no need to suppose that the human mechanisms by which such a Church may emerge must be other than humanly intelligible ones.

In other words, it may not take a social miracle to produce a post-Constantinian Church. In human terms, it may take no more than a change in the extent to which churches perceive that they have a stake in the social status quo.

The "Pre-Constantinian" Period

For every belief system there was a time when it had no stake in the social status quo. Before the existing society was ready to make room for it, and before it had created any social space of its own, it had nothing to gain from keeping that society the way it was. So it was in northern India at the time of the birth of Buddhism, and in Arabia at the time of the birth of Islam. Such also was the situation for Christianity in that period we call the pre-Constantinian era—or at least at its outset.

For every belief system, being socially an outsider or an insider also makes a great difference to the message preached. Sociologically it is not to be wondered at if Buddhism, Christianity, and Islam have in certain respects been at their most uncompromising in relation to the societies they first faced. It would obviously not have been possible for later forms of these religions, as represented, say, by Japanese Buddhism, Renaissance Catholicism, and Indonesian Mohammedanism, to have made history in the way history was in fact made vis-à-vis the caste society of late Vedic India, the imperial power of pagan Rome, and the animism and polytheism of seventh-century Arabia.

There are, however, both positive and negative sides to a religion's being a social outsider.

On the positive side, in relation to existing injustice, oppression, corruption, and stagnation, the new religion's hands are clean and untied. Insofar as it stands apart from society, it is not inhibited in judging it. Like communism in relation to nineteenth-century capitalism, Christianity in relation to persecuting emperors could well have felt that it had "nothing to lose but its chains."

On the negative side, a judgment made from a marginal position in society may be quite simplistic, and even quite myopic, concerning the central realities of that society. As early as the Book of Revelation in the first century, there was a strong perception of conflict between the values of Christianity and those of Roman imperial absolutism. Yet (to take just one example) there was no such strong Christian perception of any need to make Paul's radical non-recognition of slave–free distinctions any part of the basis for the confrontation of Christianity with the society of that century, or indeed of at least seventeen centuries after it.[12]

What this shows is that any standing apart from society on the part of a belief system is illusory to the extent that the values involved on both sides are not brought out in the open. From the moment they take on a social dimension, and even before they consciously seek social acceptance, all religions tend to be simply mirrors of the existing society in all respects in which they do not consciously take a socially deviant stand.

In the case of Christianity, when we consult its early spokespersons, we must not expect to find ancient answers to modern questions—though we may well expect to find ancient answers to *perennial* questions. We may also expect these answers to have more of the kind of single-mindedness that goes with relative freedom from social aspirations, social responsibility, or vested interest. Thus, for more or less radical denunciations of institutionalized poverty, we may turn more confidently to Saint James in New Testament times, or even to Saint John Chrysostom in patristic times, than to Saint Thomas at the height of the Middle Ages or to Saint Antonino at its close.[13] But we need look neither to the Fathers nor to the Schoolmen for the kind of insight into the workings of society that was not available even to social insiders until society had evolved toward self-organization and self-awareness.

The "Constantinian" Period

By the time the self-awareness of society had evolved far enough to found the social sciences as known today—having absorbed en route the influence of Renaissance thinkers like Macchiavelli, Reformation leaders like Calvin, and heirs of the Enlightenment like Adam Smith—Christianity had been a social insider in the West for a millennium and a half. For better or worse, the world is still in the shadow of that long interpenetration of the social and the ecclesiastical systems of Western civilization.

Legend has it that Julian the Apostate brought to a close the last stand of imperial paganism in the fourth century with the words, "Thou has conquered, Galilean!" A certain kind of hindsight in a new pagan of the nineteenth century (Swinburne) gave these prophetic words a further twist:

> Thou hast conquered, O pale Galilean,
> And the world has grown grey with thy breath!

But the truth was still more complex than that. In terms of what Christ was taken as standing for during the Constantinian period, there had indeed been a kind of conquest, but at its heart there was also a defeat. The Church that had moved from the margin to the center of society was in a better position both to understand and to manipulate the workings of society—but only at the price of ceasing to be free to concern itself exclusively with the priorities of Christ. With every century that passed after that first church-state entente, the world the Church saw itself called to be "in but not of" (John 17) was more and more a world of its own making, a world in which it had too great a stake to part from without pain. The very success that had given the Church the knowledge and power of an insider had muted its voice.

In this process of increasing implication of the Church in the prevailing social system, only a couple of significant stages can be noted here. It is notable that as long as the social system was feudal rather than capitalist, and as long as the Church's leaders were more involved in land than in trade, the Church retained its power to criticize the abuses of usury longer than it retained its power to criticize serfdom.

In neither of these areas of society was the "Christian" ideal ever given up. Strictly as an ideal, it was still as "communist" in the *Decretum Gratiani* of the twelfth century as it had been in the original fervor of Pentecost in the first century. Yet in that same *Decretum* the system of serfdom appears as having the force of canon law. This reflects a society in which the Church had long been a leading landlord—and a landlord that was in due course shown to be just as much hated as all the others.[14]

Thus far had the Church accommodated itself to the rural world it had lived in during the first millennium. It was only when the Church was halfway through its second millennium that a break began to be made with the solid stand of the moralists against that sin of the cities, usury; and it is not surprising that the break is associated with the theologian-archbishop of "the business capital of fifteenth-century Europe," Florence.[15] More properly, it was only with John Calvin, the sixteenth-century reformer, that the traditional Christian curse on capitalism began to be lifted and gradually turned into a blessing.

The question of the cause-effect relationship between the Protestant ethic and the spirit of capitalism has been a subject of controversy ever since Max Weber first wrote of it. But it is not in doubt that the Puritan strand in Protestantism did play a leading role in disarming the misgivings of Christendom over the new capitalist ferment in its midst.

Puritanism put a new complexion on the gospel paradox about the shrewd use of the mammon of iniquity. It found in its stern faith a religious sanction for a sense of this-worldly calling, at a time when religious sanction still carried much weight in the world of affairs. Eventually, the world of affairs went its own way, and what was left of the Puritan sense of calling became better known as rugged individualism and ruthless acquisitiveness.

By the nineteenth century, the Church that had made its peace with feudalism had also made its peace with capitalism. The record is there to show how Christendom put up its own fight for centuries against what Marx was to call "the cash nexus." It is also there to show how hostility was turned into ambivalence and ambivalence into acquiescence under pressures from within and from without. When Marx's indictment of capitalism came, it caught Christians of all kinds on the anti-Marxist side of the argument about his labor theory of value, almost as if they had never had a labor theory of value of their own.[16]

The Period of Confrontation with Marxism

It is in terms of this historical background that one must judge how revolutionary or reactionary the Marxist protest really was. Was Marx actually as radically in rupture with the Judaeo-Christian tradition as he and his atheist followers have asked to have believed? The question will probably long continue to be a subject of Christian-socialist-capitalist polemics.

On the one hand, it is understandable that Christians should be more conscious of the element of rupture: after all, Marx attacked their theism at a time when they saw no similar threat to that theism in their concessions to the capitalist spirit. On the other hand, it is understandable that later Christians eventually found cause for new misgivings about Christian concessions to capitalism, and for second thoughts also about Christian objections to Marxism. It is even to be expected that there should be some wide swings in the pendulum of Christian opinion in the search for a new balance. So it has proved, in proportion as Christians have engaged in the novel exercise of actually reading the Marxist critique of capitalism, and of rereading their own tradition with the hindsight of the late twentieth century.[17]

Today, any Christian consensus about Marxism is still in the future. It is beyond our scope here to anticipate what form such a consensus might take. We may only note, with Weber,[18] that historical reality will always be more complex than the abstractions captured in our dichotomies between material and spiritual factors and between causes and effects. One thing is clear in any case. The vehemence of the Christian-Marxist polemic has delayed for at least a century, for Christians and Marxists alike, the possibility of giving undivided attention to those goals that are genuinely common to both. If there are such goals, they were lost to view during most of that time.

During Marxism's first century, all statements by church leaders have had to take account of its unfolding history. In particular, they have had to take account of the developing confrontation between the capitalist and the socialist blocs in the wake of the Russian and the Chinese revolutions and the division of Europe after World War II. Faced with a choice between the two sides, Christian leaders overwhelmingly leaned toward the former, rejecting Marxist sociology along with Marxist atheism and Leninist-

Stalinist regimentation, and often implicitly accepting the Marxist premise that the defense of the Christian heritage was bound up with the defense of the bourgeois model of society attacked by Marx. To this extent the first effect of Marxism on the churches, Catholic, Protestant, and Orthodox, was to reinforce enormously their post-Reformation accommodation to the political, social, and economic values associated with that form of the modern world that seemed least hostile to what the churches stood for.

However, as the confrontation developed into a deadlock, and as the world's leaders began to search for ways to break out of it, Christians began to look further, both into the future and into the past. Geographically, the impetus came from all three of the groups into which the world was divided by the middle of the twentieth century.

As Marxism-Leninism came to claim the allegiance of about one-third of the world, and as this Second World proved that it was a factor to reckon with for the foreseeable future, pragmatism modified the attitudes of church leaders toward it, beginning with those who lived under it, and communicating itself to the others, especially after the Orthodox churches entered the World Council in 1961, and after the Second Vatican Council opened in 1962. This fait accompli was dramatized in 1978, when a Christian who had lived under Leninism was shown on the state television of his native Poland as he assumed the position of the first non-Italian pope in 455 years.

The Third World began to emerge on the basis of refusal of alignment with imperialism. In that world, imperialism was perceived more as something already suffered from the First World than as something to be feared from the Second. That perception began to be communicated from the Christians of the Third World—newly conscious as they were of constituting the Christian majority of the future—to the declining though still dominant Christians of the First. A turning point in this development was reached and shown in the stand taken at the Conference of Medellín in 1968 by the ecclesiastical leaders of Latin America, that continent where Christianity had most adherents and where imperialism most distinctly retained a First World face. Medellín stopped well short of endorsing the world's dominant socialist system, but it set a trend in official Christian repudiation of the world's dominant capitalist system.[19]

As the First World came to terms with the fact that it lacked the power to eliminate the Second or to absorb the Third, First World church leaders sought to envisage a Church that would not act as if its whole future depended on First World dominance. There was a reciprocal influence in this direction between politics and religion. It was in the year, and indeed in the very month, of the opening of Vatican II—October 1962—that the two superpowers drew back from the nuclear brink in the Cuba crisis. Throughout the next seventeen years there was no return to the worst tensions of the Cold War, either in the political decision-making circles of Washington or Moscow, or in the ecclesiastical decision-making circles of Geneva or Rome.

A "Post-Constantinian" Period?

These events of 1962, of 1968, of 1978, would have been unthinkable less than a century before they happened. Before they could happen, the world and the Church, and Marxism too, had to take on new shapes. Once these events had happened, it was no longer enough to look to the patterns of the past in order to determine what was predictable for the future.

It would be obvious to all that the Church had lost its pre-Constantinian innocence and could never recover it. It would seem obvious to many that it had also lost its Constantinian mandate, if indeed it had ever had any legitimate one. If the Church had any future, other than as part of a rearguard action by the world's haves before the advance of the world's have-nots, it would have to be in *some* sense a post-Constantinian future. At least in terms of the global situation (the three-world division), whether judged in the light of the professed priorities of Christianity (for example, taking the side of the poor rather than of the rich), or weighed in the scales of a new kind of *realpolitik* (for example, taking the side of tomorrow's masters rather than today's), the first condition for far-reaching change in the churches' relations with society was already realized. The Church no longer had a long-term stake in maintaining what had been the global status quo of the third quarter of the twentieth century.

Notice to this effect was being served throughout the latter half of that quarter century. It was served in the most general way through the traumatic change of consciousness brought about in the Catholic Church in the world by Vatican II. This change of consciousness carried forward the social concern of the popes (itself an early response to the Marxist challenge), and put that concern on the agenda of the whole Church. A new chapter in the relations of the Church with the world was opened in the first words of one of the major documents of that council:

> The joys and the hopes, the griefs and the anxieties of the men of this age, especially those who are poor or in any way afflicted, these too are the joys and the hopes, the griefs and the anxieties of the followers of Christ.[20]

This was still a statement of what should be rather than of what was; but at least it represented a new declaration of Christian intent—an intent that was represented also in the trend of thinking and speaking of the World Council of Churches in that decade and after.

The change could have remained at the level of lofty generalities; but something more than lofty generalities did follow, and not only in the positions taken by one denomination or in one continent. In the years after Vatican II and after Medellín, there was a newly reciprocal influence between the new kind of social thinking in Rome and Geneva and the new social thinking among Catholics and Protestants in Latin America. For the first time in modern Roman Catholic experience, a strong impetus from the periphery began to set the pace for the center in terms of theological reflection as well as of action. A measure of the extent to which globally representative leaders were now prepared to recognize a transformed sense of Christian social responsibility can be found in the Declaration of the 1971 Synod of Bishops on "Justice in the World":

> Action on behalf of justice and participation in the transformation of the world fully appear to us as a constitutive dimension of the preaching of the Gospel, or, in other words, of the mission of the Church for the redemption of the human race and its liberation from every oppressive situation.[21]

That manifesto could still be considered only a matter of words, words that still had to meet the Christian and the Marxist test of practice. For much of the world, when it came to a question of effective social concern, a century's experience had made it seem that Marxists meant business in a way that Christians did not. True, a tradition of Christian socialism was old enough to be scorned in the *Communist Manifesto* as being merely "the holy water with which the priest consecrates the heart-burnings of the aristocrat." It lived on beyond the time when aristocratic motivation would have sufficed for it, but it could continue to be treated dismissively until quite late in the twentieth century.

For social concern as voiced by the churches to be taken seriously as a threat to the capitalist system, the alarm had to be sounded from within the system itself. Such an alarm was sounded in 1969, the year after Medellín, in the *Rockefeller Report on the Americas*.[22] Ten years later, by the time of Medellín's successor conference at Puebla, it was commonplace among bishops of both left and right in Latin America to say what sounded so radical when Tawney first said it in 1922:

> Compromise is as impossible between the Church of Christ and the idolatry of wealth, which is the practical religion of capitalist societies, as it was between the Church and the State idolatry of the Roman Empire.[23]

In sum: in terms of church thinking on social matters, there was a noticeable shift in the 1960s and the 1970s in positions taken in the name of the Christian churches around the world. The pace was set in those continents where the need for social change was most evident; that is, the "underdeveloped" continents, and in particular the one "underdeveloped" continent (Latin America) that was also a Christian continent.

In a world system in which support for social stability had been for some time synonymous with support for capitalism, the spokespersons of world Christianity had begun to reconsider their options.

2

THE ASIAN BACKGROUND

The General Asian Background

Roughly a quarter of the surface of the globe is land, and roughly a third of that land surface constitutes the continent of Asia. But when we single out Asia for special attention, we are singling out something more than a twelfth of the world, more than the largest of the continents. If numbers of people matter, in Asia we have to do with the majority of humankind. Even if numbers were regarded as not all that important, it is still true that in Asia we have to do with a continental area which, more than any other single area in the closing decades of the twentieth century, makes a plausible center of gravity for the world's affairs.

It is not new for Asia to deserve to be central to the attention of world-minded people. It is merely new for it to be given its deserts in the estimation of those who have done most of the writing of world history. For a relatively short and recent period in that history, this writing concentrated on the European spur of the Eurasian landmass, or on the main overseas area of transplantation from that spur in North America. Today that period can be seen as an interlude of Western dominance, lasting only a century or two, between a much longer period before it and a new period that is now in the process of taking its place.

At least fifty centuries passed after the rise of civilization in the valleys of the Nile, the Euphrates, the Indus, and the Yellow River, before European dominance became a global reality with the spread of industrialization from Britain. For as far back in that period as information goes, Asia has had a certain preponderance both in numbers of people and in elements of civilization. On the eve of European expansion in the sixteenth century, and even on the eve of the Industrial Revolution in the eighteenth, there was little indication of how the West would dominate the East in the nineteenth and the early twentieth centuries. This domination was like a tide that had arisen and had already begun to ebb within a tenth of the time in which history has been in the making.[1]

17

It need not seem strange, therefore, that around A.D. 1980 the Asian homelands of some 2.7 billion people could once again look like a natural focus for most of the action affecting the 4.4 billion people in the world. We are not free to forget the rest of the world when we focus on Asia, for the eras when human communities could develop in isolation have been at an end since travel, trade, industry, communications, and armaments have brought all parts of the globe within reach of one another. But Asia is too vast a subject to be introduced in more than the roughest outline in the space here available. We must content ourselves here with the minimum summary information that will serve to put Asia in context among the continents, and Asian Christianity in context among the Asian religions, and both in some fashion in context within the general global and the general Christian situation in regard to social protest and social change.

Asia among the Continents

Among the continents, only Africa and North America are more than half the size of Asia: these two have enough physical unity to justify their being regarded as continental geographical units. But in terms of what passes for a continent in the case of Australia, Europe, or South America, it would make more sense to distinguish five or six continental regions in the case of Asia.

Geography and history have linked most of the northern half of Asia with Russia and its contemporary geopolitical frame of reference, the Soviet Union. Similarly, West Asia is linked with the Arab world of oil and of Islam. East Asia, for its part, has remained the homeland of the Chinese culture: linguistic and other links still underlie the differences between China, Japan, Korea, and Taiwan. South Asia, geographically marked off by mountain ranges, is more heterogeneous in its historical heritage, but is also not without a common fund of cultural and political experience. Indeed, it was held within the framework of a single raj as recently as a generation ago. The region called Southeast Asia is defined by exclusion: it consists of those mainland and island areas left over when the Chinese and the Indian culture areas proper have been marked off. That is not to say that it lacks distinctive features of its own, apart from reflecting a varying mix of influences from both China and India.

Such is the broad pattern. The details can be and are debated. There are borderline areas where classification can only be somewhat arbitrary— Afghanistan, for example, between South and Southwest Asia, and Burma between South and Southeast Asia. There are other points of debate with more important implications. Thus, some would count a sixth subcontinental region within the East Asian realm: "High Asia," including the western half of China in Tibet, Sinkiang, and Tsinghai, and also including Mongolia.

Some would even put High Asia first on the list of Asia's natural realms, as the one that is not only the most central and the most distinctive (there is nothing quite like it anywhere in the world), but also the most decisive influence informing the character of all the other regions. For High Asia, together with the mountain chains of Southwest Asia, physically separates Asia's northern lowlands from the plains and plateaus of the three great peninsulas on its southern side, thus determining the extremes of cold and heat, and of dry and wet winds, among the many other climatic variations of the supercontinent as a whole.

Physical features have determined Asia's climate. Both physical features and climate have determined the distribution of its population, giving the human map of Asia a shape notably different from the physical one. The human map of Asia is largely a map of alluvial valleys and plains, covering only fragments of its territory in the east and the south. The heaviest concentrations of population are found in plains of this kind in eastern China and northern India; the only comparably heavy concentrations are found on some of the islands, notably in Japan and Indonesia. In contrast, more than half the area of Asia, mainly in the north and on the plateaus of the center and west, has a population density of less than two persons per square kilometer.

Physical and human geography and history, in their turn, have left their marks on Asia's political shape. In 1980 three-fifths of Asia's 2.7 billion people were accounted for by two giant nations—China, with a population close to one billion, and India, with close to 700 million. Two-thirds of Asia's total population are accounted for if we add the two next largest national populations—the 155 million of Indonesia and the 118 million of Japan.

When we take economic production into account, it becomes clear why no list of nation-giants in Asia could omit Japan. In the mid-1970s Japan became the third nation in history (after the United States and the Soviet Union) to reach an annual gross national product (GNP) of US $500 billion. This was more than the combined production of China, India, and Indonesia. On a GNP chart of Asia, all countries except Japan, China, and India would fall far short of an annual rate of $100 billion—a rate reached during the 1970s by Australia while its population was still under 15 million. On a GNP per capita chart, all Asian countries except Japan, Saudi Arabia, and certain micro-states would fall far short of the rate of $4,000 per capita surpassed in the same decade by Australia and New Zealand.

Thus, even the most cursory survey of Asia brings us quickly to one truly characteristic feature: its poverty. The continent that gave the world its cradle of civilization is today linked by its overall poverty with the underdeveloped continents, Africa and Latin America, not with the rich continents of the West.

The main departures from the pattern of poverty in Asia have hitherto been no more than marginal in terms of the vast populations involved. Japan remains the largest single departure, but the population it has lifted up to the level of the West still represents less than 5 percent of Asia's total. Soviet development has raised average income for about half as many more people in Asia to a point about halfway between that of the Third World and that of the West. Oil has brought sudden relative prosperity to certain states in Southwest Asia embracing some further tens of millions of people. But even if this last form of prosperity were assured of being both broadly diffused and long-lasting (and it is not assured of either), the sum of the national or regional populations escaping overall poverty would still be less than a tenth of Asia's total. Asia is not only one of the poor continents: with 63 percent of the world's population, it supports, or rather it fails to support, more than 75 percent of the world's poor.

The case of Asia confronts us with the question of why world development should be so lopsided.

One part of the answer evidently lies in certain natural handicaps existing in advance of any attempt to take cognizance of the question. Obviously a certain lopsidedness must result from the fact that there has never been any overall planning of the diffusion of world population and of human communities. Presumably the world will long have to live with an arrangement in which over 60 percent of its people are confined to little more than 30 percent of its land area and to considerably less than 30 percent of its at present usable land.

Migration offers the hope of only gradual change in this regard, even if the whole apparatus of separate national sovereignties did not now exist to block it. Discovery of new resources, of new uses for wasteland, of new technologies, is a much less predictable factor, as is shown in the history of such discoveries so far. The demonstrated possibilities of increasing the productivity of resources already being exploited, such as farming and fishing, make the land-to-people ratio a much less limiting factor for the Asia of the 1980s than would appear at first sight.

There are limits to growth; but among the points clarified in the controversy surrounding the question of growth, there is the point that a continent like Asia, even with half the world's population, contributes less to the problems of growth than a country like the United States, with less than a tenth of Asia's population but consuming resources at more than ten times the overall Asian per capita rate. In a world in which figures show 200 million Americans consuming about four times as much of certain basic resources as 2 billion Asians, it is clearly not enough to study the problems of growth in terms of global statistical aggregates without regional breakdowns.[2] Some would even say it has proved illusory to aim at any such global perspective without regional bias. In that case the least distorting regional bias on humankind's predicament will presumably be that of the region where most of humankind is found.

It is not really a matter for surprise if a balance is not to be easily found between global and regional considerations in the study of the problems of growth. What is important is the growing awareness that neither the whole nor any part can any longer be studied in isolation. Nobody would deny this point now, least of all those who provoked the controversy that clarified it—the authors of the *Club of Rome's Project on the Predicament of*

Mankind. Something of the developing focus of the discussion is reflected even in the titles in that series: *The Limits to Growth; Mankind at the Turning Point; Reshaping the International Order; Beyond the Age of Waste; Goals for Mankind*.

What is the relevance of this point for us? We have already noted that part of the problem of the lopsidedness of world development, shown at its extreme in the case of Asia, can be attributed to natural handicaps existing in advance of any attempt to take cognizance of the question. What we must now note is that this is *only* part of that problem. The other part is the fact that Asians, handicapped by having less to live on to begin with, cannot even enjoy full control of what they have.

This handicap is not at all due to the blindness of human diffusion, and it is only residually due to the naked force of old style colonialism. Instead, it is due to the internal logic of the world market, whose only blindness is with regard to the boundaries between continents and countries and to the human consequences of its genius for making all the world's wealth flow more and more into a single pool. Because of this factor, there can be no serious study of the crisis of change in Asia that is not set in the context of the late twentieth-century global crisis of change.

Asia in the Global Crisis of Change

It needs little reflection to see the explosive implications of a continental situation in which more than three-quarters of the world's poor, representing more than half the world's people, and concentrated on less than a quarter of the world's usable land, are systematically deprived of control of much of the little they have.[3] Yet the situation had to exist for some centuries, and to have been notorious for some decades, before the necessary reflection was forthcoming.

Two centuries of social upheaval, carried on a wave of economic growth and greed, lie between those milestones of reflection marked by Adam Smith and Gunnar Myrdal. Smith looked at late eighteenth-century Europe and set a trend in economic thinking about the wealth of nations; Myrdal looked at late twentieth-century Asia and set a new trend in economic thinking about their poverty.[4]

There is food for thought in this shift of attention from Europe to Asia, from wealth to poverty, from development to underdevelopment and to what is more recently labelled "the development of underdevelopment." What is coming to light is that there exists an insufficiently scrutinized relationship between the wealth of some nations and the poverty of others. It has been a sort of relationship for which scrutiny could only spell trouble.

The trouble eventually had to come. We have noted earlier that the changes in human society have changed the terms of the debate on social order, putting the need for some kind of change beyond debate while sharpening differences of opinion as to what kind of change it ought to be. We have found, in this newly interdependent world, a recognition even in the rich North that there is a limit to the extent that it can continue to grow richer on the back of the poor South.

It is one thing to have broad agreement on the facts of inequality, on the interdependence of world wealth and world poverty, on the need for a more sustainable relationship between North and South than the widening gap between the rate at which the rich grow richer and the rate at which the poor grow less poor. It is another thing to get agreement that the existing world system can only continue to make things worse. Even where there is formal consensus that things must be made better, it remains the prevailing thesis of the rich world that the rich must go on growing richer precisely in order that the poor may grow less poor.[5]

Others have thought otherwise; and it has been Asia's fate to provide the world's largest testing ground for the rival theses. Seven decades after the *Communist Manifesto*, the revolution it proclaimed had captured its first country, Russia; and thus at one stroke its ideology became the official one for more than a third of Asia's territory. Three decades after the Russian Revolution, the Chinese Revolution had put almost all the rest of continental East Asia under the same banner. Three decades later again, the red flag flew over three of the nine countries of Southeast Asia, making the total of Asians placed on the socialist road to development come close to half of Asia's population, and to more than a quarter of the world's.

In no other age had any continent known an upheaval on such a scale. In little more than an Asian lifetime, a number of people comparable to the whole of humankind a couple of lifetimes earlier had been recruited or impressed into a movement aimed at nothing less than the total overthrow of the existing order of relations between nations and within them. If anything could banish complacency from the theories of history rooted in the origins of the Industrial Revolution, it should be the spectacle of those masses of humanity in twentieth-century Asia erupting out of misery in the midst of all the horrors that accompanied that process.

Asia's message to the world, conveyed through that upheaval, was that there were other voices hitherto unheard in the debate on the world's future, and that now these voices would not wait to be assigned a time to speak. They would command attention by making it impossible for any present agenda to proceed without them. Sooner or later the Asian contribution would have to be considered on its own merits.

It was not to be expected that one lifetime would suffice before this message was fully accepted. In fact, the first effect of the Asian upheaval was to turn the continent into two armed camps—or, rather, to break up and immediately realign the two armed camps of World War II.

In World War II, an imperial coalition led by Germany in Europe and Japan in Asia was crushed by an antifascist alliance that had seen the forces of the Soviet Union and of Communists and Nationalists in China fighting on the same side as the democracies of the West and their dependencies in Asia. Though World War II dwarfed all wars before it in its scale and cost to both victors and vanquished, it was as if it had only cleared the way for confrontation on a still larger scale. The first real global war was no sooner ended than the first global "cold war" began. The elimination of the victors' common enemy, the Axis, came to seem only a temporary diversion from the real trial of strength between the global forces of capitalism and communism.

In the Cold War, Asia was only one of the areas of confrontation. While the fate of Europe hung in the balance, the fate of Asia was of secondary concern to the superpowers. At one period in the 1950s, the confrontation united Russia, Mongolia, continental China, North Korea, and North Vietnam on one side, while all the rest of East, South and Southeast Asia was claimed in the name of an equally solid front representing the "Free World" on the other. The most prominent Asian leader of the period, Mao Tse-tung, said the only thing about the situation that seemed true to all concerned at that time: that there was no third way between what he called revolution and what he called counterrevolution; that political loyalty was entirely a matter of leaning to one side out of two.

But that did not long remain a very complete description of the Asian situation. In the 1950s the appearance of Free World unity dissolved with the rise of the movement of nonalignment (led in Asia by Prime Minister Nehru of India), while the communist bloc also came apart in Asia along the line of the China-Soviet dispute. Asia was a multipolar continent by the time of the new communist conquests in Indochina in 1975. Mao's own country, after Mao, seemed to be taking sides anew with its former enemies, the United States and Japan, and against its former allies, the Soviet Union and Vietnam. All this could not but blur the original postwar line of confrontation, complicating the options even for those who still thought in terms of revolution versus counterrevolution.

What did remain true was that the great question in Asia was still the question of change—not whether there had to be more change, but how much more and how soon and according to what model. The originally imported capitalist and socialist models still loomed large on the Asian scene, but there was a new proliferation of Asian variants.

On the capitalist or free enterprise side, the world market economy continued to sink its roots and extend its reach even within the socialist countries, seeding such economic growth as was compatible with its essential law of profitability: that is, capital-intensive, export-oriented growth, tending to the creation of economic enclaves.

Within Asia, Japan remained the first Asian economic success story: a story of mass prosperity free from gross subjection to foreign control or domestic coercion, but a story that was raising new questions of viability and justifiability even as it answered others.

Taiwan, South Korea, and the countries of the Association of Southeast Asian Nations (ASEAN) were moving at variously accelerated speeds into the same world market, at corresponding prices to their populations in terms of economic dependence, political repression, and enforced deferring of the full sharing of prosperity.

This pattern was still further accentuated in the oil-rich nations of West Asia, which in the 1970s left the rest of the world far behind in rates of income growth. At the same time they left the mass of their populations far behind in income distribution.

On the socialist or centrally planned side, North and Central Asia had a less unbalanced share in the development achievement that made the Soviet Union the world's second richest nation—though national statistics did mask a certain pattern of regional imbalance unfavorable to the Asian quarter of the population.

China, for its part, had been the great Asian laboratory of a distinctively Asian socialism; and the shock waves were all the greater for that, throughout Asia and the world, when much that had been most distinctive about its development approach began to be reversed or called in question after the death of Mao in 1976.

A third major socialist variant was Vietnam. A land with a generation of war behind it, it was still embattled up to the early 1980s, still affirming its separate strength as a communist power in Asia. But the crowning drama in its dramatic history since World War II was the change in the identity of the enemies it was confronting by 1978: after its "imperialist oppressors," France and the United States (eliminated respectively in 1954 and 1975), it had taken on its fellow communist neighbors, China and Kampuchea.

Such was the flux of alignments in Asia after the communist victories in Indochina and after the passing of Mao Tse-tung. It is misleading even to speak of the "capitalist" side and the "socialist" side, unless it is noted that not every country in Asia would accept a single label.

Besides those that are categorical in professing some form of socialism— the Soviet Union, Mongolia, China, North Korea, Vietnam, Kampuchea, Burma—there are several that have borrowed the language of socialism to a greater or lesser degree. The term has appeared at one time or another in national constitutions, as in those of Iraq, Sri Lanka, and Bangladesh.

Among the first countries professing to favor a "mixed" economy, and by far the most notable case (if only because of its size), is the Republic of India. India has been seen by some as the one great test case, on a scale comparable to China's, of whether there is a way out of the poverty trap that might leave more room for individual freedom and a private economic sector than the "democratic centralism" of the communist countries. After five five-year plans India was still an uncertain contender, not least because no other contender had proved decisively less uncertain.[6]

The Asian Christian Background

Christianity among Asian Religions

The continent that has given the world most of its people has also given it most of its traditional cultural heritage, insofar as this is embodied in the great world religions. If we confine ourselves to those religions and quasi-religions whose followers are numbered today in hundreds of millions, it is well known that all of them are Asian in origin. Indeed, of the five cases conventionally cited—Hinduism, Buddhism, Confucianism, Christianity, and Islam—only the last two have any major part of their following outside of Asia.

Herein lies the crux of the problem of the relationship of Christianity to Asia. The other main traditions have less difficulty in establishing their Asian credentials.

The problem is least in the case of Hinduism and Confucianism, each being identified not only with one continent but also with one ethnic ensemble, and almost with one country, India or China. Buddhism has had a wider diffusion both inside and outside Asia, while remaining overwhelmingly an Asian phenomenon. Islam, from its birth in seventh-century Arabia, always remained an Asian religion even as it became a non-Asian one; its followers today are mainly concentrated in a belt crossing northern Africa and southern Asia from Morocco through Indonesia. By comparison with all these, Christianity can make a much more plausible claim to worldwide diffusion throughout every continent except, precisely, the largest one.

If we give credence to Christianity's claim to continuity with the Old Testament tradition, that makes its Asian roots no less deep and ancient than those of any other religion. But the point is hardly significant, since ''Asia'' is an abstraction, its boundaries being ultimately a matter of arbitrary convention. The area called West Asia or the Near or Middle East, which gave the world Judaism, Christianity, and Islam, can just as well be considered (and commonly is considered) a cultural watershed between East and West, or a natural region in its own right between the regions of further Asia, Africa, and Europe, as it can be considered part of a geographical unit called Asia. What matters is that Christianity, unlike Islam, did not spread eastward during its first two millennia on the same scale in which it spread westward.

There was indeed an early eastward expansion of Christianity before and even after the rise of Islam; there was even a period when the future might have gone in that direction rather than in the opposite one. Around the middle of the first millennium, Christianity was finding its earliest important footholds outside the Roman Empire—in a Roman form in the west in Ireland and in a Coptic form in the south in Ethiopia. It was at the same time moving out in a Nestorian form in the East from a foothold in the Persian Empire along the trade routes through central Asia and through the Persian Gulf and the Indian Ocean.

Christianity had reached as far afield as China and Sumatra as early as the seventh century, and had taken root on the Malabar coast of India as early as the fourth century (or even as early as the first century according to the tradition of the Thomas Christians of India). There was a period when the Nestorian Christianity of western and central Asia may well have been

the most flourishing form of Christianity in the world. It was the period of
the Dark Ages in the West; but by the time the Christianity of the West
emerged from its Dark Ages, early in the second millennium, the promise of
Nestorian Christianity was fading.

Islam was the crucial factor in this change of fortunes—first because
Islam dominated the region from its rise in the seventh century, breaking
the links between the Christian populations of Europe and far Asia; but
more because its tolerance towards its Christian minority turned to active
persecution after the crusades. Long before the advance guard of the modern missionary movement reached Asia in the sixteenth century, carried on
the wave of European expansion, the Nestorian heritage in Asia had
vanished from sight everywhere except among the Syrian Christians of Saint
Thomas in India and in its own Mesopotamian homelands.

Herein lies the handicap of Christianity in Asia. Offered to Asia originally in a form untainted by Western dominance, it was eclipsed when
might became right on both sides of the Fertile Crescent. Reduced to a remnant in its oldest homelands in West Asia, given a new lease on life only on
the European spur of the Eurasian landmass, detoured in its expansion
around the west and south of Asia's Muslim shield, Christianity had to
make a new beginning in Asia. And this time it arrived late, a stranger and
in unwelcome company—the company of Western might and dominance.[7]

Christianity had arrived late, of course, in other continents also, and in
the same unwelcome company; but that was to become less an issue in the
other continents in the measure that they became de facto Christian. In Asia
the difference was that even Western dominance failed to make Asian
Christianity a large-scale fait accompli. By the time the quarrel about colonialism was deepening the divisions between the continents, Christianity
had still not become as undeniably Asian as it had become European or
American or Australasian or even African. It could therefore only resign
itself to being held at arm's length in Asia until such time as it might live
down its alien and imperialist image in Asian eyes.

After nearly two millennia, Christianity's net gains in Asia amounted to a
number of footholds on its fringes. It could indeed count certain Asian
achievements that it might prize: its half-hold on Lebanon, surviving as that
did from the earliest centuries; its long roots in one part of India, the single
lasting legacy of its earlier expansion; its mass success in the Philippines, the
single Asian case where a country as a whole was won to Christianity during
its later expansion. It might well cherish these achievements not least because it had no others like them, and because without them its following in
Asia today would be not much more than half its present 140 million. As for
the other half, they have represented national minorities of nowhere more
than a tenth (except possibly in North Asia), tracing their origins back no
farther than the sixteenth century (except in West Asia).

In short, as an Asian religion or as a force of any kind in Asia, Christianity has more than its share of reasons for a certain diffidence.

Numerically, Christianity's strength in Asia is less than a sixth of what would be a representative global share. In a world over 60 percent Asian, Christianity is only 10 percent Asian. At the same time, in a world over 30 percent Christian, Asia is only 5 percent Christian.

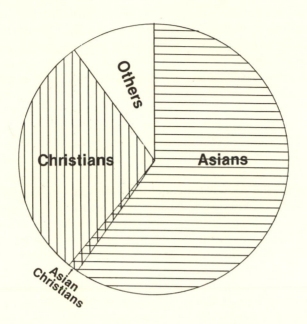

On top of that, Christianity is much more compromised by its colonial background in Asia than in any other continent, even Africa. Though its following in Africa is not very different in absolute terms, it encompasses a much larger share of the continental population and is confident of encompassing an even larger share in the future.

On top of that again, Christianity is overshadowed in Asia more than elsewhere by alternative religions and ideologies having more plausible claims to represent authentically Asian mass movements.

Clearly, on the basis of its Asian strength alone, Christianity in the early 1980s was not equipped to be a major actor on the Asian scene. At the same time, given Christianity's global role, and given the global scale and relevance of Asia's problems, the role of Asian Christianity could not fail to have some special significance for Christianity as a whole, for Asia as a whole, and for the world. It is not in itself a disadvantage for a movement to be the world's most conspicuously transnational religion when the world itself is entering a new transnational era.

Christianity in the Asian Crisis

Any special significance of Asian Christianity, or any special limitations on it, must be sought in its historical background, in its present extra-Asian

connections, and in its geographical location and institutional insertion in
Asia.

The measure of the importance of Christianity in Asia is greater than the
5 percent of the 2.7 billion Asians represented today by its 140 million followers there. There is the fact that Christianity came with the Western con-
queror, except in West Asia. There is the fact that it found its still surviving
footholds in far Asia in close association with Western power, except in
certain pioneering ventures in pre-modern India, in the pre-conquest Mo-
luccas, in pre-conquest Vietnam, in Japan, in Korea, in pre-treaty-port
China. There is the fact that its extra-Asian connections today dwarf those
of every other religious or cultural movement in Asia, and that its access to
Western financial resources had no counterpart among other faiths until oil
revenues in West Asia and North Africa began to show what money could
do for the promotion of Islam. All this has served to give Asian Christianity
a special visibility from which it has not ceased to profit, though at a cost
that in post-colonial times has threatened to outweigh the benefits.

Political decolonization in Asia has now created strong pressure for the
decolonization of Asian Christianity. To this extent Asia's colonial background has become more a liability than an asset. But it has not proved
possible for a Christianity of footholds to stand immediately on its own
feet.

At the most general level of Asian Christian policy, there was once much
talk of "missionary adaptation," and there has more recently been much
talk of "indigenization" or "contextualization." The level of practice is
another matter. In the era of adaptation, the churches in Asia never in fact
managed to be culturally much more than replicas of the parent churches.
Without a change in that pattern, the intercontinental connection in Christianity could only serve to reinforce the North–South dependency relationship, at a time when everyone is at last aware of the need to counteract it.
That need is acknowledged in the present-day acceptance on both sides of
the more radical ecclesial goal of indigenization. Once again, however, it is
one thing to agree that it should be Christian policy to counteract the dependency of the South on the North, but it is another thing to ensure that Christian practice does not in fact still reinforce it.

What has been said above about Christianity in general in the period of
confrontation with Marxism (pp. 13-14) may be applied to Asian Christianity, though of course with appropriate differences.

Given, in particular, the extremely weak and derivative character of
Asian Christianity on the one hand, by contrast with the extremely strong
and dynamic character of Asian communism on the other, it was only to be
expected that the shift in Christian attitudes from "Free World" anticommunism to Third World anticapitalism would take longer in Asia than in
Latin America. At the same time, what had happened in Vatican II, in the
World Council of Churches, and in the Latin American churches in the
1960s and 1970s (pp. 15-16 above) could not but eventually have Asian

Christian repercussions. It could only be a matter of time until Asian Christian spokespersons made their own contribution to the reconsidering of options between conservation and change that was going on all around them in their dual Asian and Christian fields of reference.

These Asian contributions would be localized according to the geographical pattern and the institutional form of the Christian presence. In practice this meant that they would be limited to some of the Asian territories on the fringes facing east and south—Korea, Japan, Hong Kong, the Philippines, Indonesia, Singapore, Indochina (for a time), Thailand, Sri Lanka, and India.

Insofar as state toleration of any social role for the churches was a precondition for such contributions, their chance had passed by 1949 in all of North and Central Asia, and in all of continental East Asia except the tip of the Korean peninsula. The Marxist judgment on the churches was that they had proved incapable of being other than instruments of reaction. Having appeared ineffective against past oppression, they were now to pay for it by being made more captive to the communist political establishments than they had ever been to the capitalist or the feudal ones. In this way social protest was excluded as a practical option for some 5 million Christians in China, and for perhaps over 12 million on the Asian side of the Soviet Union.

In a less absolute manner, social protest was also excluded as a practical option for another 5 million Christians in West Asia and in Muslim South Asia. This was a region of the Muslim world where Christians were about as small a minority, in the region as a whole, as they were in communist Asia as a whole: a minority of perhaps 2 percent. (The one exceptional case is that of Lebanon, where more than half of the 3 million people have been credited to Christianity. In the 1970s, these Christians, by an oversimplification with a factual basis, were cast in the role of reactionaries against the social radicalism of the Muslim half.)

There remained the rest of South Asia, exclusive of the Himalayan states; the countries of Southeast Asia, exclusive of Burma and Malaysia; and the rest of East Asia, exclusive of Taiwan. The exclusions were cases where Buddhism and/or Hinduism, socialism, Islam, and anticommunism, respectively, were in various degrees effectively intolerant of any critical social role for Christianity.

It will be seen that the exclusions are the most conspicuous thing about the social role of Asian Christianity. The effect of these inhibiting pressures of communism or anticommunism, of Islam or another of the prevailing religions, was to make Christian social protest a fairly total irrelevance for more than four-fifths of Asia's territory, for more than half of Asia's people, and for about one-fifth of Asia's Christians. When we speak of Asian Christian social protest, we are speaking of a phenomenon essentially restricted (and duly chastened by its restriction) to a minority within a minority—a Christian minority drawn from some 100 million Christians, among an Asian minority drawn from some 1.1 billion Asians, concentrated on less than a fifth of Asia's territory forming a crescent on its southern and eastern sides.

Among the states in that crescent of Asia where at least a limited possibility existed for Christian social protest at the outset of the 1970s, the Christian proportion of the national population was not nearly as low as it was in the rest of Asia, except in Thailand, Laos, and Kampuchea, where it was 1 percent or less, and in Japan, where it was less than 2 percent by official count and more than 3 percent according to censuses and surveys. Even in giant India, with its overwhelming Hindu majority, 27 million Christians representing 4 percent of the population retained in 1980 a precarious freedom of action. In the other countries in question, apart from the Philippines, Christianity represented a less minuscule minority, ranging upwards from about 7 percent to about 15 percent of the population in Vietnam, Sri Lanka, Singapore, Hong Kong, and Indonesia, more or less in that order, and to perhaps over 20 percent in South Korea. In terms of absolute numbers, the most substantial of these Christian minorities around 1980 were the 17 million Christians of Indonesia, the 11 million of South Korea, and the 4 million of Vietnam. These were in turn dwarfed in numbers by the nearly 50 million Christians of the Philippines, the one country in Asia where Christianity dominated the religious field.[8]

Our direct concern, therefore, will be with the countries of this Asian crescent. It is these that we must observe at closer range, though never to the exclusion of the others. We are not free to forget the rest of Asia when we focus on the areas of more significant Christian presence, any more than we are free to forget the rest of the world when we focus on Asia. We are faced everywhere with the fact of interdependence.

There are implications for history in the very unevenness of the Christian presence in Asia—in the fact that, to begin with, Christianity represents only 5 percent of Asia's population while representing about three-quarters of the rest of humankind; in the further fact that Christianity is proportionally even weaker in Asia's and the world's two largest national populations, those of China (less than 1 percent Christian) and of India (less than 4 percent Christian), and also in Asia's most economically advanced nation, Japan.

To be still more specific, there are implications in the fact that after two Christian millennia there was less than a 1 percent overlap of the most numerous single race on earth, the Chinese, and the most numerous body of believers, the Christians. If one may suppose that things could be notably different after three Christian millennia, it follows that only provisional generalizations can be made at present as to what constitutes the characteristic features of these two groups. What we have seen so far may represent only a larval stage, relatively speaking, in the evolution of the historical identities of the Christians or of the Chinese. And for all we know the same might need to be said of the Indians, the Russians, or the Japanese. The changes all these peoples have undergone in the twentieth century alone could hardly have been imagined in any previous century.

Christianity in the Asian National Security States

We are not free to forget the rest of Asia for another reason—that is, not only because it may interact differently with the Christian element in Asia tomorrow, but also because its shadow falls darkly over even the strongest redoubts of Asian Christianity today. Blurred though time has made it, the line of confrontation in Asia between the partisans and the enemies of revolution still underlies all the lines of proliferation. Without a sense of apocalyptic crisis, of "a life-and-death struggle on which the fate of the whole world depends" (to use a Chinese Cultural Revolution way of putting it), Asian history could not have been the same on either side of the line in the generation after World War II.

Nothing looms larger in that stretch of history, after the rise of the People's Republic of China, than the Korean War and the Vietnam War. They are a measure of the hardening of positions on both sides, which in turn gave substance to the charges exchanged—charges of blind intransigence, of mass hysteria, of totalitarian terror. On the communist side, the sense of siege was intensified by the break between the Soviet Union and China in the 1960s; this helped to give the Chinese Cultural Revolution its singular virulence. On the other side, the sense of siege was intensified by the ebbing of the American military presence in Asia in the 1970s; this accelerated the process by which, after Taiwan in 1949, South Korea in 1961, and Indonesia in 1965, one state after another in Asia suspended one or other or all of the forms of democracy.

This last trend of events has come to be spoken of as the rise of the national security state. As befits a phenomenon overtly related to "the threat of communism," there is nothing peculiarly Asian about it. It has been not without its effects even within the Western democracies, notably in the United States during the period of the McCarthy campaign against "Communist infiltration," and in the West Germany of the "*berufsverbot*" or security screening of state employees. But the conditions that best suited its development were found only in the Third World, where government was still traditionally the preserve of the powerful, and where democratic ideas were not yet deeply rooted.

In the Third World, restrictions that would be intolerable to Western democratic instinct gained Western acquiescence, or connivance, or protection, or even instigation as the lesser evil, for countries supposed to be vulnerable to communist influence.

So it was that Latin America—a continent that had known one Marxist government that lasted (in Cuba from 1961) and one that was forcibly overthrown after three years (in Chile in 1973)—became the continent most systematically submitted to the ideology of national security.

So it was also that the United States responded to the communist challenge in Asia—by arming Chiang Kai-shek in Taiwan, Syngman Rhee and Park Chung Hee in South Korea, Suharto in Indonesia, and a series of similar strongmen in South Vietnam, Laos, Cambodia, and Thailand.

So it was, finally, that when it became U.S. policy from 1969 to phase out U.S. troop involvement on the Asian mainland, the power vacuum quickly began to be filled by regimes armed with new emergency powers in the Philippines, in South Korea, in Thailand, and also, under the further stimulus of other local crises, in Pakistan, Malaysia, Sri Lanka, Singapore, and Bangladesh. By mid-1975, when India entered a period of emergency rule (terminated by elections in 1977), the only fully functioning democracy left in Asia was Japan.

This trend of events confronted the churches with the spectacle of "free world" alternatives to communism that had come to look more and more like mirror images of the tyranny they claimed to oppose. Thanks largely to their confrontation with communism, the churches were already in the business of denouncing political repression. Now they were faced with the fact that the repression they felt called on to denounce might be found as well on the right as on the left. They were still accustomed to the assumption that the preponderant threat to society lay more on the left than on the right. But the way was now open to call even that into question.

As it happened, reasons for such a calling into question were not far away. Besides the overt justification for "free world" restrictions on freedom (that is, "the communist menace"), examination showed other functions, less easily avowable, that were being served by the emergency regimes.

In an earlier stage of the relations between the industrialized and other nations, finished goods were traded for raw materials in a pattern of exchange that gave an entrepreneurial minority in the preindustrialized countries a vested interest in becoming those countries' new power elites. In a later stage of these relations, within the framework of the transnational corporations, it was found more profitable to transfer the simpler forms of industrial production to the preindustrial countries. The pattern thus created was one of industrialized enclaves based on cheap labor and relatively primitive working conditions, whose maintenance became a shared vested interest for the transnational corporate head offices and for the branch countries' new elites.

To the extent that this system could not be shown to benefit more than a minority, its continued functioning required coercion of the majority. Hence the new line of confrontation that was becoming more manifest in the 1970s in the southern and eastern countries of Asia—between a modernizing minority on one side, whose interests lay more and more in the world market, and a marginalized majority on the other, who now needed the persuasion of the police and the army to keep them cooperative as long as their marginalization was to last.

As long as their marginalization was to last? Was there, then, a fair prospect that it would not last indefinitely? Did the capitalist horn of plenty have plenty still in store for everyone? Or could it promise at best to bring prosperity eventually to the *majority* in the poor world, as it had brought prosperity to the majority in the West and in Japan?

Or was the latter achievement bought strictly at the price of leaving a poor majority in the world as a whole? Or were capitalism's recurring crises—and especially its mid-1970s crisis, touched off when a part of the poor world learned to play the capitalist game by charging what the market would bear for oil—sufficiently damaging to the performance and promise of capitalism to make the socialist alternative take on a newly competitive appeal? Or was the socialist alternative itself too compromised, first by the legacy of Stalinism in Russia and elsewhere, then by the disconcerting swings of the Chinese ideological pendulum, then again by the degeneration of international relations within Asian socialism into international wars?

Or, if these questions admitted of no easy or immediate answers, what in the meantime was the responsibility of Christians in Asia, confronted with (or rather, immersed in) the ordeal of Asia's two thousand million poor?

Such were the questions that confronted the Asian churches as they proceeded in the 1970s to take their own part in the worldwide Christian reconsideration of options between social stability and social change.

3

THE COLONIAL ANTECEDENTS

Attitudes toward change among Asian Christians have obviously shifted in some way along with those of other Asians and other Christians. Asian Christians could not have stood entirely apart from the ferment that has affected the rest of the world. What we need to examine at closer range is the particular kind and degree of shift that is observable in Asian Christian attitudes, as compared with the change observable in its Asian and in its Christian fields of reference, and as compared with its own point of departure.

More must be said first about this point of departure. To know something of the setting of Asian Christianity is not necessarily to know much about Asian Christianity itself. We are given an idea of what to expect from it, by way of its response to the crisis of change in the 1970s, when we examine the wider Asian and the wider Christian context of that crisis. But within the limits set by that complex of contexts, we still have to ask what is there that has been particularly distinctive about Asian Christianity and that might give us some further idea of what to expect from it. We must then examine more particularly some precedents and counter-precedents for a critical social role for Christianity in Asia, before seeking to identify any new turning points in its experience in the 1970s.

Some Features of Asian Christianity as It Has Been

We have seen how much the geographical pattern of Christian distribution in Asia differs from the pattern of population distribution. In more intrinsic ways also, the profile of Asian Christianity is something other than a miniature of the profile of Asia as a whole. As its history has led us to expect, Asian Christianity counts among its adherents a larger-than-typical minority of Europeans and Eurasians, a higher-than-typical level of education, a larger representation in the cities and towns than in the country, and a larger representation among some ethnic minorities than among most national majority races such as the Han, the Hindi-speaking, the Javanese, the Thai, the Burmese, the Malays, and the Taiwanese.[1]

A Double-Edged Marginality

It would be a fair enough conclusion from all this to say that Asian Christianity is marginal to Asia in many ways. However, it should also be clear that it is not always marginal in ways that detract from its potential. In level of education and degree of urbanization, for example, it is untypical in ways that put it on the cutting edge of modernization.

There are two sides to the urban bias of Asian Christianity, as indeed there are two sides to the urbanization process itself. The facts of the case are clear-cut enough: in Asia, the countryside is still where the people are, generally in a measure of over 70 percent of the total population; the city or town is where the Christians are concentrated.[2] Therein lies a particular weakness of the Church in Asia, inasmuch as it is not where the people are today. Therein also lies a particular opportunity of the Church in Asia, inasmuch as it is where the people are likely to be tomorrow.

In Asia it is certainly too soon to discount the importance of the peasant. If the Chinese revolution is any indication, the West has learned from the East (and Marxism has learned from Maoism) that sometimes the levers of history can lie in the countryside. If the wars of Indochina had proved anything by 1975, it was that superpower force and skill can avail nothing against peasant determination and endurance. The mere fact that people in Asia are still mostly peasants should be reason enough for peasants to get priority in movements like Christianity, which claims to give priority to people, regardless of their degree of importance in global politics.

However, if Christianity ever lives up to that claim in Asia, it will perhaps be less because it has taken deeper root among the peasants in the country than because the peasants have uprooted themselves from the countryside. For the fact is that the world as a whole is on its way to town, under capitalism and under socialism alike. The world's urban population is nearly 80 percent in the industrialized market economies, and nearly 60 percent in the centrally planned economies outside the Third World. Even the Third World is on its way to town, though starting from far away from it. Indeed the pathological pace of its urbanization is one of the most conspicuous symptoms of its mal-developing condition.

Is the urbanization process reversible? There are those who believe that the telecommunications revolution will reverse it; but such a source of relief will surely not be effective in Asia very soon. In Asia recourse has been had to some forceful government efforts at dispersal of population—in the Soviet Union, in China, in Indonesia. The effect has scarcely anywhere been on the scale of the problem. In any case, since it has been shown that less than 5 percent of a population is needed to produce its food, there is no long-term prospect of a real return to the land.

The situation, then, is that the average Asian is on his or her way to town, with the average Asian Christian a bit ahead. In another respect, however, closely related in its implications, Asian Christianity is still where the rich world was yesterday and where the poor world remains today. In the industrialized countries, including the centrally planned ones, only a shrinking minority live by farming; moreover, only a minority are by any definition young. In Asia as a whole, however, the peasant-born majority must remain a majority at least for this generation, since the bulge in its population structure has not yet moved up beyond the earliest decades.

In other words, as if it were not enough for Asia to be producing more than its share of the world's job seekers, it is doomed to increase their numbers at perhaps twice the rate of the West for at least the rest of this century.

A Politically-Patterned Conflict of Creeds

A minority of 5 percent in Asia as a whole; a minority of about 9 percent on the southern and eastern fringes of Asia; a minority of some 15 percent on the fringes exclusive of India (though of only 6 percent on the fringes exclusive of the Philippines); a minority distinctively tinged with Western ways, distinctively rarer in the countryside than in the towns and cities, distinctively marginal ethnically as well as numerically and geographically, and distinctively youthful by comparison with Western Christians, though not by comparison with other Asians—these are some characteristics of Asian Christianity that keep that term from being a mere abstraction.

And here is another. If the average Asian Christian is marginal in ways not common to Christians of other continents, and young and poor and trapped in poverty in ways shared at least with two other continents, she or he has inherited one more characteristic shared by all Christians everywhere: the characteristic of being more or less grievously at odds with half or more of all the other Christians in the world.

The two main historic splits in European Christianity—between East and West in the eleventh century, between North and South in the sixteenth—have had the effect that twentieth-century Christians have generally identified themselves not as Christians but as particular kinds of Christians: as Catholics, in a global proportion of about 56 percent; as Protestants or Anglicans, in a proportion of about 33 percent; as Oriental (mainly Orthodox) Christians, in a proportion of about 11 percent.

This pattern has been reproduced in Asia, with about the same proportion of Oriental Christians (mainly in Soviet Asia, India, Lebanon, and Syria), and with a smaller proportion of Catholics (about 50 percent), who constitute nearly 90 percent of all Christians in the Philippines and Vietnam alone. These two countries together contribute about two-thirds of the 70 million Catholics in Asia. The countries of Protestant strength are chiefly Indonesia and South Korea, where Christianity is about 75 percent Protestant and where about half of Asia's 50 million Protestants are concentrated. For the bulk of the remainder of the Protestants, one must look to India, the Philippines, Japan, and Taiwan. (Here and elsewhere, if only three categories of Christians are distinguished, we count as Protestants all those not categorized as Catholics or Orientals.)

Thus has Asia inherited the family quarrels of Christendom along with much else that has come to be thought of as more Western than Christian. Political power rather than theological reflection determined that Catholicism would have a head start in the ex-colonies of Spain, France, and Portugal; that Protestantism would prevail over Catholicism in the Indonesian archipelago when the Dutch superseded the Portuguese there; and that Christianity would take a mainly Orthodox form where the Russian flag flew across Siberia.

To be sure, the pattern of Christian belonging did not follow the flag with equal predictability everywhere. There were other factors. It could happen that an Asian colony remained beyond the immediate reach of any Western flag. Such was the case of Korea, whose colonial masters were Asian instead of European. Or it could happen that the colonial power itself ceased to attach political importance to religious belonging. Such was the case in British South Asia in the nineteenth century.

Wherever modern Christianity entered Asia without having overriding political power behind it, perhaps the next most decisive single factor for its fortunes and forms was the presence or absence of powerful opposition. In all of monsoon Asia, where this opposition existed, it was held in check by the colonial power to a sufficient extent to enable Christianity to put down roots, survive independence, and generally prosper as much or as little afterwards as before. Opposition existed also in the case of Korea; but its effect there was counterbalanced by the exceptional revolutionary role played by Protestants, including Protestant missionaries, in the anticolonial struggle.

Korea was the Asian country where Christianity was least associated with Western imperialism. It was also the Asian country where Christianity was most associated (certainly in its Protestant form) with the nationalist struggle against a colonial power (in this case Japan). It thus provided one of those rare cases in Asian history in which nationalism worked in favor of Christianity rather than against it. For it was in Korea, to a greater extent than in any other Asian country, that Christianity (again mainly in its Protestant form) gained a share of public influence out of all proportion to its share in the national population.[3]

A Beginning of Ecumenical Convergence

As the age of colonialism was coming to an end, the age of ecumenism was being inaugurated. Having bequeathed its denominational divisions to Asia, Western Christianity began to put its own house in order even as it was ceasing to have full control over anyone else's.

Ecumenism was partly a lesson learned in missionary lands. Since it was as novel for the parent churches as for their offspring, the latter were enabled to contribute to it on a less unequal footing. Most of the early national unions of Protestant denominations took place in Asia—in China in

1927, in the Philippines in 1929, in Siam in 1934, in Japan in 1941. The formation in 1947 of the Church of South India, a more far-reaching ecumenical venture, was a milestone for all non-Roman churches on all continents. The formation in 1959 of the East Asia Christian Conference (renamed the Christian Conference of Asia in 1973) gave the non-Roman Christian world another lead from Asia, this time on a continental scale, in the task of bringing Christians together.

The EACC/CCA idea did not long remain the novelty it was in 1959. Another continent took a similar path when the All Africa Conference of Churches was formed in 1963. The other half of Asia's Christians were put on a parallel path when the Federation of Asian Bishops' Conferences (FABC) was formalized in 1972. The lead the FABC was following had been given by the Catholic hierarchies of Latin America in the formation of CELAM in 1955.[4]

A parallel path? At the point of departure of this path in 1972, the isolation of the Catholic Church and the Protestant churches from each other in Asia was about as complete as it could well be twenty-four years after the formation of the World Council of Churches and seven years after the close of Vatican II. It was not to be long, however, before the paths of the CCA and FABC showed some signs of converging.

The state of official relations did not always reflect exactly the state of relations at the grassroots: these conditions could vary well beyond the current officially approved range of firmness and flexibility. The impetus for change came not so much from ecumenical negotiations between Christian bodies as from the pressure of forces from the larger society. And what force could have exercised greater pressure than that which overshadowed all others in the later decades of the twentieth century—the force of the movements for social change?

Here we touch a reality whose implications have yet to be fully assimilated. Even in its internal relations, even in its self-understanding, Asian Christianity was to be profoundly affected by its immersion in Asia's struggle for self-realization. Ecumenical barriers that seemed impervious to direct penetration often seemed to be simply left behind for those Catholics and Protestants who found themselves side by side on the social front.

People with such experience might be pardoned for feeling that direct efforts at self-understanding on the part of the churches had created more problems than they solved. The assumption that many Christians were led to act on, rightly or wrongly, consciously or otherwise, was that the true role of the Church, the role in which it could both be itself and understand the world, lay much more than had previously been thought in turning outwards to the world, and much less in turning inwards upon itself.

Some Precedents and Counter-Precedents for a Critical Social Role

In the matter of social attitudes the background of Asian Christians is as varied as is their national and denominational background, within the limits

of what is common in the Constantinian heritage. To consider what Asian
Christians have brought with them to the social confrontations of the 1970s
will require taking some account, in the general context of the social role of
religion in Asia, of the social attitudes rooted in the Catholic and the Protestant experience in the West and in Asia.

The Social Role of Religion in Asia

Understood in [a] realistic and comprehensive sense, religion usually acts
as a tremendous force for social inertia. The writer knows of no instance
in present-day South Asia where religion has induced social change.

The writer was Gunnar Myrdal. The judgment was set down in the period
from 1960 to 1967, the period of the drafting of *Asian Drama*. The statement introduces a section on "the role of religion" (p. 103) under the
broader heading "the wider field of valuations" in the general introduction
in Volume I.

It has the merit of giving us a clear-cut point of departure. On the face of
it, it is a devastating judgment on the social role of religion in Asia.
Whether it is ultimately justified or not, it cannot be dismissed as ill-
informed or ill-considered. On the contrary, it would be hard to think of a
more obviously appropriate source of judgment on such a question than
this classic survey of the problem of socioeconomic change in Asia in the
period immediately prior to the decade that concerns us. If it is not a true
judgment, the question is nevertheless posed as to how it came to appear
true to one of the most careful investigators of the broader theme.

Myrdal himself makes it clear that the judgment is not made on religion
as such. As he puts it (p. 105), "no religion on the 'higher' level need be in
conflict with the modernization ideals." Without going as far as that in
open-mindedness on the subject, even those theories of society that expect
least from religion would have recognized the antecedent possibility that in
one context or another religion might be a force for social change, or at
least an agent of social protest, rather than a force for legitimation and
reinforcement of the social status quo. Marx was explicitly allowing for that
possibility when, in the same passage in which he called religion "the opium
of the people," he also called it "the sigh of the oppressed creature."[5]

Is Myrdal, then, telling us not to expect to find in Asia even the minimal
degree of religious influence for change that might be expected on the most
negative hypothesis? On the face of it, that seems to be the general implication. Research on the broader background of religion and social protest in
Asia is sufficiently scarce to leave room for a range of opinion on the point.
However, a survey of religion and "pre-capitalist modes of production"
does find material for inquiry on religious movements of social protest in
some of the main religious traditions.[6]

As it happens, the findings here are also fairly consistently negative. Historic Hinduism is seen as the legitimizing ideology of the archetypal caste

system. Historic Buddhism, in whatever form, is found incapable of providing a basis for social protest. Contestation in general is seen as having gained religious sanction, as a rule, only in an elitist or an ineffective popular millenarian form.

The one significant exception identified in this analysis (a professedly Marxist analysis) is the case of Judaism (and, by implication, the Judaeo-Christian tradition in general). For reasons that are explained in terms of history, this tradition is seen as having a unique prophetic strand strong enough to bear the weight of a genuine movement of social protest.[7]

These findings are defined as applying more properly to religion in *precolonial* Asia. What has been the effect on the social role of religion in Asia, of the experience of colonialism and nationalism, of capitalism and socialism? It has been a disruptive effect, though not in the same way in each case.

What is perhaps best known to the world at large is how the colonialist-nationalist struggle has injected a new political dimension into the Asian religions, dramatized in Buddhism in phenomena like the self-immolations of monks and nuns in embattled South Vietnam, and in Islam in the resurgence of Muslim fundamentalism, one of whose most sensational feats was the 1979 toppling of the Shah of Iran. In fact one could speak of a "new face of Buddha"[8] in countries of Theravada and Mahayana, and for that matter of a new face of Islam in both Sunnite and Shiite lands.

What concerns us here is whether there has been anything that could be called a transformation of the social role of religion in the direction of making it something more than the "tremendous force for social inertia" of which Myrdal wrote. It does not appear that the evidence on this has been persuasive to those who have examined the ferment in the main Asian religions with a critical eye from the outside.

Hinduism, Buddhism, Islam, Confucianism, Shinto—all can be cited in particular circumstances as having been effective as vehicles of *nationalism*. But only Islam and Buddhism have lent themselves significantly to the rhetoric of *socialism*, and in both cases the shift in preaching has been more noticeable than any shift in practice.

Thus, Holmes Welch, a Buddhist and an authority on Buddhism in China, while strongly discounting assertions of decline in Chinese Buddhism in late traditional China, is rather inclined to believe the worst about Buddhism under Mao, both as to the credibility of its conversion to socialism and as to its hopes of a socialist future.[9]

Similarly, Maxime Rodinson, a Marxist who writes with some authority on Islam, has this to say on what he calls its "inconclusive correlation" with "any particular economic system":

> In India, it is true that the Hindus threw themselves with more ardor and earlier than the Muslims into the adventure of capitalism, as in Europe the Protestants before the Catholics. But it was not religious precepts in

the pure state that were involved here. . . . God and the gods, rules for living, sacred or semi-sacred moralities, all in turn bow down and in the end prostrate themselves before triumphant Mammon.[10]

As observations on the social role of religion in Asia, the above are not necessarily either definitive in themselves or representative for Christianity, precisely inasmuch as it has been so marginal to the Asian mainstream. They do serve, however, to put us on guard against any easy assumption that the Asian Christian experience would not be open to similar criticism. If it is to be shown that the Christian God in Asia does not "bow before Mammon," there is a weight of evidence to be confronted for which another sentence of Rodinson (otherwise far from being the most doctrinaire of Marxists) may serve as a summary:

What is most likely is that, once again, the religious authorities will follow the movement of society, and will supply their governments with ideological justifications in strict conformity with the requirements of the economic policy these governments will have chosen.[11]

The Critical Dimension in Catholicism

In one sense, the last thing that medieval Catholicism could be accused of was forgetfulness that God judges all human systems. Even its involvement in temporal affairs was its way of affirming the kingship of Christ over the whole of creation. It was this critical principle that made a pope humiliate an emperor at Canossa, a bishop challenge a king in the person of Thomas Becket, a laywoman defy a political-ecclesiastical alliance in the trial of Joan of Arc.

Even where the roles of Church and State were most comfortably concerted (and in Catholicism the accommodation to the secular power did not generally go as far as it did in the Church-State relations of the Orthodox churches), there was always an assumption of accountability before a higher power. Even where the Church seemed to serve for little more than blessing the swords of the conquistadors, it always represented at least a feeble reminder to these latter that they could never be entirely a law unto themselves. Such work as was done for social amelioration, in Europe and in Asia, was mostly done within the limits of implicit acceptance of the prevailing European or Asian temporal order.

In another sense, of course, it can be said that the medieval Catholic confidence in the redemption of the temporal order led directly to the imprisonment of the Church in a particular temporal order, one from which the Reformation later fought to set it free. Historically the Reformation was the largest-scale demonstration that an ultimately irrepressible dimension in the Church had been repressed to a point where restoration of the balance had to take an explosive form.

In the short run, this explosion could only have the effect of walling what was left of the old Church behind even more unyielding institutional ramparts. The habits of power, and of partnership or rivalry with power, remained the most natural reflexes of the missionary extensions of the Catholic Church, as long as the existing political power had a place for such partnership or rivalry. As a whole, the institutional Church proved no exception to the rule that power is never given up freely, but only yielded under pressure of *force majeure*.

In 1511, the Portuguese admiral Albuquerque, who was the founder of the Portuguese empire in Asia, struck the keynote for most of the modern missionary movement when he said:

> As the King of Malacca . . . makes no endeavor to negotiate with us, . . .
> Our Lord is blinding his judgment and hardening his heart, and desires
> the completion of this affair of Malacca.[12]

Four centuries later, in 1898, the same keynote was still being struck in the very last days of the Spanish empire in Asia, in the words of the representatives of the main Spanish religious orders in the Philippines, which had been the most effective agencies of religious and political control in that colony. In a memorial addressed to the colonial minister in Madrid, these representatives made their last stand in the name of "the just and benevolent, and Catholic and Spanish regime," affirming it as their obligation "to watch over Spanish interests, which are not at variance, but perfectly amalgamated, with religious interests," and on these grounds demanding the crushing of sedition by unrelenting refusal of the freedoms denounced in the papal Syllabus of Errors of 1864.[13]

Was this the best that could be hoped for from medieval or Counter-Reformation Catholicism by way of a critical attitude to a social or political status quo? Even if it were, perhaps the mere fact of its arrogating to itself the role of an independent guide to the uses of state power planted a creative tension at the heart of Western civilization that played a part in the dynamism of the West at a time when the Muslim and the Chinese civilizations seemed to have passed their prime.

But there had to be something more than a parallel power structure in a form of Christianity that had a place for Old Testament prophets as well as kings and for New Testament saints and sages as well as political prelates. There was in fact more even to a pope like Hildebrand (the pope of Canossa), to a bishop like Becket, and certainly to a phenomenon like Joan of Arc than could be accounted for simply in terms of political Catholicism.

The prophetic dimension in historical Catholicism, inhibited in hierarchical structures, found its main institutional outlet in the religious orders and congregations. Like Chrysostom in fourth-century Asia, Las Casas in sixteenth-century America could thunder against abuses of power more freely outside the hierarchy than inside. When the friar-missionaries reached Asia, the tradition of championing the oppressed returned to Asia with them. It remained with them as long as their identity was not entirely bound up with that "perfect amalgamation" of "religion and the fatherland" of which the friar memorial was to speak. In the early years, the role of the "voice of the voiceless" could be played as well by Bishop Salazar of Manila in the Asian part of the "Indies" as by Las Casas in the American part.

Much more diffuse was the paternalistic social concern expressed in the kind of missionary community building that sought, rather generally throughout the Spanish empire, to make the missionary Church the exclusive screen and filter between the imperial power and the native populations. This took its extreme form in the Jesuit reductions of Paraguay. This too could be called a form of social protest; but in practice, while it combatted exploitation, it only reinforced dependency.

Would something similar need to be said about the most diffuse institutional influence of all the churches in all the empires—that of their educational institutions?

Within the Spanish system, the only protests these institutions could utter against the ills of society were those that were part of the official policy of the Royal Patronage. Within all the colonial regimes, colonial control tended to keep them forcibly within the limits of colonial policy. Where they existed beyond the limits of direct colonial control, as in China, Japan, Korea, Siam/Thailand, and Iran, they were limited by national policies of their host governments without being altogether free from state influence from home countries.

Under post-colonial regimes, church school systems had to pay the price of having conspicuously too great a potential, whether as thorns in the side or as tools in the hand of the powers that be, to be left to their own devices by these powers. Where they were not simply nationalized, the threat of nationalization or of crippling taxation could normally be counted on to neutralize them as possible threats to the existing balance of social forces.

In general, then, Catholic school systems in missionary lands fell into the pattern that eventually brought a radical criticism of the whole school system to the point of finding the only hope of social salvation in the "deschooling" of society.[14] A similiar pattern could be found in Catholic medical services and communications media—in short, in all those areas where Catholic institutional influence was particularly effective. It was precisely their institutional prominence, set in sharper relief by their top-heavy structures of authority, that exposed them to the possibility of being coopted as agents of social consolidation and control.

The Protesting Tradition in Protestantism

It might be thought that the "protesting" principle in Protestantism would make for a substantial break with the Constantinian heritage. But we have already noted the role of the Calvinist tradition in the evolution of capitalism; it is also well known that all the mainstream traditions of Protestantism have in some ways lent themselves even more than the Catholic Church to an accommodation with the powers that be in state and society. Historically, it can now be seen that there was both loss and gain for Christian freedom in the repudiation of a supranational center of religious authority—loss of the check it could provide on national political power and local narrowness generally, and gain in terms of relief from abuse of the supranational power itself.

It might still be thought that Protestantism would prove more fertile in protest than Catholicism, in virtue of its capacity for producing, or provoking into existence, a constant stream of new sects rejecting ties with all established institutions, Protestant or Catholic, ecclesiastical or political. Again history has unfolded a pattern not quite predictable on the basis of any simple theory. As noted earlier (p. 10), in practice it is not enough for a movement to be marginal to a society in order to be more a force for social change than a force for social inertia. On the contrary, a movement that opts out of social and political concern tends quite naturally to reinforce the social or political status quo.

It is not by accident that the two words conventionally combined to describe some of these "reformations within the Reformation" are the words *conservative* and *evangelical*. The words describe accurately, even in ways that were hardly intended, the tendency shown by most movements that have sought to bypass human tradition in order to link up directly with what is taken to be the word of God. Unless these movements find motivation for social radicalism in the gospel message they affirm, their professed unconcern with institutional forms and forces turns out to be the surest prescription for the most rigid and reactionary kind of institutionalization.

It has been argued that this historical link between biblical fundamentalism and sociopolitical conservatism is a historical accident, and that its "great reversal" of the radicalism of the gospel, which admittedly occurred in the evangelical movement in the course of the last hundred years, could be reversed in its turn.[15] Certainly that stream of world Christianity conventionally called "evangelical" has not managed to remain unaffected by the later twentieth-century pressures for greater Christian recognition of social concern. It has, however, offered greater resistance to these pressures—a resistance that has tended to range its more fundamentalist representatives among the most categorical supporters of right-wing regimes.

Occasionally, as in Chile and South Korea in the 1970s, manifestos to this effect have complicated matters still further by identifying their stand as *the* Christian stand. Such claims do not bear close investigation. As a rule, these fundamentalist church groupings, even when they represent a majority in the list of churches in a country, represent only a minority of the Christians there, and are not represented at all in the national or international ecumenical network.

The Social Gospel in Colonial Asia

It is clear that all the main historical forms of Christianity, whether they found their point of reference in Rome or Constantinople or Moscow or Geneva or Canterbury, were unfavorably preconditioned in regard to any critical social role in the missionary world. But what has been said about the survival of a critical dimension in Catholicism and a protesting tradition in Protestantism does not exhaust the record of precedents provided in pre-1960s Asia for a critical social role for Asian Christianity. The most obvious precedents predating the Latin American contribution come from the very muted influence of a socially conscious Catholicism arising out of post-Revolution France and the post-Risorgimento papacy, and from the much more tangible influence of "the social gospel" in Anglo-Saxon Protestantism.

In the eighteenth century the Enlightenment had polarized Protestantism between a pietist instinct to turn inward and let the world pass by, and a rationalist instinct to seize the leadership of modernizing change. The latter tendency had an ambivalence of its own. An earlier form of it had produced the Puritan accommodation to capitalism; and now a post-Darwin, post-Wellhausen, post-Marx form of it produced, via Ritschl, Harnack, Troeltsch, and interpreters like Kingsley in England and Rauschenbusch in America, a new enthusiasm for Christian socialism and the social gospel. A Roman Catholic counterpart of the same modernizing tendency was driven underground by Pope Pius X in 1907, and kept there by his successors until 1962.

In Protestant preaching, the gospel in Asia on the whole had a pietist accent in the nineteenth century and a rationalist accent in the early twentieth.

The pietist, fundamentalist strain was not without drastic social effects. It could be the bearer of nationalism, as in Korea,[16] of an evangelical work ethic, as in Iran,[17] or even of a genuine social revolution, as in the Taiping rebellion in mid–nineteenth-century China.[18] It has never been sufficiently marvelled at that a fundamentalist form of Christianity has been the professed ideology of that largest of social upheavals in Asia before the twentieth century. Had it achieved its aims, not only China and Chinese Christianity, but Christianity in general and the world in general, would wear a very different face today. Protestant China today might have far outweighed even Catholic Latin America in the world scales of Christianity. Up to half the world might have been aligned with a truly multiracial and intercontinental Christianity. No more than a fraction of the other half, and presumably no more than a negligible fraction of the Asian half outside the Soviet Union, might have been aligned with atheistic socialism.

The reason all this is not marvelled at, of course, is that the final defeat of Taiping Christianity was so overwhelming as to ensure that the next Chinese revolution would seek a different inspiration, and even to ensure that the next wave of Protestant missionaries would have little temptation to look back to its example. In China, moreover, even more spectacular auguries of success attended the shift in Protestant missionary emphasis from fundamentalism to what one of its historians calls modernism. Protestant fundamentalism could claim the Hungs, the leaders of a great if abortive rebellion; but Protestant modernism could claim Sun Yat-sen and Chiang Kai-shek, two of the three chief father figures acknowledged in one or both of the Chinas to this day.[19]

In the end the Christianity in Sun Yat-sen's legacy was repudiated by his communist heirs, and that of Chiang Kai-shek's was banished with him to Taiwan in 1948, where its appeal remained quite limited. But in the Nanking decade up to 1937, when Chiang's writ ran on the mainland without major challenge from the communists or the Japanese, much had been hoped for from the modernizing influence of the Christian colleges, from the Mass Education movement of the YMCA, and from the rural reconstruction pursued with Chiang's blessing by Y. C. Yen.

Given the odds against it in China—in particular, given the fact that relative normalcy ended in 1937 there, as the Japanese moved in force to take over the whole country—it seems fair to say that the social gospel never got a real chance in China to show what it could do. In Meiji Japan it got a better chance, and for a time enjoyed a rosy promise. Perhaps nowhere else in Asian Christian history can we find a movement that bears closer comparison than Meiji Christian socialism does with the Christian social protest of today.

It is not as if the odds against Christian socialism in Japan were not also overwhelming. A century ago, when the movement began, Christianity in Japan looked even more like a drop in the ocean than it does today.[20] Even among its .2 percent of the population in the 1880s, the vast majority of the people, including the pietist Protestants and the new and old kinds of Catholics, would have been quite out of sympathy with it. In the nation as a whole it found itself confronting a military-industrial establishment in the making.

Yet in the liberal Protestant "New Theology," bequeathed especially by American Unitarianism, the inspiration was found for Japan's first socialist party in 1901 and its first socialist premier in 1947. In the period from 1880 to 1910 especially, this Christian socialism was "a *primum mobile* in the agrarian, labor, and socialist movements in Japan."[21] It has not ceased since then to leave some mark on opposition politics in Japan, though from a position more convergent with that of Christians in democratic politics elsewhere in the world in the middle decades of the twentieth century—that is, on the left of the prevailing center, but on the right wing of that left.

4

THE POST-COLONIAL SETTING

Tomorrow began yesterday, as the aphorism has it. If this holds true for Asia and for Christianity, then by our rapid review of what their yesterdays have been, at a point about two-thirds of the way through the twentieth century, we have already learned something of what the future then held in store for them—something that could not be learned simply by looking at the subsequent record.

If we can keep in mind those overlapping backgrounds—the global, the Asian, the global Christian, the Asian Christian—we shall be better prepared to take a closer look at the Asian Christian experience of social protest after the mid-1960s. We shall be less likely to forget how diverse are the tributaries that have fed the river of that experience—some of them distinctively Asian, many derivative from outside the continent, and many others showing in various measures a cross-fertilization of Asian and Western influences.

By the same stroke we shall be prepared to see how the Christian movement, already transnational and even transcontinental and transhemispheric to an extent not paralleled in any other of the major religions, could find a place of its own in a new era of nationalism and transnationalism in Asia.

The Postwar Generation in the World and in Asia

There are watersheds in history as well as in geography. World War II is the historical watershed that lies across the middle of the twentieth century like a ridge of scar tissue, dividing what went before from what came after as markedly, in its way, as the geographical watershed of Eurasia divides north from south, or as that of the Americas divides east from west. As we have already seen, the global society that gradually took shape after World War II did so in a new, post-imperial, post-colonial setting, and also developed new political fault lines of its own.

If we try to take a bird's-eye view of the global historical landscape in the

47

generation after World War II, ignoring all but the most towering historical peaks in that landscape, and taking no particular account of either Asia as such or Christianity as such, what are the unfolding features that thrust themselves first on our attention?

If we had to answer this question in a paragraph, we should have to single out for special mention the new bloc confrontation in Europe marked by the rise of the NATO alliance and the Warsaw Pact; its broadening into an East-West conflict with major flash points in Korea and Vietnam; the re-sounding advances of communism in Eastern Europe, in China, and (by 1975) in Indochina; and the eventual fragmentation within the socialist bloc that set China at odds with the Soviet Union and later with Vietnam.

However, lest we should make it appear that all postwar developments are related to only one line of division, the East-West one, we must mention in the same breath the emergence of a new consciousness of North-South separation. This follows a vast process of decolonization and the rise of a nonaligned bloc; it is complicated by an endemic Arab-Israeli conflict and the rise of an oil cartel in a region vital to the West because of oil; in its turn it complicates the tensions between the splintered East and the faltering West as the flash points shift to Iran and Afghanistan.

If we had to chart the postwar scene in further detail, while still confining the record to developments of major global historical salience, we should have to draw up a set of chronologies along the lines of Appendix 1 of this study. It might then be instructive to find out to what extent the continent called Asia and the religion called Christianity naturally find places in such a record.

With this question in mind, let us look first at the first quarter century of the postwar generation.

It turns out that Asia is a looming presence in it, while Christianity is an inconspicuous one. So large does Asia loom already in contemporary history that, even in this quarter century, most events of major global reverberation turn out to be events that occurred in Asia.

In the case of Christianity, perhaps no more than three distinctly church-related developments in the same period pass the same test of global political salience. These would be the formation of the World Council of Churches in 1948, the galvanization of Roman Catholicism through Vatican II from 1962 to 1965, and the emergence of the new Christian social concern reflected in the international church assemblies of Beirut, Uppsala, and Medellín in 1968. But these events alone were portentous: they set the scene for a return of world Christianity in the 1970s to a higher and sharper profile in world politics than it had had for some hundreds of years.

Let us next look at the political record of the period since 1969.

In this period too, even when viewed in a global perspective, it is clear that key world events turn out to be Asian events in a majority of cases.

As for developments in the churches in the same period, perhaps only two are on a comparable level in terms of deep and lasting public impact. These would be the papal succession that ended a centuries-old Italian monopoly in 1978, and the continental confrontation of Christian social attitudes in the Latin American church assemblies of Oaxtepec in 1978 and Puebla in 1979. But then again, these alone suffice to certify the return to high-profile visibility of Christianity in general and of Roman Catholicism in particular as an actor on the global political stage.

With these considerations we have enough data to place post-colonial Asian Christianity in transcontinental perspective. It is clear that we are not dealing with a marginal continent or with a marginal movement in world affairs. We are not at all leaving the center of the world stage when we focus on Asia. We are hardly doing so even when we focus on the Asian prolongations of the movement called Christianity.

"Prolongations" is the word to bear in mind, for the sake of a realistic appraisal of Asian Christian social protest in its earlier manifestations. As we have seen, there is little Asian Christian social protest to report before 1965, except by way of the prehistory of the subject. There is little that was not heavily dependent on extra-Asian Christian influences for another decade after that.

Asian Christianity is derivative in this respect as it is in so many others. It would be strange if it were otherwise. One does not normally look to marginal minorities in a population for a lead in social protest, any more than one looks to the passenger nearest the water to be the first to rock an overloaded boat.

One does not look either for such a lead to a putative Christian majority, if it is found only in a small country like Lebanon, when that country itself is on the fringe of a Muslim mass. One does not look for it even from an overwhelming Christian majority, if it is found even in a fair-sized country like the Philippines, when that majority is alone in its relative Christian strength, and is dwarfed by the Asian mass to whose margin it clings, and is marginal even in relation to the Latin American mass to which it is culturally more akin.

The wonder is that it was not later when the phenomenon surfaced, and that it did not take longer to acquire some distinctively Asian features. The wonder is that there is so much to report so soon, as can be seen from the Asian items in the lists of "Other Events Relevant to Asian Christian Social Protest" in Appendix 3.

We have here, in fact, an illustration of a phenomenon now widespread in world affairs—namely, acceleration in the diffusion of transnational influences—when we observe that Christianity in Asia had already developed transnational organs of its own, for militant social concern, at high and low levels alike, not within decades but within years of the upsurge of social ferment in the great Christian clearinghouses of Geneva and of Rome and in the awakening Catholic heartland of Latin America.

The Rise of Transnational Christian Bodies in Asia

The postwar proliferation of transnational linkages in Asian Christianity
—for communication, for consultation, for financing, for reflection, for
action—goes well beyond the scope of a summary such as this one. Even a
list of all kinds of transnationally organized expressions of Christian *social*
concern, from "relief and rehabilitation" through "development" to "con-
scientization," would be too inclusive for our purpose. We shall have to
confine our attention to two categories: the most representative bodies generally and the most representative ones on the social protest front specifically.

In Asia, by the middle of the 1970s, there were three organizations that
between them aspired to represent all kinds of Christians in all parts of the
continent: the Federation of Asian Bishops' Conferences (FABC), the
Christian Conference of Asia (CCA), and the Middle East Council of
Churches (MECC). All three had been formed within the previous two
decades—the CCA in 1958, the FABC in 1972, the MECC (at least under
that name) in 1974. Except as an illustration of this transnational trend, the
MECC need not concern us further; its (non-Roman) constituency is too
tiny and too intimidated by circumambient Islam. As for the other two,
their story is inseparable from the story of the Asian rise of militant Christian social concern.

Because of the breadth of their claims to representativeness, and because
of their identification with the institutional side of the Christian movement,
the FABC and the CCA raise plausible questions as to the depth and
strength of their roots in the Christian communities. A priori it is quite
conceivable that they are following a social line of their own, at their rare-
fied national and transnational altitudes, without organic relationship with
anything that is really germinating at the base.

To check on this possibility, we need to look in two directions: on the one
hand, at the FABC and the CCA, as the most widely representative bodies
at the highest institutional levels within Asia; on the other hand, at movements representing Christian activists (workers, peasants, students, intellectuals, religious, clergy), as the most widely representative ones at levels
closer to the Asian grassroots.

In fact, due regard for chronological order in recording the rise of Christian activism, at least on the Catholic side, requires us to give first place to
certain transnational initiatives at levels no loftier than that of a particular
religious order or that of pastoral clergy in general. These go back in their
origins as far as the CCA. They antedate the FABC by more than a decade.

In 1962, the year of the opening of Vatican II, 40 million Asian Catholics
made up about one-fourteenth of 540 million Catholics then in the world.[1]
They were represented at the first session of the Vatican Council by some
three hundred prelates, themselves making up about one-eighth of the 2,540

Council Fathers actually present.[2] Those 40 million Asian Catholics were as little involved in the preparation of the council as the faithful elsewhere, and social activism is as little in evidence in reports of their activities up to that time as it is in those of the other 500 million Catholics.[3]

In short, there were few ripples on the surface of Catholic life in Asia in 1962, either when the bishops went to Rome or when they first came back. They returned to a church whose social role was seen by friends and enemies alike as that of a minor bastion of the prevailing order, feudal though that was;[4] to a church seen even by the occasional church leader as preyed on by the demons of power, prestige, and property.[5]

How isolated, at such a time, any struggle for social justice had to be, if it really sought to strike at the roots of injustice, is illustrated by the case of Father Joseph Vadakkan of Kerala. His struggle against peasant eviction and landlordism (by his own estimation in 1961) ranged "90 percent of the bishops against" him, while only one Kerala bishop spoke openly in his favor.[6]

Such was the pattern in South Asia. In East Asia too there were those who were prophets before their time. One of them was Walter Hogan, the prime mover in the pioneering Jesuit social action network, Socio-Economic Life in Asia (SELA). SELA dates back to 1959, anticipating by a decade the establishment of the more general Jesuit transnational Asian network, the Bureau of Asian Affairs (BAA). Here already we have the beginnings of a new pattern, a pattern of transnational thinking deriving its urgency from social concern, and expressed in the rationale that "national boundaries could no longer be the only basis for effective work in Asia."[7]

Activists of this vintage—prophetic and ahead of their time—whether they were Asian-born like Vadakkan or missionaries like Hogan, were to find that they would have to spend a time in the wilderness before receiving a kind of vindication in the 1970s.[8]

Is there a single date that can be said to mark the turning point, the point at which the social action scene in Asian Catholicism became something more than a silence broken here and there by voices in the wilderness? Insofar as there is such a date, it might best be set in 1965.

This was a landmark year in many fields. In the East-West conflict it was the year of a fateful escalation of the Indochina war. In China it was the year of the launching of the no less fateful Great Proletarian Cultural Revolution. In global Catholicism it was the year of the ending of Vatican II—an ending that was really a beginning for so much more than was then foreseen. And in Asian Catholicism it was the year of the launching, in Hong Kong, of the first transnational movement involving Asian diocesan priests in social action.

This was called PISA, or Priests' Institute for Social Action. It was one of the earliest initiatives sponsored by SELA.

The PISA meeting was something less than a media event.[9] No one would have been surprised had it proved as modest in its fruits as in itself. As

things worked out, however, it was not destined to sink into oblivion, not at
least for another couple of decades. A whole series of developments related
to Christian social protest in these decades gave proof that PISA represented something more than a passing trend. It has a logical place at the
head of a list of some dozens of these developments in Appendix 3.

With PISA, social concern found a point of entry into the mainstream of
the Catholic apostolate. Many scattered initiatives of Catholic inspiration
now began to come into their own: farmers' and workers' movements, research and training centers, a Brotherhood of Asian Trade Unions, a
Federation of Free Farmers, an Asian Social Institute, an Indian Social
Institute, an Institute of Social Order.

By 1966, as a direct result of PISA, the Philippine half of Catholic Asia
had its NASSA, or National Secretariat of Social Action, which was later to
play a crucial role in the social struggle. By 1967, training courses had been
held in the Philippines for the first set of diocesan directors of social action.[10] By 1970, when the Asian bishops met in Manila for the first Asian
assembly in their history, some winds of change were blowing not only from
Rome, Geneva, and Medellín, and not only from the fronts of hot and cold
Asian wars, but also from the Asian Catholic grassroots in the Philippines,
Korea, India, and Vietnam.

At least they blew strongly enough to evoke from the bishops assembled
in Manila the commitment to be more truly, in Asia and with the Asians,
"the church of the poor . . . the Church of the young."[11]

The Representative Asian Body for Rome-Related Christians: the FABC

What has already been said about the Federation of Asian Bishops' Conferences (p. 38) shows the sense in which the FABC can be called the representative Catholic body in Asia.

In the absolute sense there is no such thing, of course, as a truly representative body for the Asian majority of humankind, or for the followers of
any religion in Asia. Catholics in particular have long been accustomed to
being represented by church leaders in whose selection they have had no say
whatever. In the fifth century Pope Leo the Great could say that people in
charge in the Church should be subject to acceptance by all those they were
in charge of (*"Qui profuturus est omnibus ab omnibus eligatur"*). By the
twentieth century, at least up to the twenty-first Catholic Council, this tradition had long been lost sight of, and neither pastors nor flock saw a need
for any mandate for the former from the latter beyond a passive assent to a
particularly authoritarian ecclesiastical system.

The Catholic pastors in Asia, however, did have that kind of unques-
tioned mandate from the Catholic faithful. They were also much better
organized to make use of their mandate in the 1970s than they had been
before.

The case of the FABC presents us with another of our transnational nov-

elties. Neither in Asia nor elsewhere have Catholics been accustomed to
having levels of representation above bishops but below the Holy See. For
most countries the development of even national conferences of bishops
does not date back much further than the middle of the twentieth century;
and the development of continental federations of bishops is more recent
still. The Latin American bishops were breaking new ground when they
formed their own transnational structure, CELAM, in 1955. The Asian
bishops, for their part, had never gotten together en masse anywhere before
the 1960s, when they did so during the four sessions of Vatican II. They had
never gotten together in Asia before 1970, when some 180 of them gathered
in Manila in advance of Pope Paul VI's Asian-Australasian tour.

Formal approval of the FABC by the Holy See did not come until 1972.
Strained exchanges behind the scenes reflected an awareness on both sides
that something substantive was at stake. As an innovation in horizontal
communication in the Church, the FABC had to overcome formidable
obstacles of distance, of differences in language and culture, and even of
Catholic and of Roman conditioning; for it ran counter to a structure in
which, even at the level of bishops, communication was almost exclusively
vertical.

Thus, the mere birth of the FABC was a portentous change in Asian
Christian history. Once that change had come about, the whole outlook for
change was no longer the same.

So signs of change began to multiply. For data on them we turn to three
sources, in descending order of institutional authority: the contributions
from Asia at the Synods of Bishops in Rome; the general assemblies of the
FABC; and the field of action of the FABC social office. But we shall have
to go beyond the public record of all of these for evidence of an important
rift in the FABC on the social question.

Asia at the Synods of Bishops

The Synods of Bishops in Rome were another novel transnational ecclesiastical structure of the post-conciliar period. Inaugurated in 1967, preoc-
cupied with internal problems in 1969, the Synods began to look outward in
1971.

The session of 1971 was on justice and ministry; that of 1974, on evangelization; that of 1977, on catechetics; that of 1980, on the family. The
score or so of Asian bishops present each time amounted to only about 5
percent of the FABC and only about 10 percent of the Synod participants;
but the overall evolution of the Synods was a primary reference point for
the overall evolution of the FABC. Thus, the 1974 FABC Assembly cited
the 1971 Synod, as we shall see; and the 1978 FABC Assembly was careful
to note that it defined "liberation" according to Pope Paul's *Evangelii
Nuntiandi*, which filtered and synthesized the findings of the 1974 Synod.[12]

Among statements emanating directly from the Synods, we have already seen (p. 16) the landmark formulation in the declaration of 1971 affirming "action for justice . . . as a constitutive dimension of the preaching of the Gospel''; and in the 1974 declaration we are given a reaffirmation of this, reworded as "the intimate connection between evangelization and liberation.''[13] Among statements made by Asian bishops at the Synods, two in particular were widely noticed and have particular relevance for our inquiry —one by Cardinal Kim of Seoul in the 1974 Synod, and one by Archbishop Binh of Ho Chi Minh City (Saigon) in the 1977 Synod.

At the 1974 Synod Cardinal Kim stated the case for wholehearted church commitment to action for social change in perhaps the boldest terms yet heard from any Asian hierarchical source. Let us hear him at some length, remembering that these words have not come cheaply from a churchman whose government was holding one of his fellow bishops in jail at the very time he spoke in Rome.

> We are here to seek ways of making the "Christ-event," the reality of Christ, a reality in the hearts of the people of this age, in such a way that our world is really transformed by the Gospel. . . . Evangelization in any given historical context must always be conceived in such a way that it really corresponds to the needs and aspirations of the people of the period in question.
>
> When we apply this to Asia . . . [with] its daily increasing multitudes . . . it is unthinkable that this most urgent of tasks (promotion of social justice) should be treated as peripheral, or as secondary to "direct evangelization," since in fact it is the chief demand made of the church of our time. This task was already declared by the 1971 Synod of Bishops "a constitutive dimension" of evangelization; still better, it must come to be seen as the concrete actualization of the sacramentality of the Church.
>
> That the Church may be really the "great sign of credibility" spoken of by Vatican II, it must become more and more a Church not for itself but for the life of the world. Especially in Asia it must be manifested to all, and especially to the poor and to the young, as a community that voluntarily exposes its own life to the greatest damage and danger for the sake of meeting mankind's most pressing needs. . . .
>
> As the miracles of Christ were signs of reconciliation and salvation, so also the promotion of justice in the world today can manifest the power of the resurrection of the Lord, and can reconcile all men and make all things new. This is in fact a sign of great credibility; it is the true Gospel; it is real evangelization. . . .
>
> This is the unanimous view of the Episcopal Conferences of Asia as reflected in the statements made [in this Synod]. . . .[14]

At the 1977 Synod it was the turn of a church leader from the other side of Asia's ideological line of confrontation to contribute a notable statement—one of the few statements, in fact, that made a jaded public take some notice of that Synod. Archbishop Binh undertook to speak to and for those who have to address the gospel to a milieu dominated by Marxism. Nobody at such a level had yet spoken on that topic as forthrightly as he did. For Catholics "impregnated with Marxism-Leninism," he said, there should be no hesitation about translating the gospel into Marxist terms, any more than there was hesitation about translating it into Aristotelian or existentialist terms.[15]

Binh's voice was not only a lonely one for that Synod or any other. It was a lonely one even among the voices of bishops in Vietnam itself. As can be seen from a glance at Appendix 3, a solitary supporting voice, that of a fellow archbishop in Hue, had changed its tune from support to criticism of the government that same year. Of course the Binh manifesto had enormous significance for Christians already looking forward to seeing the "new leaven" (of Marxism) "at work in the Church." Such at least were the terms in which Canon François Houtart of Louvain congratulated the clergy and religious of Binh's diocese the following year.

> More than any other church which is living the beginning of socialism, you here in Vietnam bear the hopes of millions of Christians throughout the world.[16]

It will have been noticed that a claim to wide representativeness is made in connection with both Synod speeches. For our purpose here, representativeness is not the point. The word *unanimous* actually disappeared from the translation of Cardinal Kim's speech when it appeared in an FABC-sponsored collection. When questioned about it, the cardinal conceded that his original *sensus unanimus* had been a bit too strong.[17] Similarly, for better or worse, it would be hard to prove that "the hope of millions of Christians throughout the world" has been invested more in the Church of Vietnam than in, say, the Church of Poland. But both Synod speeches are of some consequence even if taken only as high water marks of boldness in Asian ecclesiastical statements.

The FABC Assemblies

Apart from the Manila meeting of 1970, there were only two occasions in the 1970s when the FABC spoke as a body. Its two plenary sessions of the decade were held in Taipei (1974) and in Calcutta (1978). The Manila statement spoke for all who were present. With 180 bishops present, that assembly was the largest Asian episcopal gathering up to that time. The Taipei and Calcutta statements were endorsed by the voting participants, who had a well-defined mandate from all the bishops (about double the Manila number) in fourteen Asian countries.

What line, then, emerged as the voice of the FABC? In the texts of 1974 and 1978, the commitment of 1970 to be "the Church of the poor and of the young" was "wholeheartedly reaffirmed."[18] The 1974 document included in this reaffirmation the conclusions of the first Bishops' Institute for Social Action (BISA)—the only BISA that had taken place by that date. No BISAs were mentioned in the 1978 document, which was concerned with prayer (the 1974 meeting had been concerned with evangelization) and which in any case "wholeheartedly reaffirmed" the recommendations of 1974.

The statements thus endorse both the prevailing line of the BISA meetings and the prevailing social emphasis of the episcopal voices emanating from Rome, Medellín, and Puebla. Thus, the 1974 statement, citing the 1971 Synod on "action for justice . . . as a constitutive dimension of the preaching of the Gospel," went on to say:

> We affirm this teaching again, for we believe that this, in our time, is part and parcel of "preaching the Good News to the poor" (Matt. 11:5; Lk. 4:18). . . . Engaged in tasks for justice in accordance with the spirit and the demands of the Gospel, we will realize that the search for holiness and the search for justice, evangelization, and the promotion of true human development and liberation are not only not opposed, but make up today the integral preaching of the Gospel, especially in Asia.[19]

Similarly, the 1978 statement related its topic, prayer, to the concern for "total human liberation" in these words:

> Far from alienating us from sharing in man's responsibility for the world and for the establishment of just and loving relationships among men and groups in society, prayer commits us to the true liberation of persons. It binds us to solidarity with the poor and powerless, the marginalized and oppressed in our societies. It is prayer which brings us to the understanding of how injustice is rooted in the selfishness and sinfulness of men's hearts. It is prayer which will help us to discern the tasks and deeds which can call on the Spirit to create within us both the courage and the love to bring about conversion in men's hearts and the renewal of societal structures.[20]

To be sure, it is only realistic to reserve judgment as to how seriously these words were meant, or as to whether the FABC could ever live up to them even if it were unanimous in wanting to do so. It was never to be expected that church leaders, in the Asian Catholic or in any other church, would suddenly make the break that had been promised in 1970 with the "compromising entanglements" of the past.

The weight of the past was in fact to lie heavily on them. The choice of Taipei as the venue for the first assembly meant that the FABC would make its debut before the world as the honored guest of Asia's longest-running martial law regime. Nobody could pretend that this had not been foreseen.

Similarly, the choice of prayer as the topic for the second assembly was bound to be interpreted by some as masking a retreat from social commitment, assertions to the contrary notwithstanding.[21] And the country-by-country record of the hierarchies left plenty of room for skepticism about that commitment.

All this is only to say that the FABC was taking shape in Asia, not on the moon. The assemblies could hardly be blamed for taking account of the fact that Asia was still politically polarized in 1974, or of the fact that it was still the continent of the great religions in 1978. We must look further before forming any firm impressions as to what was the overall tilt of the FABC by the end of its first decade.

The FABC Office for Human Development

The outlook for change was itself changed by the mere establishment of the FABC, and it was on the social front that change went furthest in the first years. Among the specialized service agencies set up by the FABC, the first to move into action and generate a whole series of further actions was the one called the Office for Human Development. It was an idea whose time had clearly come, thanks to the intercontinental Christian *prise de conscience* focused for Catholics in Vatican II and in the Synods of Bishops, and thanks also to the specifically Asian conditioning already outlined.

True to the pattern we have seen already—new breakthroughs in transnational thinking spearheaded by urgent social concern—the FABC Office for Human Development (OHD) was organized and ready for action before the FABC itself was formally constituted. A survey tour in 1972 by its first chairperson, Bishop Labayen of the Philippines, found something to report by way of church structures for promoting development in Hong Kong, Vietnam, Malaysia, Singapore, Bangladesh, and Sri Lanka, but more particularly in Indonesia, the Philippines, India, and Thailand. An overall appraisal by the OHD's first executive secretary noted the presence of "three perspectives of social welfare"—relief, development, and liberation. As for the liberation perspective (the only one involving social protest in our sense), the secretary found that, with scarcely an exception,

> . . . there is no national committee [of the OHD] where the "liberator" feels at home in a development office or atmosphere. . . . Hardly ever will a committed liberator accept a function in development work. . . . It is hardly possible to obtain funds from funding agencies for liberation work.[22]

Why the uneasiness about the "liberator"? It is worth pausing on this question, since it highlights the interplay of international influences we have been considering in the Asian context.

Fundamentally the reaction in question must be seen as the stiffening common to all social institutions when faced with a substantive threat to the social status quo in which they have been rooted. More specifically in the Asian Christian case, it must be seen as the fear of the concrete social alternative.

In no country in the region, and at no time in the period in question, does the institutional Christian leadership cease to look over its shoulder at the "menace" of communism. Where the menace has been felt to loom largest, as in South Korea, Taiwan, Thailand, and Indonesia, Christian leadership attitudes will range from firmly to obsessively anticommunist. Elsewhere outside the socialist states, as in the Philippines, India, Sri Lanka, and Japan, an anticommunist priority among church leaders will still command solid national majorities, but no longer entirely to the exclusion of minorities who rate the need for social change above any risk of "communist infiltration." On occasion, as attested by the Houtart citation above, a minority among these minorities will make an explicit option for a Marxist or a Marxist-Leninist political model. But few among these will claim that their hour is near to striking.

If the period has witnessed any letting down of the guard of "the Church" in this sense, that probably happened before the mid-1970s rather than after. With the dismantling of the mystique of Maoism in China and the outbreak of intersocialist wars in Indochina, it was as if some scales had fallen from Christian eyes on Asia's maritime fringe. In the matter-of-fact words of the General Secretary of the Christian Conference of Asia in 1980, "today it is harder to sell Marxism to Christians in Asia."[23]

But let us return to the 1972 appraisal by the OHD secretary. At the time it was written, seven years remained of the 1970s. In that period, if the OHD made a mark on the Asian Catholic consciousness, it is safe to say it was made mainly through the five seminars held in that period in the series called the Bishops' Institute for Social Action (BISA) on the Social Dimensions of the Gospel.

BISAs I through III were held on a sub-regional basis in 1974 and 1975. Together they involved over 60 bishops from over 20 countries and a total of 147 participants. Feedback from BISA I showed that the idea that had sunk in best was "the need to be a Church of the poor."[24] Further feedback was made possible by the Asian Seminar held near Bangkok in 1977, in which sixty-one people involved in Catholic social action in ten countries discussed the practical application of the "BISA document" summarizing the thinking of the first three BISAs.

What emerged was that, while no one quarreled openly with the theory, all countries had some trouble with the practice, including those where the action groups were most committed. Thus, a Korean consensus reported "deep doubt about the possibility of realizing this ideal in practice," while the Thai group tempered its "eager welcome" for the ideal with the still bleaker comment, "The teachings seem unrealistic." The Thais confessed to a time-honored concern that church social work should be done "equally with the rich." The Koreans touched a nerve less often probed: "The present church structure cannot be poor."[25]

BISA IV was held near Manila in 1978 with thirty bishops present; BISA V in 1979 in Baguio with thirty-seven. Each of these meetings originally aimed at representing the entire FABC region, as well as including observers from outside the region; each also provided for exposure of bishops to conditions of poverty in several countries.

The overall effect was a deepening of commitment and a deepening of interconfessional and intercontinental solidarity. In their final statement after BISA IV, the participants echoed the theme of the 1977 CCA Assembly of their Protestant Asian counterparts, Jesus Christ in Asian Suffering and Hope. They recognized the risks of both solidarity with the poor and the gospel command "to risk everything for the growth of God's Kingdom." In their final statement after BISA V, the participants echoed the consensus of their Catholic Latin American counterparts (reaffirmed in the 1979 Puebla Assembly) "that our preferential option should be for the poor." They proposed Human Rights in the Contemporary World as a theme for the Synod of Bishops.[26]

The BISA seminars had involved about one in four of the FABC bishops. These bishops were not necessarily simply the left wing of the Asian episcopates; the selection process ensured a certain representativeness that in fact excluded a certain number of the most socially radical bishops. At the same time, some consideration had to be given to involving bishops who were positively interested in being involved; and this opened the way for a "BISA line" to emerge which might not be representative for the FABC as a whole.

It was on a geographical basis, however, that the clearest evidence of strain emerged in the relationship of the OHD to its parent body.

The East-West Rift in the FABC

Historically, in Asia, the chief rivalry for influence has come from the two giant cultural ensembles, China and India. The cultures of these two countries dominated the regions now called East Asia and South Asia, and carried into the space between them a competition for cultural dominance reflected in geographical terms like *Indochina* and *Indonesia*.

In postwar Asian Catholicism the pattern had to be different, given the relative weakness of Catholicism in East Asia and its lopsided strength in the Philippines. Hence the main polarity that developed was between India and the Philippines. Two factors combined to sharpen it.

On the one hand, the social question took on an urgency in the client-state, martial-law Philippines that was partly deflected in India by the professed nonalignment and eclecticism of that country in relation to the capitalist and the socialist blocs. At the same time, the majority status of Catholicism in the Philippines made for a relative boldness in prophetic social witness by its church leaders, as compared with that of church leaders in continental South Asia. There the leaders tended to be cowed by minority insecurity into toeing the line of whatever regime was in power.

The moment of truth came in each country with the assumption of emergency powers by its current chief of government—by Ferdinand Marcos in 1972 in the Philippines, by Indira Gandhi in 1975 in India. When the dust settled, a certain distance had developed between the political responses of Filipino and Indian church leaders, both Roman and non-Roman.

There were other factors—notably the greater Indian predisposition to favor the contemplative over the active dimension in religion, and the factor of caste. It could only be a matter of time before the tensions would come to a head. They were already present among the Asian theologians when they met at Wennappuwa in January 1979 to formulate a common response to the Asian challenge. They had come out in the open in the OHD by May 1979, when a chapter of semi-accidents ended in switching the site for BISA V from India to the Philippines, and in the concerted though not quite complete abstention of the South Asian episcopates from participation in that seminar. There followed a four-year hiatus before a sixth conference in the series was successfully assembled in 1983.

No hint of this high-level dissension can be seen directly in the record of the common organs of the FABC—*FABC Newsletter* and *Info on Human Development*. To know of it, one would have had to hear the copious private comment on both sides from 1979 on. It was like the rift that developed the following year in Latin America between the Brazilian episcopal leadership and the official CELAM leadership; it was an open secret, but it was in nobody's interest to make it more official than it had to be. The furthest that any side went towards formalizing it was in the following, from "The Report of the Standing Committee" in the record of the biennial meeting of the Indian bishops of October 1979:

> . . . The first meeting . . . of Bishops of the South Asian Region (India, Sri Lanka, Pakistan and Bangladesh) from March 24–27, 1979 . . . offered the occasion to consider the forthcoming BISA V and the slanted composition of the panel of animators.
>
> The Bishops of India declined to take part in . . . BISA V. . . . The non-participation of the Indian Bishops raises the important question of the way the entire FABC is organized and the weightage to be given to the pronouncements and doings of its subsidiary organizations.[27]

Clearly this was not a happy moment for the FABC dream of 1970. Must we read in these words the thud of a heavy body coming back to earth after a doomed attempt to take to the air?

Before we do that, we ought to take account of subsequent attempts to patch things up, both through new protestations of unity and through further efforts to make OHD pronouncements and doings (and personnel) more representative of the whole FABC region. Let us therefore reserve judgment until we can put both the early euphoria and the later malaise into a larger perspective.

The Representative Body for Other Christians: the CCA

We have noted that Roman Catholicism accounts for about half of all Asian Christians. About two-thirds of the remainder are Protestants, leaving some millions of Oriental Christians. These latter are not found in significant numbers in the crescent of countries relevant to our inquiry, except in the case of the couple of millions of Syrian Christians in India.

We have noted also the rise of an organization representing Christians in Asia not in communion with Rome—the organization known today as the Christian Conference of Asia (CCA). When launched in 1959, this structure was something new on the non-Roman horizon, just as the Latin American CELAM, when launched in 1955, had been something new on the Christian horizon. Both were not only transnational but also transcontinental.

CCA and FABC: Comparisons and Contrasts

The FABC and the CCA are only roughly comparable, even in geographical scope. Like the FABC, the CCA excludes the countries of Southwest Asia; unlike the FABC, it includes Australia and New Zealand. If these latter are not counted, the CCA had in the 1970s an Asian constituency of about 40 million Christians.

Other parallels also are only approximate. As the FABC finds its chief extra-Asian point of reference in the Vatican, in the Second Vatican Council, and in the Synods of Bishops, so also, but in a much looser way, the CCA finds its chief extra-Asian point of reference in the World Council of Churches, in the WCC General Assemblies (Amsterdam 1948, Evanston 1954, New Delhi 1961, Uppsala 1968, Nairobi 1975), and in the interim activities of WCC bodies.

We shall give some prominence to that point of reference, partly because Asians are prominent in their own right on the transcontinental Christian scene, and distinctly more so in the Protestant world than in the Catholic one. At the same time we must bear in mind that, true to their stronger sense of ecclesial autonomy and Asian equal dignity, CCA leaders would be at pains to correct any impression that the CCA is in any sense a branch office of the WCC.

The dissymmetry shown in the comparison of the CCA with the FABC goes still further. The linkages in the CCA are no more hierarchical in relation to local churches than in relation to transcontinental bodies. The FABC, for its part, has no collective binding power over its constituent churches beyond what its members have individually; but Catholic bishops and hierarchies do have more local leverage over the implementation of their collective resolutions than CCA delegates have. A certain feeling of being relatively rootless and free-floating is in this sense more characteristic of a Protestant than of a Catholic transnational structure.

The negative side of this relative freedom in the Protestant structure is isolation from the mass base (though only in terms of formal power). The positive aspect is the freedom from inhibition that goes with lack of formal jurisdiction. A General Secretary of the CCA, unlike a Secretary General of the FABC, has no difficulty in remarking casually and cheerfully:

> We're not so clear as to what we're for. . . . We're not so concerned about what was said before. . . . We're more concerned with action than with spinning phrases.[28]

That "spinning phrases" suggests a still more crucial dissymmetry. The great phrase-spinner of the CCA was its Sri Lankan father figure, D. T. Niles. His phrases continue to adorn CCA information folders and to inspire its orientation. His vision of the CCA would make of it an institution dedicated to going against the grain of institutions:

> The churches as institutions are geared more to conserving the gains of the past than to attempting the tasks of the future. The necessity, therefore, is for the churches to have those frontiersmen who are willing, as it were, to venture into uncharted territory, whether of thought or action or organization. To give these frontiersmen a sense of solidarity, encouragement and sharpened insight is a prime concern for such an organization as the CCA.[29]

Brave words, these! Some would even call them quixotic on the part of an enterprise that after two decades had yet to raise a tenth of its annual budget from within its constituency.[30] But the enterprise bears watching all the more because of that. It should give us a chance to see whether there is such a thing as an institution capable of defying successfully the supposedly iron laws of sociology and economics.

The CCA counted six assemblies by the end of the 1970s. As in the case of the FABC, there was an "antenatal" assembly two years before the CCA's formal inauguration; as the FABC idea was launched in Asia's country of chief Catholic strength, the Philippines, so the CCA idea was launched (though under mainly South Asian leadership) in Asia's country of chief Protestant strength, Indonesia. The inaugural session of the CCA was in Kuala Lumpur in 1959; it was followed by two assemblies in Bangkok. The 1970s assemblies took place in Singapore in 1973 (when the present name was adopted) and in Penang in 1977. The seventh assembly was held in Bangalore in 1981.

CCA Christians on the World Christian Scene

Can we trace a shift in social attitude in the CCA as in the FABC? The question is complicated by the dissymmetries referred to above. Assemblies representing Christians other than those in communion with Rome cannot speak with one voice in the way that has been possible for representative Catholic bodies. There is nothing on the Protestant side to compare with the organic development of official Catholic social teaching in a series of papal, conciliar, and synodal pronouncements.

But that is not to say there is any less evidence of a shift in social attitude in the global Protestant leadership than in the global Catholic leadership. On the contrary, the winds of change on that front have blown more strongly around the churches linked with Geneva than around the churches linked with Rome. The more participatory structures of Protestantism have left doors and windows wide open to them.

The pressure for a more militant social stand in the WCC came first from the Third World churches. The Third World had provided an Indian chairperson of the Central Committee by 1968 and a black General Secretary by 1972. A tribute from the latter to the former, made at the 1977 CCA Assembly, provides us with one perspective on the Asian contribution to Christian social protest in the world:

> For us Christians, it was Asians, led by M. M. Thomas, who in the 1940s and 1950s started the process of analyzing the social revolution from a Christian basis and with the tools of Marxist critique, and thereby assisted us in other areas of the Third World to begin to pay attention to the justice of God as an essential part of the message of the Kingdom of God.[31]

This Third World influence reached the point in 1970 where the WCC Fund to Combat Racism began to be shared with black guerrilla movements in Africa. Throughout the 1970s, despite vehement controversy, there was no retreat from this policy.

Third World militancy, however, is only one of the pressures at work in the WCC. Another pressure has been brought by the Orthodox churches since their entry in 1961. This has tended in the direction of keeping social concern from going "too far," especially wherever it has involved any criticism of the policies and practices of the Warsaw Pact.

Moreover, among the Protestants themselves, there has been a sizable minority that has rejected altogether the conciliar-ecumenical-activist tendency in favor of a conservative-evangelical-pietist spirit. This minority found its rallying point in the World Mission Congress of Lausanne in 1974—which nevertheless expressed "penitence" for having formerly opposed evangelism and social action, and affirmed instead that both were "part of our Christian duty."[32]

These tensions remained unresolved throughout the decade. They were reflected starkly in 1980. Before that year was out, the increasingly shared desire for a common world congress on mission had resulted not in one but in three international mission congresses: a Roman Catholic one in Manila in December 1979, a WCC-sponsored one in Melbourne in May 1980, and a Lausanne-inspired one in Pattaya, Thailand, in June of the same year.

It is notable that all three congresses found some common ground in the notion of a providence that privileged the poor. In Manila the poor were called "ultimately the privileged community and agents of salvation." In Melbourne the participants declared themselves "challenged by the suffering of the poor." Even in Pattaya the idea surfaced, though more obliquely, that "God is biased in favor of the poor."[33]

What is the clue to the future here: the persistence of divisions, or the emergence of this overarching consensus on the providentially privileged role of the poor?

Only the future can answer that question. If events should show that the apparent consensus transcended not only national and confessional boundaries, but even the chasm between ecumenicals and evangelicals within the confessions, that would have truly major social implications. Certainly events showed no such thing within 1980—not at least within the American heartland of evangelicalism, where in that same year a self-styled Christian Moral Majority resoundingly repudiated any departure from the Puritan spirit at Pattaya or elsewhere.

But let us return to the ecumenical mainstream. As in Catholicism, so in Protestantism, the new language in high places on social questions took on its contemporary tone in the mid-1960s.

A measure of the willingness of the WCC to take a radical social turn was shown in the WCC Conference on Church and Society, held (with Roman Catholic participation) in Geneva in 1966. It talked of "theology of revolution," which went beyond anything that would have found such a high-level forum in official Catholic circles at that time.

Two years later the WCC joined forces with the Vatican in Beirut in an Ecumenical Conference on Development (their first on an international scale) and in the joint agency for social concerns, SODEPAX. (SODEPAX lasted till 1980; it remains to be seen whether its demise in that year was another sign of a turn-of-the-decade ebbing of the activist tide.)

Social concern loomed large in the WCC Assemblies of Uppsala (1968) and of Nairobi (1975), though by no means large enough to transcend the tension between ecumenicals and evangelicals.

Uppsala spoke of "the ever-widening gap between the rich and the poor" as being "the crucial point of decision today."[34] Nairobi's program guidelines spoke of "the basic Christian imperative to participate in the struggle for human dignity and social justice." Nairobi also gave currency to a formula that became the special WCC contribution to defining the goal of

Christian action in the world: "a just, participatory, and sustainable global society" (JPSS).

On the relation, however, between what it called "social action" and what it called "evangelism," Nairobi found nothing new to say: it simply reaffirmed both, essentially as Lausanne had done. In general, first impressions of observers tended to see the transition from Uppsala to Nairobi in terms of a shift from militancy to "moderation," from radicalism to "consolidation."[35]

The social-gospel trend nevertheless held firm in other ways. There was a continuing willingness to let the agenda of the Church be set by the world, and especially by the Third World and its major component, Asia. When the WCC held its World Mission Conference of 1973 in Bangkok, "the challenge of social revolution" was cited as one of its "starting points for a new day."[36] This was more a question than an answer in the CCA's Fifth Assembly, held in Singapore the same year, on the theme Christian Action in the Asian Struggle:

> Where should the weight of the support of the CCA, with its prophetic as well as its pastoral concerns, fall—on the radicals, on the majority, or on the silent ones on the middle path?[37]

The WCC 1975 Assembly could have been a good occasion for clarifying the matter, especially since that Assembly was originally supposed to have been held in Asia (in Jakarta), having as its theme the slogan "Jesus Christ Frees and Unites." But the organizers failed to reckon with Indonesian Muslim opposition, or perhaps rather with the capacity of Christian and Muslim fundamentalists in Indonesia to provoke each other beyond endurance. In 1974 the venue for the Assembly had to be switched to Nairobi. The embarrassment was seen by the outgoing Chairperson of the Central Committee—M. M. Thomas, himself an Asian—as "a judgment on church growth propaganda in Indonesia."[38]

The Nairobi Assembly was more representative of its constituency than any comparable Catholic body. According to figures released, of its 700 delegates (among some 2,300 participants), 40 percent were lay, 20 percent women, and 10 percent under 30 years old.[39] It also more faithfully reflected the divisions of its constituency; and these divisions effectively muffled any social clarion call that might have come from the Asian fraction (a fifth or so) of its delegates. When these took time off in Nairobi for Asian gatherings, they found unbridgeable differences precisely where a common voice seemed most urgently needed—among the Koreans, the Indians, and the Filipinos.[40]

Reviewing at Nairobi the course of recent events in the Christian world, the retiring Central Committee Chairperson claimed to find a certain convergence in the thinking represented at Rome in 1971 (the Synod of

Bishops), at Bangkok in 1973 (the WCC World Mission Conference), and at Lausanne in 1974 (the evangelical World Mission Congress). He described it as a convergence in favor of an emphasis on "the whole Gospel for the whole man in the whole world"; in favor of relating evangelical and ecclesial questions; and in favor of an "affirmation of the realities of the contemporary world."[41] Given the strains of its unwieldy constituency, it was perhaps achievement enough for Nairobi to allow that assessment to stand.

The Evolution of the CCA

All this is part of the background of the progressive *prise de conscience* of the CCA. A further part of that background is the lead given for links between the CCA and the FABC by the shared operations of the WCC and the Vatican—from 1965, a Joint Working Group; from 1968, Roman Catholic membership in the WCC Faith and Order Commission; from 1968 through 1980, joint RC-WCC sponsorship of SODEPAX.

Structures for such CCA-FABC links were part of the plan of both from the beginning—a CCA program unit for unity, an FABC Office of Ecumenism. But, in keeping with the pattern by which it has been on the social front that transnational trails have tended to be blazed, contacts were developing on that front well before the FABC Office of Ecumenism had anything to report.[42] By the time of the Penang CCA Assembly of 1977, these contacts had become accepted to the point where one of the principal addresses of that Assembly was given by Bishop Labayen, who was then the chief FABC spokesperson, not on ecumenism, but on social action.

Between Nairobi and Penang, the CCA found itself with no real reason for euphoria in its preparation for its Sixth Assembly. As a CCA commentator put it, "the Christian community remains largely a barking dog without much bite."[43] Africans and Asians had questioned the African and Asian credibility of the Nairobi slogan, Jesus Christ Frees and Unites [44]; no such questionable claim was embodied in the Penang theme, Jesus Christ in Asian Suffering and Hope.[45]

The Penang venue, like the Nairobi venue, was not the original choice; the meeting had been planned for Manila. The fact that this plan had to be abandoned is in some degree a measure of the growing divergence between political trends in regimes like Manila's and political thinking in organizations like the CCA. Even this "non-biting dog," the CCA, at this point in its and in Asia's history, could no longer easily find a place where it could feel free to bark.

The General Secretary of the CCA before and after Penang was Yap Kim Hao of Malaysia. By way of emphasizing what a long way the organization had come in its twenty years, he told the Assembly:

> In a real sense ours is one of the most important religious gatherings in Asia. . . . No other Asian Christian meeting is as fully and officially

representative of the established churches as this Assembly. No other Asian Christian group can claim as many recognized leaders as this Assembly. No other Asian Christian voice is as authentic an expression of Orthodox and Protestant views as this Assembly. No other Asian Christian conference is also as diverse in its composition as this Assembly.[46]

Of the concrete assertions here, the last two at least are beyond any serious question. What is more to our purpose is to inquire whether and how the growth of the CCA has modified its nature.

One could find a hint on this in the question cited earlier in connection with the 1973 Assembly: where should the weight of the support of the CCA, with its prophetic as well as its pastoral concerns, fall—on the radicals, on the majority, or on the silent ones on the middle path? The mere posing of this question is in itself an evidence that time had not stood still for the rhetoric of the CCA. Where the frontier image could still be appealed to up to the end of the first decade, in the second it became appropriate to speak of pastoral concerns as well as prophetic ones. Where support for the radicals would seem to follow naturally from the frontier role, it had become a question rather than a premise by 1973.

Does the CCA then turn out to be, after all, one more case of the iron Weberian law of the routinization of charisma?

One thing at least is evident and acknowledged: the concerns of the leadership of the second decade could not be exactly the same as those of the first. The Presiding Chairperson of 1977, T. B. Simatupang of Indonesia, a veteran in both military and ecclesiastical affairs, had his own way of explaining it. He had presided over the passing from a first- to a second-generation leadership in the CCA at a time when he saw Asia as a whole passing from a revolutionary to a "post-revolutionary mood"; and already in 1975 he had "called CCA to a listening and dialoguing task to balance the pioneering and initiating role it had played." Far from being a retreat from the creativity of the frontiers, this was the only way for the CCA to remain at once "a community of memory and hope."[47]

How widely this understanding was consciously shared is one thing. Not all the CCA leadership, in fact, was entirely happy with that "post-revolutionary mood," or with that "balance." How things worked out in practice was another thing.

The fact was that the CCA's leverage was limited, not only over Asia's orientation, but even over its own. Nothing in the 1977 Assembly could change that. Its members might express impatience, as they did express impatience, with "imported theologies and structures." Women and youth might struggle, as they did struggle, for stronger representation in the leadership. The leadership might resolve, as it did resolve, "to raise 25 percent of its administrative budget from the region." The program guidelines might say, as they did say, that "the CCA should continue to give priority to human rights in its programmes," and that "the major thrust of CCA-

URM [Urban Rural Mission] in the next few years should be in building up power for the powerless so that they can remedy the imbalance of power and work for a more just and humane society."[48]

The problem with all this was an old one: Penang spoke loud, but events spoke louder. Over all these conferences—Manila, Bangkok, Singapore, Taipei, Penang, and Calcutta alike—lay the shadow of what had actually been happening in Asia and Asia's churches. In particular there was the shadow of the moments of truth precipitated for these churches by the use of emergency powers in the Philippines, in Korea, in Taiwan, in India, in Indonesia, and in a dozen other countries.

What, for example, lay behind the Penang guidelines that said: "The churches have a responsibility to speak to each other in love about their perceptions of human rights violations in their own countries and in the region"? A particularly painful story lay behind it, centering on the experience of the Emergency in India (1975–77). As will be noted in more detail later, the role of the churches in that crisis was less than heroic all around. The official CCA-related leadership in India, in particular, had actually shown itself readier to criticize the CCA and WCC criticisms of Emergency abuses than to criticize the Emergency abuses themselves.[49]

In other words, for any Asian Protestant/Orthodox body, at least as much as for any Asian Catholic one, any move to come to grips with "Asia's suffering and hope" was doubly daunting. In biblical terms, it was not only the move of a David taking on a Goliath. For the Asian David, unlike the biblical one, was still entangled in King Saul's armor, and still between two minds as to the wisdom of renouncing its protection.

These difficulties continued to be highlighted in the CCA's own organ, *CCA News.* Its editor up to 1981, T. K. Thomas of India, referring to those who called on the Church to tell the State, "Thus far and no further," permitted himself no complacency on that account. "These and similar voices," he observed, "are not the only Christian voices heard in India. There are other voices, more numerous and perhaps more representative, that support the status quo."[50]

In short, divided counsels at high levels on social questions were still a major mark of Asian Christianity at least up to the end of the 1970s. This was a decade after the pledge of the Asian Catholic bishops not to "tie their hands" with "compromising entanglements"; yet Thomas could point to examples of entanglement on the FABC side as easily as on the CCA one.

How much, then, is already clear about Asian Christian social attitudes in the 1970s?

Unprecedented stirrings of change, yes; decisive overall change in one direction, no. The foregoing account of the FABC and the CCA, cursory though it has been, is still enough to show that any simple linear image of increasing Asian Christian mobilization under a banner of social protest would not fit all the known facts even for the period from 1965 to 1982. What remains to be seen is whether a "two steps forward, one step backward" model may fit those facts better.

5

THE TRANSNATIONAL
AVANT-GARDE

Scouts for the Asian Frontier

Poles and Roles within the Church

Let us pause at this point to review our concept of *the Church*. Hitherto we have made do with a designedly adjustable notion, depending for its particular focus on the context, as is customary in historical writing.

Only one piece of terminological shorthand has been consistently employed. The term *the Church* is used only where there is question (at least in the minds of agents of religion whose positions are being reported) of the ecclesial phenomenon as a whole, complete with its claim to be something more than a mere historical phenomenon, though always without judgment as to the validity or invalidity of that claim. Otherwise we speak only of *the churches*—concrete historical realities, occupying a determinate social space, inseparable of course from their theological pretensions, but considered only in the light of whatever is their empirically verifiable interaction with their economic, social, cultural, and/or political environment.

What we need to do now is not only to make that distinction explicit, but also to recall that when we shift our focus from the most official (FABC, CCA, for example) to any less official embodiments of *the Church,* there is still no theological presupposition one way or another. That is to say, it is not necessarily as if we were turning from the Church to the churches or any parts thereof; neither is it necessarily as if we were moving in the opposite direction. A priori, we are in no position to say that the FABC or the CCA are more real or less real as representatives of the Church than the local churches or their activist avant-garde.

As a historical question, to ask, Which is more real? is to ask, Which has played a more significant role in history? The answer may vary from context to context. For that matter, even as a theological question it is an open one, whether we take our theological criteria from Protestantism as a whole or from Catholicism as reinterpreted by Vatican II.

One thing only is clear and decisive for our inquiry. With the FABC and the CCA we have disposed of those transnational structures that claim an overall mandate from Roman and non-Roman Christians respectively in maritime Asia. In the case of all other movements or structures, we must remember, on the one hand, that they do not claim to represent the whole of the Christian community, and, on the other hand, that they may throw more light than more representative bodies on what is really happening in particular areas of Christian activity, or even at the Christian "rice roots" in general.

The point is not purely academic. When it comes to the question, Who speaks for the Christians? the historical evidence is always less categorical than the claims of the protagonists. The more exalted the status of the spokespersons, and the more they claim a mandate from God rather than from humankind, the less it can be taken for granted, on purely natural grounds, that the faith they assign or attribute to the people is the faith these actually live by.

This is not to say there is ever a total dissociation. As long as Christians even passively acknowledge the legitimacy of their spokespersons, they are signifying at least a minimal willingness to be associated with the positions taken by these latter, and even a preference to be represented by these spokespersons rather than by any others.

The essential point is that we must avoid prejudging the question of what Christians *effectively* stand for. To do this we must work with a less tidy mental model of the Church than that which is implicit in the view from the top or from the center. We must also avoid prejudging the relative importance of one or other of the poles of activity in the Church. To do this we must bear in mind that at any given moment there are several poles and several roles, some being at cross-purposes with others, but all having some share in determining any overall orientation the Church may have.

In general, for the purposes of the historian, the sociologist, or the political scientist, it is simply not useful to think of the Church as a fixed point in the firmament. *That* Church, if it exists, is not accessible to empirical study. What we have under actual observation is more like a rather scattered moving pilgrimage in the midst of a larger mass of people also on the move. Working with this pilgrimage paradigm of the Church, we may well recognize a certain unity in the procession, or at least a certain will to unity, but only within the limits of a permanently precarious distance between the head and the tail of the procession, and between the standardbearers and the scouts.

Standardbearers and Scouts

We have seen something of the standardbearers in the post-colonial pilgrimage of Asian Christianity at the transnational level. Though they see themselves as being at the head of the procession, it remains to be seen whether they are nearer its head or its tail. To balance any bias inherent in the view of the standardbearers, we must now try to see how the situation looks from the vantage point of the scouts.

Scouts, of course, are essentially the very kind of people we have heard of already—the people on the frontier. We have seen how that role was projected explicitly on that out-of-the-ordinary church body, the CCA, by its own chief assigner of roles. Some speculative theology in Catholicism would go further: it would assign the very same ideal role to the ordinary church officebearer, referred to in some places in scripture as the *episcopos* and in some streams of church history as the bishop. In sum, for CCA and FABC alike, a theory exists that would situate their leadership precisely on the frontier between the Christian community and the wider world.

That may be the theory, but even the short history of the CCA shows that there is a long step between it and reality. The broader sweep of church history in general (see pp. 9-16) conforms even less convincingly to that ideal pattern. We must pause on this discrepancy, because it goes to the heart of the problem of Asian Christian social protest. For the heart of the problem of Asian Christian social protest is that it seems to involve a basic contradiction in terms.

Call them what you will, define their mandate as coming from God or from humankind, mandated church representatives are still essentially persons invested with responsibility for the institution. Accordingly, the measure in which they gain access to the levers of power in the institution tends to be precisely the measure in which they put the interests of the institution above all other interests. In other words, the measure in which they get to be in positions to make the institution serve society tends to be precisely the measure in which they are committed to make it serve itself first.

Conversely, the measure in which other church members are disposed to make the church institution serve any object beyond itself tends to be precisely the measure in which the institution will seek to deny them access to its levers of power. Far from being in a good position to combine the roles of scout and standardbearer in the pilgrimage, the church standardbearer seems foredoomed to bear the standard away from its front and its flanks toward its place of greatest safety—its rear.

Hence, if we were depending exclusively on Asian standardbearers, and despite anything they might say to the contrary, we should have good grounds for skepticism about any proclaimed or apparent departure from the traditional pattern of their relationship with power in the institution and in society. It is not merely a question of historical improbability, that is, the unlikelihood of any sudden change in the habits of centuries in the history of the Church. It is even arguably a question of sociological impossibility—the impossibility of any deliberate break between a large social body and the social power center on which its survival depends.

To be sure, presumption must yield to evidence, and evidence may force a redefinition of probabilities and possibilities. But where are we to look for that evidence? Short of a social miracle or an overall change in the perception of institutional interests (see pp. 10f.), we are compelled to look for it among scouts who are *not* standardbearers, that is, among bearers of religious influence whose role is not effectively circumscribed by responsibility for the interests of the church institution.

That word *effectively* leaves open the question of whether on occasion church officebearers may also play a pioneering role, even to the extent of subverting institutional interests. For it is not the individual but the system that tends to push the standardbearer to the tail of the procession, thereby creating an innovation vacuum that tends in its turn to be filled by individually and corporately different scouts.

Scouts for the Asian Frontier

On the Asian Christian scene, then, where are the scouts? We must look for them on those fringes of the Asian Christian pilgrimage where movements originating within that pilgrimage encounter the flow of Asian life around it at those points where that flow is most truly and densely representative of Asian life. In one word, that encounter will be with the poor; in two words, with peasants and workers; in four words (covering overlapping categories), with peasants, workers, youth, and intellectuals.

To speak of the first three categories is to cover the overwhelming majority of Asia's people; to speak of the fourth is to speak of the meaning-makers, of those who give voice and direction to that otherwise impersonal millionfold mass. The workers were put on the map by Marx; the peasants, by Mao; the youth, by the Chinese Cultural Revolution and the worldwide student upheavals of the late 1960s. The intellectuals, by their nature, have been recognized historical forces ever since such things were first thought of. Marxism only changed the direction of the crucial role it acknowledged in them by seeking to steer it or suppress it.

Doubts might remain about the importance of the youth role. After all, youth is a very recent and untried invention as a social category.

Doubts remain too about the relevance of the intellectuals. Myrdal, no Marxist, could plausibly say that "the volatility of the intellectuals in some of the South Asian countries certainly does not reflect the mood of the masses."[1]

Doubts also remain about the historical potential of the masses themselves, and particularly of the rural masses, even after the evidence of China and Indochina, and despite the fact that the rural population in Asia accounts for about three-quarters of the total. Much of Marxism still takes its cue on peasants from Marx's own expression, "rural idiocy"; and Myrdal, looking at South Asia, insisted that "poverty, inequality, and a lack of development have no foreordained and definite roles in the process" (of modernization).[2]

However, there is evidence of change here. We may speak of a genuinely significant rise in the dammed-up waters of rural discontent in Asia in the decade after Myrdal wrote. That was a theme often on the lips of the World

Bank president of that period. Another reluctant witness to it is the report on the first decade of the Asian Development Bank (1967–76), which professed to see "the impetus for equality . . . rapidly becoming . . . a revolutionary force."[3]

To elicit such an admission from such a source the evidence had to be compelling. It was read as an indictment of the Bank's own policies and a vindication of the Bank's critics. Except by repudiating it, the Bank could no longer treat the notion of "economics as if people mattered" as if it were romantic and impractical. The premise of the humanists now had certification from the technocrats.

To this kind of Asian frontier, let us now see the approach of the Christian frontierspeople.

Urban Rural Mission

As noted earlier (p. 35), while the average Asian is still in the country, but beginning to get on the way to town, a larger proportion of Christians are in town already. This urban bias of Asian Christianity and its ambivalent implications are reflected in the nomenclature used for what has been the main social arm of the CCA. Originally known as Urban Industrial Mission, it has from time to time or from place to place had other labels, such as Christian Industrial Mission or Christian Industrial Committee. Only since 1973 has it settled at CCA level for the more inclusive label Urban Rural Mission (URM).

The reality covered by these labels has varied widely too—from pietistic evangelism among urban workers, through an approach sometimes called in-depth evangelism, which is conservative evangelical with a social emphasis (a significant minority trend in both Latin America and Asia), to ecumenical concentration on social justice issues in relation to workers, peasants, minorities, women, youth, and, most recently and problematically, power.

Power for the Powerless

To speak of power, of course, is to go to the heart of the matter. The question is, in the popular phrase, to what extent did the CCA put its money where its mouth was?

If one were to consult only the evidence of overall financial accounts, it is welfare that loomed largest on the CCA horizon through its first two decades. Over the period from 1974 to 1976 (a period straddling the change of power in Indochina), close to half of total CCA expenditure went for the Indochina program called Asian Christian Service.

This need not have had much to do with standing budget priorities. More perhaps than most other budget items, it reflected (current) availability of (designated) funds. If we remove the ACS account from the total, we find that in the same period expenditure for URM rose from a quarter to a third of total payments, becoming the leading item. Thus, if we compare the funding situation of URM within the CCA with that of the OHD within the FABC (judging by whatever is informally known in the latter case), it would be similar on two counts. On the one hand, for all funds involved, the origin was overwhelmingly non-Asian. On the other hand, from all non-designated funds the lion's share went to the agency on the cutting edge of social action.

Within the URM account, the largest single item of expenditure was the Asian Committee for People's Organization (ACPO).[4] ACPO, as the name implies, was the focus for organizing the powerless for power; here again the CCA's budget priorities can be considered consistent with its policies. By focusing on power, it was touching a raw nerve; this accordingly produced a violent reaction in places where it was strong enough to be a threat, as in South Korea.

A Strong-Minority Pattern: the Korean Case

Let us look briefly at the case of South Korea, as a test case of where organizing the powerless for power in post-1965 Asia was likely to lead.

South Korea was one place where URM had muscle to flex and judged that it could dare to flex it. It was also a place that could claim an indigenous Christian practical ideology of its own—*minjung* or "people's" theology, defining itself over against Western bourgeois theology, Latin American liberation theology, and the Marxist *inmin* ideology from North Korea.[5] Furthermore, it was a place where support for militancy from the Christian community was more broadly based than elsewhere in Asia, as shown by the fact that only in South Korea did repression need to be extended to the sentencing and jailing of interdenominationally representative national Protestant leaders, as well as of a Catholic bishop.

What actually happened in Korea was traumatic, and the question must be asked whether it had to be as traumatic as it was. On the one hand, URM in fact made use of imported techniques such as Saul Alinsky's confrontation-oriented Community Organization. Its way of doing this was discriminating according to its partisans, but not so according to its critics, though some of these latter were themselves Christian activists. On the other hand, whereas by 1979 the Christian activists and the Park regime had to some extent taken each other's measure, and knew what to expect from each other, nobody foresaw the ferocity of the regime that eventually consolidated power after Park's assassination.

Ever since World War II the Korean peninsula has been a major flash point on the left-right line of division running through Asia. Ever since the devastating war from 1950 to 1953, a million soldiers had faced each other along a neck of land a couple of hundred miles wide. After American power lost its other foothold on the East Asian seaboard in Indochina in 1975,

Korea became even more a place of superpower stakes and terrible possibilities. It was a situation guaranteed to breed paranoia.

All this must be taken into account in assessing the political judgment of the Korean Christian activists. What, then, is the verdict on it? Three things must be said. First, on the whole their judgment, more broadly based than that of other Christians in Asia, was also more militantly critical of the regime in power. Next, apart from a couple of star performers on the Catholic side, this militancy generally was stronger among Protestants, and more particularly among URM-related ones. Last, the events of 1980 did not prove the realism of their rhetoric of the immediately preceding period.

The question is commonly posed whether the new wave of activist Christians in the Third World are not too politically innocent for their own good. The question remains posed in the light of the crisis of the Park regime in Korea more directly than it had been posed by the crisis of the Thanom regime in Thailand.

In URM circles, as things stood in the immediate aftermath of General Chun's bloody seizure of power, hindsight more easily credits the activists with integrity and courage than with shrewdness and foresight. The more militant among them were insisting at the end of 1979 that the tide of popular demand for democratization could not be turned back; and even among the more temperate of them there was no anticipation of the way in which their hopes were to be devastated in 1980.[6]

Setbacks like these provide occasions for patient endurance, a virtue in which Korean and other Christians have much practice. Setbacks also provide lessons, and not only for Korean Christians, in the novel exercise of adapting Christian social idealism to the refractory realities of history and politics.

A Weak-Minority Pattern: the Indian Experience

The Korean pattern was of course not the only URM one. There are lessons to be learned too, for example, from the URM experience in Hong Kong, where it has been not a negligible force, and in India, where it has been quite marginal.

The Indian case is illustrative less of URM as an organization than of ACPO as an idea. Nothing could have been more relevant than the notion of "organizing the powerless for power" under the Indian Emergency of 1975 to 1977. There was even an Indian Christian ideology to embody it, or at least an Indian mix of Gandhism, Marxism, and liberalism, articulated by a voice of World Council fame, that of M. M. Thomas.[7] Under his inspiration, via the challenge of the Emergency, there came into being a national Fellowship of Justice Concerns with local constituents such as the Delhi Forum for Christian Concern for People's Struggle. Meanwhile another ecumenical figure in the ACPO framework, M. A. Thomas, launched a continuing movement and bulletin called "Vigil India."

The thinking of these movements may or may not have reflected Myrdal's "mood of the masses," though roots in the villages were not at the outset the most evident thing about them. In any case it is clear that these movements did *not* reflect the mood of the officebearers in the Indian churches— Protestant, Catholic, or (with one partial exception) Oriental. Instead, the Church leadership came close to assuring the leader of the Emergency that they would not complain about whatever happened to human rights in general, as long as nothing happened to their minority rights in particular. They came close to acting accordingly in the way they successively propitiated the Emergency regime, the Janata government, which dismantled the Emergency measures, and the restored Indira government of 1980.[8] This was in stark contrast to their response to a direct threat to their minority rights two years after the Emergency, when massive Christian mobilization against discriminatory proposed legislation brought tens of thousands of Christians out on the streets.

When Christ sent his apostles "like sheep among wolves" (Matt. 10:16), he told them to be "as clever as snakes and as simple as doves." A certain redistribution of these qualities, as between India and Korea, might well have been desirable among the Asian apostles of "power for the powerless."

But the differences were not only in the Christians, or only in the degree to which their assessment of their minority status permitted them to be "prophetic." There could be no Christian realism or idealism that would not take account also of the differences in the internal and external challenges these countries faced. Given the complexity of any people's predicament, there could never be any a priori criterion of whether it was better to play the dove by flying in the face of the obstacle (in the manner of the activists among South Korea's strong Christian minority), or to play the snake by wriggling round it (in the manner of the spokespersons for India's weak one).

One thing, however, remained clear in Korea and became clear in India: Christians could not ultimately separate their own fate from the fate of the whole people.

There was food for thought for Christians everywhere in the heartsearching that followed the Indian Emergency, no less than in the sacrificial suffering that accompanied the Korean one. Faced with the manifest mix of wheat and cockle inside the Church as well as outside it, some of the reflection harked back to "the hidden brotherhood of Christ" implied in Matthew 25, and spoke of "a double election of the Church and of the poor as instruments of God's Kingdom," while some went so far as to redefine the Church itself as being precisely that "emerging paradigmatic fellowship" of faith and solidarity which "can speak to the powers critically and prophetically" in the name of the powerless. For where else could the true Church be found, given "the abdication by the Indian church bodies of their position as 'the Church in the power of the Spirit' "?[9]

We have heard of a "Church of the poor." Are we now hearing of a

"Church of the pure"? That is one way of reading this line of thinking; it would have plenty of Latin American parallels. Another way of reading it is in terms of the political reality underlying it. In any struggle of the powerless for power, the churches as power structures could no more claim immunity from internal strains and stresses than could any other part of the fabric of society.

We have seen this verified in CCA as well as in FABC circles. At the transnational level, the Protestant/Orthodox pattern differed from the Catholic one in that no conflict came out in the open between URM and the CCA like the conflict that surfaced in 1979 between the OHD and the FABC, or at least the South Asian side of the FABC. This was evidence of the relative success of the CCA in identifying with the scouts rather than with the standardbearers. But that is only to underline the fact that in neither case could the main transnational body escape the necessity of some taking of sides.

The alignments might differ, but the source of conflict remained. Once again it was South Asia that provided the most clear-cut example, this time ranging the powers in State and Church together against the WCC, the CCA, and the local defenders of the powerless. For that was what was spelled out during the Indian Emergency most explicitly at the level of the National Christian Council of India (NCCI), when on the one hand, in 1975, "about 90 percent of the assembly were for going the whole way with the P. M." (i.e., Prime Minister Gandhi), while on the other hand, in 1976, notice was served on the CCA and the WCC that "the Churches of India are mature enough to handle a matter like this on their own," and that "outside help need be offered only when the Churches here ask for it."[10] The words might have been borrowed from the national spokespersons of the Russian Orthodox Church or the Chinese Three-Self Movement, inasmuch as they represented an option coinciding with that of the local political power rather than with that of any churches abroad.

Youth and Student Movements

We have singled out the URM as the particular continentally commissioned front of Asian Christian social protest ambitious enough to extend its reach in principle to the entire nine-tenths of Asians who are rural poor or urban workers. It is logical to look next for something with a similar continental reach or mandate, this time extending to the seven-tenths of Asians who are still in the first half of an average human life span: the youth.

Young Christian Workers

The majority of youth and peasants or workers are the same people. Accordingly, we must look first for forms of the Christian social apostolate that give their range of concern the double demarcation of rural youth or young workers. Both in fact figure in the Life and Action programs of the CCA. The ecumenical convergence on this frontier is such that a Catholic nun has headed the CCA program for Asian women workers.

Politically, however, the highest profile in this area belongs to the movement called Young Christian Workers (YCW) or *Jeunesse Ouvrière Chrétienne* (JOC or Jocists).

We have considered URM at the transnational level as the CCA's counterpart of the OHD, mainly in view of the comparable breadth of its social mandate and the contrasts in the structure and evolution of its relations with its parent body. We could consider the YCW at the local level as the Catholic counterpart of URM; here again both comparisons and contrasts would be in order, and in fact are commonly made, where both movements have struggled on more or less equal terms on the same front, as in South Korea or Hong Kong.

Drawing on a larger overall Christian constituency, and remaining less associated with Alinsky-style specializations in its social approach, the YCW in Asia tends to claim greater overall effectiveness than URM (though in fact any difference is dwarfed by the marginal character of both movements in the vast world of Asian workers). It is not for nothing that the YCW figures repeatedly in the earliest events relevant to Asian Christian social protest (Appendix 3), notably in South Korea and South Vietnam.

Perhaps the chief interest of the YCW for an inquiry into the workings of Christian social protest is the precarious balance it endeavors to maintain on the frontier between "Church" and "world," while keeping one foot in each.

The URM experience fails to pose this problem sharply because, while URM gets its mandate from the CCA no less directly than the OHD gets its mandate from the FABC, and acquires a certain transnational identity and consistency through the same connection, the CCA could never operate as an ecclesiastical superbody (even if it did not repudiate any such pretension) in the way the FABC embodies and deploys the institutional authority of the Catholic hierarchy. URM, as we have seen, meets quite enough ecclesiastical resistance at national and sub-national levels; but the YCW meets resistance both there and transnationally.

The YCW carries the blessing and the burden of having pioneered in the world of Catholic Action on the industrial scene. Having grown up in and survived through the period between the repression of Modernism and the Second Vatican Council, the YCW painfully earned the respect and the sanction of the ecclesiastical authorities. Its founder was even named a cardinal in 1965. But from the point of view of the workers' struggle, this official ecclesiastical mandate might be said to have strengthened its right arm while tying its left behind its back.

In the post-conciliar period the YCW became a microcosm of the tension between the jealous embrace of a parental institution and the consuming demands of the human promotion to which the institution is supposed to contribute. More particularly, it became a focus for the tension between the intersecting transnational forces of Catholicism and Marxism. Further-more, because of the Marxist factor, it was guaranteed an uneasy relation-ship with the governments of the national security states. But since that problem is common to the YCW and other youth movements, it can be considered in common for all of them.

Schools and Students

To speak of the student world is to speak also of the intellectuals—especially if we take account of the Gramscian connotation, which tended to bestow the title of intellectual on worker and peasant leaders, and the Chinese Cultural Revolution connotation, which tended to bestow it on all students from the secondary level up. Certainly at the university level, no Asian government of the period could afford not to monitor the goings-on in student circles, any more than it could afford not to keep an eye on any organized activity among farmers and workers. Whether in professedly socialist countries like China or Burma, or in professedly anticommunist ones like South Korea, Thailand, or Indonesia, it was on the student scene that mass discontent could be most easily ignited.

To speak of the Asian student world is also to speak of an area where Christians are not as marginal as they are among peasants or workers—not merely because Christians have more than an average share of education in Asia, but because the churches have had more than an average share in the provision of education for Asians.

We touched earlier (p. 43) on the ambivalence of the role of Christian schools in colonial and post-colonial Asia. On the Catholic side, we have noted that it was precisely their institutional prominence, set in sharper relief by their top-heavy structures of authority, that exposed them to being coopted as agents of social consolidation and control. It is only against such a background that one can understand, for example, the drama that rocked Hong Kong in 1978 over the alleged misuse of funds at the Golden Jubilee School.[11]

A similar furor could not have arisen over the Protestant schools, which were much less authoritarian and much more concentrated on the university level. But in the last analysis the price of institutional prominence has to be paid by the Protestant schools no less than by the Catholic ones. As a group, as a system, they all constitute levers of institutional power; and in the very measure in which they are levers of power they can only tend to imbed themselves in the strata where power is to be found. For this reason the institutional side of Christian education in Asia is not the side on which to look first for a significant social protest role.

The side of the students is another matter. Whatever else may be said of the nebulous phenomenon known in the 1970s as the emerging youth cul-ture, its very existence implied that youth, including students, were no longer deriving their values exclusively from institutions such as school, church, and home.

True, students could never escape completely the built-in consequences of their dependent, transient, and middle-class status. True, the majority would always be apathetic toward politics unless they were actually pressed into politics. Even the activists among students would always include large constituencies in favor of major traditional institutions, religious or political or cultural.

Despite all this, the stereotype of the student of the late 1960s and early 1970s, on both sides of the ideological line in Asia, was politically radical. In that period there was hardly a country that did not feel the tremors of student activism, sometimes building up into political earthquakes that actually left a changed political scene, at least for a time, as in China after 1966 and in Thailand after 1973.

Where were the Christians on this student scene?

The majority of them could be found with the student majority in general—on the sidelines. It would in fact be common to say of them, as their own activists said of the East Asians among them, "most Christian students are more conservative than other students"[12]—as indeed one might expect from their minority status and from their exposure to the additional conservative influence of their local church institutions.

When we speak of activists we are never speaking of more than minorities among minorities. Nevertheless, it is such minorities that have set the pace among Christians at least as much as among others. "In Asia," we are reminded in the same activist circles, "the strongest and most organized elements of the extra-governmental sector are the Christian Voluntary Agencies."[13]

IMCS and WSCF

At the transnational level, the organized presence of Christians on the Asian student scene has been represented by the International Movement of Catholic Students (IMCS-Asia) and the World Student Christian Federation (WSCF-Asia).

The IMCS is synonymous at the student level with Pax Romana (a name it prefers to forget in the measure that it takes its anti-imperialism seriously, as it does in Asia perhaps more than elsewhere). The WSCF covers the same ground as the Student Christian Movement (SCM). Thus, they are both not only transnational, but, like the YCW, transcontinental, and, to that extent, Asian only by import. However, they can count among distinctively Asian achievements the holding of a joint WSCF-IMCS Pan Asian Assembly in Hong Kong in 1976—the first such joint assembly for these bodies or any similar ones.

What can we learn from the proceedings of this Assembly?

First, the ecumenical sharing goes further here than anywhere else at the transnational level. In other instances of sharing, either the group is small, unstructured, and of debatable representativeness (as in the case of the Third World theologians group), or, if it involves major established structures, ultimate control usually remains firmly in the hands of one side or confessional family. In this case, over eighty participants from fifteen Asian political jurisdictions, operating out of two established church-related structures, carried through a ten-day meeting as a fully shared enterprise.

Second, the choice of topic (The Struggle for Self-Reliance in Asia Today) put the Christian students not only on the social protest front, but on a particularly contentious outpost of that front. Though there is no unanimity even about the slogans, there is a more receptive forum here than elsewhere for the language of anticolonialism, anti-imperialism, and anticapitalism. The Christian task is seen as one of building people's power and self-sufficiency; the student Christian task, as one of joining forces toward this end with the majority of people who are peasants and workers; and the Asian student Christian task, as one that "critically considers all non-indigenous inputs,"[14] whether of capital or of culture, or, for that matter, of Christianity.

Third, even the question of the concrete socioeconomic alternative does not prove too hot for the students to handle. Though the East Asians speak of "a dilemma between Christianity and socialism," and only the South Asians affirm explicitly "a responsibility . . . of building socialist society," it is notable that the only Catholic bishop among the resource persons (Bishop Leo Nanayakkara of Sri Lanka) was the Asian Catholic bishop best known for commitment to socialism, and that the one keynote speaker invited was a Marxist-Leninist ex-M. P. of India, an ideologist contemptuous of reformism, categorical as to the superiority of "the world socialist system," committed to work for a "seizure of State power" in the name of that system, and not surprisingly banned from leaving India to deliver his speech in person.[15]

In all three respects, whether rightly or wrongly, the students were grasping nettles impossible to touch at more "responsible" church levels. The most that gets sanction at these latter levels amounts to a kind of programmed ecumenism that enjoys little credibility among students, a kind of anticolonialism that pulls some punches in the ecclesiastical arena, and a kind of anticapitalism so carefully matched with anticommunism that they tend at best to cancel each other out and to hold the Church indefinitely on the fence.[16]

Our concern here is not to judge between the church leaders and the students, but to demonstrate the point that without a plural-role and even a multi-polar church community the issues and options can hardly even get considered. The monolithic church structure so dear to conservative church leaders is truly a guaranteed force for social inertia; and the pious hope cherished by some other church leaders that the Church can be a force for change in the world's power structure, while leaving intact the status quo in its own, is a wish not rooted in the evidence of experience.

It is one thing to say that a judgment must eventually be made between the church leaders and the students; obviously they cannot all be right in all respects. It is another thing to say that the existence of differences between them is itself a symptom of disintegration in the Church. When, as commonly happens, the latter idea is imperceptibly substituted for the former, it is clear that the pilgrimage or procession model of the Church is being rejected in favor of the funnel or pyramid model. It should also be clear that the pyramid model does not correspond with the way things can actually be seen to happen in the life of the churches.

We must reserve for later consideration some of the ways in which scouts like the YCW, the WSCF, and the IMCS have tended to carry the logic of Church of the poor and power for the people further than it has tended to be carried by the standardbearers in the FABC or even the CCA. In practice this divergence throws up some crucial issues, such as those of the internal power structure, the transnational and transcontinental center-periphery relationship, and the transnational and transcontinental Church-and-Marxism relationship, of the Christian communities in Asia.

It must suffice here to draw attention to some immediate consequences of the political polarity between the institutional centers of gravity in the churches and the edges along which they encounter the world around them.

For one thing, the relationship of these groups with the church hierarchy is an arm's-length one, and seems doomed to remain so. The 1976 assembly record speaks of "pressures" from a "nonsupportive" church establishment seen as "resistant to change." The testimony of Asian-level leaders several years later shows no significant lowering of the guard on either side.[17]

In this connection, one must learn to expect a higher decibel level in the rhetoric of advocacy by students, by other youth spokespersons, and by other frontierspeople. Up to a point this must be considered a normal and functional part of the role. Occasionally it is even tacitly acknowledged as such among the *responsables* (to use the word in the French sense) in the Church and other groups out of power. In Indonesia, for example, the relative impunity with which students could voice criticisms of the regime in power enabled them to serve at times as stalking horses for more inhibited critics. In the middle and later seventies the student leaders in Indonesia, including the Catholics among them, said things in public that others would not dare to say but were not necessarily unhappy to hear said.[18]

A second notable effect of the polarization or specialization of the frontierspeople is that their activity significantly widens the range of access to documentation by all those who wish to understand the issues. In any field of inquiry concerning social struggle all words are weapons, and "subversive" documentation is inevitably "fugitive" documentation in more than one sense. Given this situation, objectivity is not a matter of according equal weight to all viewpoints competing for attention. To be objective is to try to compensate for the factor of sheer power in the production of documentation. In practice this requires systematic critical resistance to "establishment" data and corresponding critical openness to sources of data that are unfashionable or even literally unmentionable.

To this task the WSCF-IMCS Assembly made its own contribution. Some of the more practical strategies emerging from that Assembly were those that concerned "communication links," "a regular vehicle of communications," and "interregional exchange of information and documents."[19] These strategies found implementation in two notable series of publications, of independent IMCS origin, called *Interflow* and *Document Reprint Service*. Such publications may be expected to serve a purpose, not at all necessarily as representative records of the struggle for self-reliance in Asia today, but as alternative sources of the sort of documentation that more "representative" records prefer to leave in the shade.

There is a third direct effect worth noting here of the out-on-a-limb situation of Christian militants making common cause in social protest with the mass of farmers, fisherfolk, workers, women, youth, and intellectuals. This is the tendency of transnational headquarters of movements and transnational centers of documentation to cluster in the few Asian havens of relative political freedom.

Not always necessarily for this reason, but in many cases at least partly for this reason, the following agencies of Christian activism, to mention only some of those with transnational horizons, have found their Asian haven in Hong Kong: URM, the WSCF, the IMCS, the Protestant-sponsored Asia Forum on Human Rights, and the Catholic-sponsored Center for the Progress of Peoples.

Hong Kong, though itself no democracy, has been sufficiently insulated from the left-right polarization of the rest of Asia (as a result of a convergence of interest between Beijing and London) to be the only place in the continent besides Japan that could afford a relatively free haven to activist headquarters throughout the 1970s. (Since Asian headquarters also need to be more or less central geographically, at least in terms of air travel around the maritime crescent, the other favored locations have been Bangkok and Singapore.)

A particular form of this migration of agencies in search of freedom of action is the practice of basing a center in one country for dissemination of information about repression in another. Japan has played this role for South Korea through the Japan Emergency Christian Conference on Korean Problems and the Japanese Catholic Commission for Justice and Peace. Hong Kong has played it for the Philippines, notably through a Resource Center for Philippine Concerns.

The same role, of course, has been more extensively played outside Asia for countries of both left and right within the continent. Historically the role was introduced to Asia in the 1950s by the "China watchers" in Hong Kong and elsewhere. Among church people, and in reaction to right-wing repression, it is more properly a phenomenon of the 1970s.

In these ways—through driving activist headquarters and communication systems beyond national borders—the authoritarian regimes of left and right in Asia made their own unplanned contribution to the transnationalization of Asian Christian social protest.

Radical Religious Meaning-Makers

Peasants, workers, youth—we have seen these as the broadest (overlapping) categories into which Asians fall, and at the same time as the broadest potential and actual sources of social discontent. Another overlapping category, also a potential source of social protest, has been mentioned so far only in passing: the category of women. When we speak of peasants, youth, and women, we are in each case speaking of a category constituting an actual majority in most Asian countries, and a majority in one way or another excluded from the mainstream of Asian public life.

It is only with our last category of Asians important to a study of social protest—the category of intellectuals in the stricter sense—that we are treating of a group that is marginal in actual numbers, and numerically marginal at the level of membership and leadership alike.

By defining intellectuals earlier as those who give voice and direction to the mass, we have left room here for both speculative specialists and pastoral agents in the category of radical religious meaning-makers. By the transnational test, we need not expect to find too many of these in Asian Christianity, any more than we have found any great multiplicity of leading Christian elements in the other categories.

Christian-inspired movements of farmers or fisherfolk, for instance, are scarcely in view in Asia on the transnational horizon, though the Federation of Free Farmers in the Philippines has a relatively long history on one national horizon. As for Christian-inspired movements of workers, we have met these in the YCW and in URM; as for Christian-inspired movements of students, we have met them in the IMCS and the WSCF.

But what about Asia-wide embodiments of social protest in the ranks of the full-time personnel of the churches themselves? We met them at the outset of our survey of transnational Catholicism in Asia in the forms called SELA and PISA. There is more to be added; and since the role of religious personnel, irrespective of whether it is a ministry of word or of sacrament, is in perceptible effect preeminently the role of meaning-makers, we may appropriately group under this heading the activities of transnational associations of religious along with those of theologians.

To complete our skeleton survey of the transnational avant-garde, since the meaning-making function in religious protest tends to culminate in the words, the symbols, and even the persons of individual men and women, who may or may not be priests or religious, we must scan the Asian horizon for transnationally salient instances of these individual voices of the voiceless.

Frontiers in Ministry, Male and Female

As noted at the outset of this study, all churches are transnational organizations at least in tendency. The Roman Catholic Church has been transnational in tendency and reality as long as there have been nations to transcend; in fact, on the scale of its history, nation states appear as a novelty and almost as an interlude. Within that Church, the Catholic hierarchy and the diocesan clergy had a transcontinental organization at least a thousand years before they had a continental one.

This transcontinental (and, in modern times, transhemispheric) organization was never stronger than it has been in the post-colonial era. It continues to play a preponderant role in global Catholicism, one that is not necessarily in a decolonizing direction in the intermediate term. This is a point that will require further examination. Meanwhile, part of the effect of the beginnings of continental organization in the Asian context has been in the direction of reducing continental dependence in relation to the transhemispheric "center."

The FABC as a bishops' organization is alive and well in the short term, as we have seen, with some signs of internal strains in the medium term, as we have also seen. The Asian diocesan priesthood has never had a comparable continuing continental organization, though the PISA meeting of 1965 gave the clergy a temporary sense of Asian identity on the social action front.

But there are also the religious orders and congregations and missionary institutes of men and women, who make up a large majority of full-time consecrated pastoral agents in Asia. What is the situation of these as regards transnational organization?

Once again history in the form of the Western background and bureaucracy in the form of Roman centralism have combined to make the dominant pattern one of transcontinental organization, with only incipient networks between the transhemispheric center and the national or sub-national Asian base. Still, it is these incipient networks that should be watched as harbingers of a new kind of Catholic transnationalism.

Let us take note of two current patterns, one among men religious, the other among women religious.

The Society of Jesus, with membership still numbered in the tens of thousands, is the largest clerical religious body in the Catholic Church. Its governmental structure provides for transnational assistencies between the Generalate in Rome and the provinces in the various countries. In the region relevant to our inquiry the most notable example is the East Asian Assistancy. This has been served by an elaborate bureaucracy, already mentioned, called the Bureau of Asian Affairs (BAA). As also mentioned, it was preceded or spearheaded into existence by one of its present component movements, an East Asian Jesuit association on the social action front, Socio-Economic Life in Asia (SELA).

Both the BAA and SELA were still alive and well in the early 1980s. At least, there was no sign that their activity would fade away in the then fore-seeable future. Indeed, they were already such relative old-timers on the Asian Catholic scene, and so strongly structured for long-term service, that they were beginning to be seen as overtaken by the Weberian process of routinization. Such at least was the feeling among some activists, including some Jesuit activists; this might be fair or unfair, but it was inevitable. For change is a battlefield on which no artillery, all the more if it is weighty and effective, can retain for long the image of being always where the action is.[20]

Men religious in Asia, in any case, have not been in the forefront of ef-forts at Asia-wide cooperation among religious institutes. For that matter, in the judgment of many of both sexes, men religious in Asia have not been in the forefront of renewal and innovation on any major front, by compari-son with their sisters in religion.[21] It was left to the women religious to de-velop in the 1970s, from a beginning modestly called Asian Service Center for Religious Women, the only transnational and transinstitutional associa-tion of religious on the Asian horizon.

This is now known as the Asian Meeting of Religious Women (AMOR). By 1980 it had met for the fifth time, bringing major superiors of women religious of twelve countries together in Sri Lanka.

Its statement there urged its members in Asia and Australia to "reeval-uate and reorient apostolates to meet the challenges of today." That was standard rhetoric in any post-conciliar gathering of religious of either sex; but the delegates of AMOR V went further. In reference to their traditional apostolates of "education, health, and social welfare," they accused them-selves of having "unconsciously strengthened the hands of the oppressors" and "actually helped to generate and perpetuate an elitist class of people." They now called for shifting "from serving the elite groups to living with the poor," for abandoning "hothouse formation methods" in favor of "the new method of learning while living with people," and for "the Sisters who opt for the poor" to be "ready to be broken and given as sustenance in the struggle of the people."[22]

What this could mean in practice was spelled out only a month later in another continent, in the shallow graves of the murdered women mission-aries of El Salvador. But in any case the women behind the AMOR state-ment were themselves no strangers to real experience of victim women and shallow graves.

Behind AMOR V stood a novel convergence of emerging forces: those of women, those of youth, those of post-conciliar religious renewal, and those of social protest in the global sense.

At the turn of the decade, the important social training center, the Asian

Social Institute in Manila, was headed by a woman, the Filipina Mina Ramirez; the Asia-Pacific Secretariate of the YCW was led by a woman, the Filipina Norma Biñas; the CCA program for women workers in Asia was under the charge of a woman religious, the Filipina Teresa Dagdag; and the head of AMOR, after the Filipina Christine Tan, was the Indian Gladys D'Souza.

None of these women was elderly; most were young; and as for being socially radical, even to the point of arousing controversy, the religious were if anything more in the forefront than the laywomen. If one were looking for signs of the distance travelled by Asian Christianity between 1965 and 1982, one could hardly find more telling ones than the differences between the Asian women religious of the 1950s and those of the 1980s, at least on those frontiers of activity occupied by contestatory superiors, political detainee task forces, and rural missionaries of various kinds.

The prominence of Filipinas and of Philippine areas of activism in this picture calls for comment. It is not that Filipino women religious had a proportion of the Asian total of nuns as large as Filipino layfolk had of the Asian total of Catholics. On the contrary, there is a disconcerting contrast between the contours of the Church of the people in Asia, as measured by the Catholic population, and the contours of the institutional Church in Asia, as measured by the numbers of pastoral agents (bishops, priests, other men religious, women religious—the women religious being always a majority of the total).

This is illustrated in Appendixes 5 and 6. There are about four times as many pastoral agents in India as in the Philippines, which has about five times as many Catholics; by a per capita index of institutionalization on this basis, the Catholic Church is more institutionalized in other countries than in the Philippines by a factor of sixty in Japan, of fifteen in India and Vietnam, of ten in South Korea, of eight in Sri Lanka, and of four in Indonesia.

How are we to interpret these figures? We must leave until later an attempt to put all the elements in the balance, and confine ourselves here to noting once more, as we have noted in connection with the FABC, the CCA, the NCCI, the YCW, the BAA, and SELA, the ambivalence of institutionalized agencies, even institutionalized agencies of change. It is clear that change does not start either from top-heavy structures, which can only fall by their own weight, or from bottom-heavy bodies, which are inert by definition. Somewhere between the extremes there is an always fluctuating optimum area of leverage for change.

The evidence suggests that change must begin from circles outside but not too far outside the centers of power.

In the context of the world order, it must begin from nonruling groups within striking or destabilizing distance of rule, such as some parties and some churches.

In the context of churches, it must begin from nonhierarchical groups in orbit between the hierarchical centers and the marginal masses, such as religious orders and some mass-based lay movements.

In the context of religious orders and congregations, it must begin similarly from groups not too near either the gravitational force of the center or the tangential force of the fringes, such as groups of women religious in not too heavily institutionalized religious institutes and national churches.

In the context of women religious institutes, it must begin in conditions where some provocation for change and some prospects for change are proffered by the forces at play in the larger society. In the 1970s these conditions were realized more fully in the Philippines than in any other country with a Christian population of a million or more.

Frontiers in Dialogue and Theology

At the International Mission Congress of 1979 in Manila, already mentioned in connection with those of Melbourne and Pattaya in 1980, the focus was on relating the three emerging themes in Asian Catholicism: justice for the poor, dialogue with religions and ideologies, and inculturation into the Asian context. Agencies to deal with the first two concerns existed in various stages of readiness in both the FABC and the CCA. As for inculturation, there was a wide gap between the degree of self-reliance assumed as a birthright by the churches of the CCA on the one hand, and, on the other, the narrow course steered by the FABC between the various Asian cultural contexts and the steady pull of centralization from Rome.

Judged by their degree of social impact, the activities of the CCA Asia Ecumenical Center (AEC) and of the FABC Bishops' Institute for Religious Affairs (BIRA) are not particularly relevant to our inquiry. Neither is the World Conference on Religion and Peace (WCRP), which under the presidency of the Catholic Archbishop of Delhi blazed some trails in meetings of the 1970s—in Kyoto, Louvain, Singapore, and Princeton. More directly relevant is the idea embodied, though on a much humbler scale, in the organization known originally as the Asian Cultural (and Religious) Forum on Development (now ACFOD).

ACFOD is another transnational and transconfessional creation of the 1970s. Launched in 1973 under the ecumenical sponsorship of SODEPAX, brought to grips with development problems in 1975 in an interreligious conference with the cosponsorship of the UN Food and Agriculture Organization (FAO), based in Bangkok with a Catholic priest and later a Thai Buddhist as chief coordinator, it set itself the task of "action, dialogue, and mutual support" linking religious and cultural groups "in a common endeavor for social justice and development."[23]

If ever there was a David taking on a Goliath, it was ACFOD undertaking to break down the barriers built by millennia of cultural conditioning among the religious, ideological, and cultural blocs of Asia. It is impossible to report anything yet from ACFD by way of significant impact on its chosen field of endeavor. Only the fact that a systematic beginning has been made makes ACFOD a possible milestone in the history of Asian efforts at social change.

Action is of the essence of movements like ACFOD. What of cooperative initiatives that concentrate exclusively on reflection? So far the Asian pattern has been for theological associations to emerge transnationally within the CCA family and in the course of time to gain Catholic participation. In these, as reflected in journals like the *South East Asia Journal of Theology*, attention to social issues has been an effect rather than a cause of social awareness in the wider world. An effort to put theology more in the mainstream of the struggle for self-reliance is represented by the CCA Commission on Theological Concerns, with its ready welcome for indigenous theological thinking.

But to touch a nerve and provoke a reaction, socially radical theological thinking in Asia had to become still more broadly transnational and transconfessional. Theologians as a group became a visible factor in Asian Christian social protest only with the Wennappuwa meeting of the Ecumenical Association of Third World Theologians (EATWOT).

Third World theologians had to become a separate association in order to get a hearing in the theological—hitherto practically synonymous with the Western theological—world. Otherwise they could never have been much more than an echo of that world's trumpet tone, or at best a very muted variation on its themes. When EATWOT held its first Asian meeting in Sri Lanka in 1979, it had already met twice in Africa (1976 and 1977). Its first Latin American meeting was held in 1980. But by 1979 its most influential input came from liberation theology, and the most influential source of this was Latin America.

By 1979, liberation theology was proving itself not merely influential but distinctly threatening to the received wisdom in theology. Its voices now came from several continents; it wore the faces of several races and of both sexes; it spoke with the accents of Marx, Ché Guevara, Gandhi, King, and (as was the case in the Philippines) Mao. It had its opponents in the Third World, and it did not easily prevail at Wennappuwa; but prevail it did in the end, as is seen in the statement cited at the beginning of this study.

Wennappuwa undertook its task with not insignificant credentials. There was a cardinal (Darmojuwono of Indonesia) and six bishops from four other countries among the eighty participants from ten Asian and several other countries. Sri Lanka itself was disproportionately represented, but none of the nonsocialist Asian countries of major Christian strength, with the forced exception of South Korea, was without representation. What the group had to say, therefore, could not be immediately brushed aside as the sloganeering of an immature or unrepresentative minority.

Where the WSCF-IMCS meeting of 1976 had spoken of the struggle for self-reliance in Asia, the EATWOT meeting spoke of Asia's Struggle for Full Humanity and saw that as "the Asian context" of the search for "a relevant theology." Its analysis of the issues in Asia accepted some basic Marxist criteria; passed a harder judgment on the role of capitalism there than on the role of socialism; spoke of "revolutionary violence" there as being "most often unavoidable"; reacted against theology's past "elitist" and "domesticating" role; and called for a theology for which, as Marx himself would have put it, the point was not to interpret the world but to change it.[24]

If getting attention may be considered a first step for a theology committed to change, the Wennappuwa statement at least met that first test. Within little more than a year Vatican displeasure had been manifested, first in a direct criticism of the Wennappuwa findings, then in an attempt to isolate the following EATWOT meeting in São Paulo. The criticism accused the Wennappuwa findings of being a warmed-over version of an already discredited trend, not worthy of the name of theology.[25]

The immediate effect of this criticism was to provoke the reaffirmation and reinforcement of the views expressed by the conference. Less immediately and more positively, the criticism may have influenced the framing of the São Paulo statement, which took more care than the Wennappuwa one to sound like theology rather than like politics.[26] In the longer term, even apart from any ultimate rights or wrongs in the case, it posed in its context a particular burning question about transnational relations.

The burning question is this: on the whole, do transnational relations make for a freer, more fraternal, more participatory, less unbalanced, more peaceful world than nation state relations do?

In the intermediate term, it is not at all certain. There is generally admitted to be a certain ambivalence in the way such relations work out in international politics in the more conventional sense. There appears to be a similar ambivalence in the way they work out in the politics of transnational relations in the churches. When we return to this, we must return prepared to look for some clarifying distinctions.

Individual Symbols of Social Protest

The meaning-making function in religious protest tends to culminate in the words, the symbols, and even the persons of individual men and women. The global record is full of religious rebels who are the hinges, as it were, on which history has turned: Gautama, Jesus, Mahomet, Luther, Gandhi, to mention only some giants. The case appears to be no different with movements that claim to have outgrown religion and outgrown individualism. Who would say that individual charisma has loomed less large in the world of Marx, Lenin, Stalin, Mao, Ho, Tito, Castro, and Kim Il Sung?

How this is explained is of course a subject of perennial dispute among social scientists. There will probably never be an end to efforts to explain one of their fields in terms of another, if only because there will never be an end to tendencies to exaggerate the role of one or the other and thus provoke a swing of the pendulum.

Marx and Engels arrived on the historical scene at a moment when the pendulum, in terms of exaltation of the role of what would come to be called superstructure, had swung to a Hegelian extreme. Similarly, Hitler, Stalin, Gandhi, Mao, not to mention more recent arrivals like Deng Xiaoping, John Paul II, and Khomeini, may yet be seen in historical retrospect as having shown in practice the inevitability of a return swing.

One might hazard the hypothesis that each age in history is liable to be dominated by that particular one of the irreducible sources of historical dynamism that has been most denied its due credit in the preceding age— whether that be the forces and relations of production and power, or the structures and dynamisms of the cultural complex, or the role of the individual human personality.

As for the personal contribution in the present age, the frontier of contemporary Christian social protest has already produced its crop of individuals who have articulated and embodied its force and direction—Martin Luther King, Camilo Torres, Helder Camara, Ernesto Cardenal, Oscar Romero. Can we find comparable transnationally salient figures on the Asian horizon? The seeds of such may have been sprouting, but within the 1970s they had not yet yielded a harvest.

As a galvanizing signal, the martyrdom of a high church leader might cross frontiers fastest. This did not happen in Asia within the 1970s, though a Korean Catholic bishop, Daniel Tji of Wonju, came close to becoming a martyr-figure in General Park's prisons, and though the general secretary of the main Protestant church in Taiwan, the Presbyterian C. M. Kao, was serving a heavy jail sentence for association with Taiwanese dissidence by the beginning of the 1980s.

The barriers are greater where the message needs to be articulated, since this requires crossing boundaries of language and culture. Neither English nor French can reach as many Asians as there are Latin Americans reached by Spanish or Portuguese; and the mass languages of Asia, led by Chinese, Hindi, Indonesian, and Japanese, are even more culture-bound.

When the articulation in question is at a technical theological level, the difficulties are compounded. M. M. Thomas of India, Cardinal Kim of Korea, Bishops Labayen and Claver of the Philippines were among the few Asians of high ecclesiastical standing whose articulation of a Christian rationale for social protest was beginning to have an international and interconfessional audience within the period under study.

Literary figures command a wider following than theologians. In a country like Japan, where the institutional writ of the churches runs no higher than 1 percent to 2 percent of the population, one arrives at a very different measure of the influence of the Christian leaven when one considers those Christian writers, such as Endo Shusaku, who have been among the most widely read throughout the population. In Indonesia, comparable national eminence has been enjoyed by W. S. Rendra, whose Christian connections are tenuous but who has been directly associated with social protest.

In the end, however, one must look to the Philippines and South Korea, the two foremost Asian countries of Christian social protest, for living symbols of protest who have some visibility beyond their own national horizons.

The Filipino example most in view in the 1970s was Edicio de la Torre, a young priest of the Society of the Divine Word. His path to radicalization came through the experience of his chaplaincy to the Federation of Free Farmers, which in the 1960s was a pioneering organization on the rural frontier. He had been preaching the need for social revolution in more or less Marxist terms before the imposition of martial law in 1972. He put off arrest for two years by going underground, then spent over five years in political detention before being released without trial in 1980. By then he had become something of a celebrity abroad as well as at home.

The conditions of his imprisonment were not the harshest or most restrictive suffered by Philippine detainees. This no doubt contributed to a notable serenity in the development of his thinking. As described by himself in the last months of his first detention (he was re-arrested in 1982), that thinking had not only gone beyond the stage where a committed Christian radical gives priority to cultural revolution within the Church, but had also gone beyond the stage where he or she ceases to be concerned for cultural revolution within the Church.

History, he felt, had already shown that, just as the Church alone is incapable of bringing social revolution to the state, so the state alone is incapable of bringing social revolution to the Church. To leave the institutional Church to its fate is not consistent either with concern for the success of the social revolution (the revolution may swallow the Church, but an unreconciled Church will stick in its throat) or with concern for the success of renewal in the Church (a Church of the people does not leave its institutional framework behind it like a used cocoon).[27]

In his pre-jail days de la Torre had promoted a group called the Theological Writing Collective of the Christians for National Liberation, a specimen of documented cross-fertilization of theology and Maoism outside China. Among products of his prison days is a collection of poems and letters by himself and others called *Pintíg*—a primary source among the mass of documentation on the jails of Marcos, and a Philippine product of the sort of conditions that produced the prison writings of Bonhoeffer under Hitler, of Gramsci under Mussolini, and of Berrigan in the Vietnam-era United States. Out of prison and out of the Philippines from 1980 until 1982, de la Torre joined the transnational dialogue on human liberation on the terms hammered out of his experience. These terms amounted to a dialogue on all fronts—with the Church, as a priest who has opted to remain a priest, and with all other forces, including Marxist and Muslim ones, which purport to offer a way to liberation by whatever means the task requires.[28]

As an international symbol of social protest in the 1970s, the South Korean counterpart of de la Torre was Kim Chi Ha.

Like de la Torre, Kim was widely read in radical theology and social thinking. Like de la Torre, he suffered political imprisonment, which in his case meant repeated jailings, extremely harsh jail conditions, and a confession of communist sympathies which he later repudiated as having been extracted by torture. Like de la Torre, he had poetic and artistic gifts; in fact it was as a poet and playwright that he came to be identified nationally and internationally. As in the case of de la Torre, his passion was for the people, and most particularly for the rural people, whose poverty and hunger had been part of his own life.

Unlike de la Torre, Kim was not a priest or even a cradle Christian. His conversion to Catholicism dated from 1971; but his life from then on was entwined with that of his local bishop in Wonju, the one bishop in non-socialist Asia who could compare notes with him on what it was like to be behind prison bars in a national security state.

Kim Chi Ha's last imprisonment in the 1970s covered almost the same years as the first period of detention of de la Torre—with the difference that in Kim's case there had been a trial, a conviction, and a sentence commuted from death to life imprisonment and later to twenty years before being lifted altogether in 1981 under the presidency of General Chun. His post-prison course falls outside the scope of this study. It must suffice to say that it began with a reaffirmation of the themes of his previous writing, and a declaration that this was "only the beginning."[29]

What were those themes? They concern us here because in them there could be taking shape, with all the crudeness and fragmentation but also with all the passion and intensity of the crucible from which they came, something that might yet be seen as an authentic Asian theology, capable of catching imaginations transnationally and of providing social protest with a vision at once credibly Asian, credibly Christian, and credible as a motive force for social change.

As for the Asian roots, we have touched on them earlier in connection with URM in Korea. These roots sink beneath the Confucian topsoil into the peasant culture that bred a century of popular upheavals against alien rule: the 1894 Tonghak rebellion against Chinese tutelage; the 1919 March 1 Movement against Japan; and the upheaval of the students, workers, and farmers who rose against the South Korean military elites of the period after World War II.

Providentially, some might say, Kim had no recourse other than this "Eastern learning" before his encounter with Christianity. By the time of that encounter, he was already imbued with an outlook at once populist, religious in both an intense personal and a broad social sense, and non-violent (in a sense that will need further qualification[30]). For him the Tonghak principle—treat people as though they were God—needed only to be given a theological rationale in the doctrine of the incarnation, and a social application by way of social theory or political strategy. On the side of social theory, however, it was still inchoate at best at the time of his death sentence.

We have mentioned how *minjung* theology, which is the theology appropriated by Kim Chi Ha and developed by some Protestant theologians such as Kim Yong-bock, defined itself over against (which is not to say in any rigid opposition to) Western liberalism, Latin American liberation theology, and Marxism-Leninism, especially as embodied in the North Korean regime. Three pressures doubtlessly played a part in crystallizing this thinking: the cultural need to affirm an indigenous identity, the hostility of the prevailing political and religious climate to anything savoring of Marxism, and the consciousness of the problems that had remained unsolved and in some ways exacerbated after twelve decades of attempts to act on the *Communist Manifesto*.

One of these problems was the catastrophic impasse, illustrated nowhere better than on the embattled Korean peninsula, in the worldwide struggle between economic liberalism and Marxism. Another problem was the seeming inevitability of the betrayal of every revolution, and above all the seeming inevitability of the betrayal of every Leninist revolution, by the newly established power elite. The question posed by the latter problem is: Is there any way to keep the needed revolution faithful to the interests of the people; and, if not, is there any strategy for coping with the inevitable betrayal? This question could not but be a constant preoccupation of Asian Christian leaders at the transnational level; and so it is not surprising to find *minjung* thinking being hopefully scrutinized in bodies such as the CCA's Commission on Theological Concerns.[31]

Kim Chi Ha has sometimes been described as Asia's Solzhenitsyn. The comparison, though suggestive, can hardly be taken too seriously. On the one hand, by 1981 Kim had yet to show that he could produce a literary work on the scale or with the universality of appeal of a major Russian novel. On the other hand, his sociopolitical thinking also had yet to show signs of the sclerosis and stridency of that of the celebrated Russian exile.

Kim, at 41 (in 1982), had already become a transnational voice of the Asian voiceless, and a symbol of Christian solidarity with more than Christian victims of oppression. Still, his ultimate stature could not be confidently predicted. As he himself said, it was only the beginning, a beginning that might or might not have an important sequel—both for his role in the history of Asian Christian social protest and for the role of Christian protest in the history of Asian social change.

6

THE UNDERLYING
LOCAL CONTEXTS

In any attempt to scan the Asian horizon in search of transnationally salient features of Christian social protest, two things most immediately demand to be noticed.

On the one hand, the multiplicity of the data, overwhelming when one recalls that it spreads over nearly two-thirds of the human race, becomes relatively manageable when attention is confined strictly to those transnationally salient features—just as it is easier to take in a map of Asia if the continent can be imagined as covered with water to a height of, say, 1,000 or 5,000 meters. At 5,000 meters, the waters would make Asia look like a cluster of islands in the vicinity of what we now call Tibet. At 1,000 meters, we would see an Asian backbone running from Iran to Mongolia, with ribs and limbs scattered as far as Turkey, Yemen, Sri Lanka, Java, New Guinea, Japan, and the shores of the Arctic Ocean. Similarly, if considered exclusively at its transnational altitudes, Asian Christian social protest takes on a certain shape—a skeletal shape, which is not entirely misleading for all that.

On the other hand, in any living body the skeleton is not separated from the flesh, and in fact gives only a very approximate idea of what the whole body looks like. In excluding from a map of Asia all land below 1,000 meters, one would in fact be excluding the Asia in which the immense majority of Asians live and have lived from time immemorial. Similarly, in excluding from the study of Asian Christian social protest the purely national or subnational processes that could be considered part of it, we risk conveying some major misrepresentations of the totality of the phenomenon.

To learn all that can be learned about the transnational level of Asian Christian social protest, while at the same time compensating for any major distortions or deficiencies liable to result from focusing on that particular level of that phenomenon, we need to put things more precisely in context in relation to a series of overlapping other contexts. One context can cover some of the same ground as another in any one of three ways: by falling wholly within the same ground, by falling partly within it and partly outside it, and by covering all of it and more. We must look for significant instances of all three kinds of contexts in relation to the ground we have already surveyed.

Let us take a closer look, then, at those national or subnational processes that belong to the underlying local contexts of Asian Christian social protest.

In the measure that global society becomes more transnational, it becomes more difficult to draw that contour line, on the map of humankind, which distinguishes phenomena that are transnationally salient from those that are not.

The distinction is at its most elusive when applied to communication. It is when one contemplates a world of mass media, satellite media, and international travel that the myth of the global village looks closest to becoming a reality. It begins to seem almost as if Teilhard de Chardin's noosphere has really become a medium spread uniformly around the globe—at least now that the various iron curtains and bamboo curtains of the first postwar generation are no longer as tightly closed as they used to be.

It is premature to think that the global village has arrived, even in respect to communications; but it is true that a certain common fund of global awareness exists today in a way that was unthinkable in earlier times. There is really something new under the sun when people on both sides of the globe can simultaneously follow space flights or sports events or the repercussions of major political developments, and be aware of being united in the activity; when the starvation of children on one side can be witnessed in living rooms on the other; and when tyrants on any side must live with the possibility of being detected in their tyrannizing by observers on any other.

Thus, in Asia, regimes that have had something to hide (and what regime has not something to hide?) have had to live with the fact that at least something of what they are up to will come to light through outside monitors of their behavior. There is ample evidence (for example, in the files of Amnesty International) that a certain amount of international political leverage has been made possible through this porosity of even the most tightly sealed interstate borders.

The fact remains that even in respect to communications there is still a long way to go before everyone in the world feels like everyone else's neighbor. A glance at the local press on any continent, including those where press freedom is least restricted, suffices to show just how insular, how positively parochial, the readers of the press are presumed to be by those whose vested interest lies in giving the people what they want. A conversation with a peasant in northern China will show in a similar way that his or her mental world map is not the same as that of a worker in southern India, or for that matter as that of a peasant in southern China. Even what is seen as the social protest experience differs drastically from country to country and from province to province.

In what respects, specifically, does the transnational picture of Asian

Christian social protest already outlined need to be corrected or put in perspective in the light of the country-by-country record?

To suggest an answer to this question, let us first examine the main events
or event-clusters that have loomed large in the record of Asian Christian
social protest. Let us look at these without particular regard for the question of what country they occurred in or whether their repercussions have
been felt beyond that country's borders. This examination alone will not
suffice to bring to light the full geographical pattern, since the underlying
processes are like icebergs that do not always show tips above water in the
temporally definable sense of "events." But it will show that the events and
processes involved do have a certain geographical concentration; and this
realization will oblige us to compensate for one major inadequacy in our
transnational picture by supplementing it with one outstanding national
case history—that of the Philippines.

Events, Event-clusters, and Their Geographical Distribution

Appendix 3 itemizes the relevant events and event-clusters over an
eighteen-year period. As a guide to the unfolding of the phenomenon under
study, it is only indicative, first because it shows only the tips of the icebergs
and second because it is only a selection among these. As far as possible the
selection is confined to events whose relevance is more or less self-evident.
In addition, the selection is biased toward events that point beyond themselves, indicating (though this is not in every case verifiable) that a whole
series of events or processes lies behind or beneath each one.

Granted its limitations, what generalizations can be made on the basis of
such a list?

About one in six of the events occurred outside Asia, either involving
Asians (as in the worldwide Catholic or Protestant meetings) or at least
affecting Asian Christian social protest (as in the continent-wide Latin
American meetings). Their field of concern extends beyond the borders of
Asian nations and of Asia itself. About one-fourth are events whose field of
concern is transnational, though not transcontinental.

These two groups of events would by themselves suffice to show what is
meant by saying that a new transnational trend, spearheaded by a new intensity of transnational social concern, has become part of the pattern of
global Christianity in the past generation, and more especially in the past
half generation. Such a list of events could scarcely have been predicted by
anyone trying to peer into the future half a century or even a quarter of a
century earlier.

Our list also shows that a clear majority of the relevant events were of less
than transnational scope. For the people who precipitated them, the precipi-
tating factor was regularly a local provocation.

Accordingly, one looks for major provocations where there have been
major reactions. These major provocations are in fact not far to seek in

South Korea, in the Philippines, and in the Republic of Vietnam, the three countries that together account for about two-thirds of the local cases on the list. However, they have also not been far to seek in other Asian countries less strongly represented, such as Indonesia, India, Taiwan, and the People's Republic of Vietnam, or in other Asian countries not represented at all, such as North Korea, China, or Thailand. So we need to take a closer look at these local cases.

There is no simple correlation between the strength of a local provocation and the strength of the local Christian reaction. The most obvious reason for this is that social protest, like human eyesight, can operate only along a limited segment of the spectrum of theoretical possibility. To put the point in Toynbeean terms, eliciting a creative response requires a challenge that is neither too crushingly strong nor too enervatingly weak. We can now attempt to define more precisely what constitutes in Asia a challenge capable of eliciting a creative response in terms of Christian social protest.

First Exclusions: Homelands of Half of All Asians (North and West)

We have had occasion already, when considering Christianity in the Asian Crisis (p. 29), to determine that Christian social protest has been excluded as a practical option and made a fairly total irrelevance over more than four-fifths of Asia's territory and for more than half of Asia's people, though these include only about one-seventh of Asia's Christians.

The first decisive factor in these areas is extreme minority status, Christians being a minority of at best 2 percent in communist-dominated northern Asia taken as a whole, and in Muslim-dominated southwestern Asia, together with Pakistan and Bangladesh, taken as a whole. The second decisive factor in both areas is the hostility of the dominant ideology to any Christian voice or influence in public affairs.

The combination of both factors makes the relations of force too unequal to permit any real confrontation between Church and State on issues of public policy. Where minority status is not extreme, as is the case in Syria, which is almost one-tenth Christian, the entrenchment of Islam in and around the country is sufficient to rule out any flexing of Christian political muscle. Where Christians are not in a minority at all, as has been the case within the very local limits of Lebanon, they are certainly involved in confrontation, as also noted earlier, but not at all in the role of social radicals.

Obviously it is not difficult in Asia to find clear-cut cases where the pressures inhibiting corporate Christian social protest are insuperably strong. Even in such contexts it will always be possible to find *individuals* heroic enough to protest in the name of justice for others; but in such contexts it is not humanly realistic to expect significant postures of protest on the part of representative *groups*, except in the face of threats to the groups' own survival.

"Of course," one could hear in 1980 from the newly mandated spokes-

person of Chinese Protestantism, "our patriotism is not without a prophetic or critical character."[1] But the mere mention of this idea is an ex-
traordinary novelty in that situation. It is not a statement of the way things
have recently been in the People's Republic; rather, it reflects a new relax-
ation inside China and a new openness to currents of thought and talk outside it. It is a novel Chinese testimony to the legitimacy of that particular
current in global Christianity. [2]

Further Exclusions: Homelands of Three-Quarters of All Other Asians (South and East)

It is not only in northern or western Asia that one can define the relations
of force between Church and State as insuperably unequal. Even in the
absence of a hostile dominant ideology, it does not appear that a Christian
minority of less than, say, 5 percent, can realistically be expected to put
itself on a collision course with state power, except where its own survival is
at stake. That seems to be the lesson of experience in the remaining parts of
Asia; and that criterion would excuse us from the trouble of looking for a
prophetic or critical Church in any country of continental Southeast Asia
except Vietnam, and in any country of East Asia except South Korea.

Or is this generalization too sweeping? It is partly a question of definition, a question as to which postures of protest are representative enough to
be significant.

On a small scale these postures can be found in embryo almost everywhere—even in Bangladesh, where Christians are only half of one percent
of the population. On a national scale they can be found in pure form
nowhere, and certainly not in the Philippines, the only majority-Christian
country, where the line between conservatism and radicalism runs through
the Church itself.

Between the extremes, we must be content to diagnose postures of protest
as representative and significant when the groups involved are somewhat
broadly based and have a degree of linkage to the institutional Church,
sufficient to modify the overall distribution of Christian weight in the balance of power in state and society. This is shown most clearly in united
stands on public issues by nationally representative church bodies that are
distinctly and riskily critical of the policies of those in power. These united
official stands usually represent a diluted response to militant pressures
from lower levels of representativeness.

Let us see in the concrete if we have excluded too much of Asia.

Japan, officially less than 2 percent Christian, might look like a refuta-
tion of the thesis, given its relatively vocal national organs of social concern
among both Protestants and Catholics. It might look like it, that is, until we
measure the element of risk. There is undoubtedly an evolution in boldness
there, especially among Catholics; but the last time it was really risky for
Christians to be critical in Japan was before and during World War II. Jap-

anese Christianity failed the test then, and it has not been confronted with any comparable test since, though it has made increasing use of its relative freedom in the meantime.[3]

Japan, along with Hong Kong, is about the only territory in Asia of which it could be said that the Church there in the postwar generation was being killed with kindness, in contrast with the pattern of crucifixion and resurrection in the Philippines and South Korea. There would still be some truth in this generalization, although, if it were entirely true, much (see pp. 83f.) would be missing from the present transnational picture of Asian Christian social protest.

Burma, no more than 4 percent Christian, might also seem to challenge our hypothesis. What are we to make of a situation where large minorities are in perennial armed revolt, and where government suspicion, in the words of a Burmese bishop, falls on "Buddhists, Baptists, and Muslims, in that order"?[4] We must be explicit here about a distinction that we shall have to consider later in the case of Taiwan: tribal or nationalist protest is not necessarily social protest, and in itself is much less securely linked with the Christian ethos, even where it speaks with Christian accents. In the judgment of the Secretary General of the Burma Council of Churches in 1980, Karen and Kachin insurgency has been largely Protestant, but its motivation has been more racial than religious.[5]

There remains the most massive national exclusion if we test the suggestion that a Christian minority of less than 5 percent is incapacitated from being a force for social protest. What about the Christians of India—27 million of them by some reckonings, and the largest national Christian community in Asia after the Philippines? They are a minority of less than 4 percent.

We have seen enough of the Indian case to know that the winds of change have blown there too, and that formidable reserves of energy can be mobilized in the face of a threat to the Christian community's survival (as in the case of the Freedom of Religion bill in 1979). But the Christian community as a whole and in its leadership, when faced with a national polarization between the powerful and the powerless (as in the Emergency of 1975–77), is not yet secure enough to dare to throw its weight on the side of the latter.

Local Sources of Militancy: The Search Narrowed Down

Once we have eliminated from consideration all Asian countries with a Christian population of 5 percent or less, we find we are left with some ten Asian territories of the 1970s that could claim a Christian population approaching or exceeding 10 percent. Eliminating further, for reasons already seen, the cases of Soviet Asia, Lebanon, and Syria, we are left with three Christian footholds in continental Asia (South Korea, Vietnam, and the British colony of Hong Kong) and four in insular Asia (the Philippines, Indonesia, Singapore, and Sri Lanka). We could count an eighth case if we

counted Papua New Guinea with Asia rather than with Australasia. However, though it would provide us with a second case of a majority-Christian
country in East Asia, it would not add to our case histories of social protest.

Seven Christian Footholds on Asia's Fringes

Seven territories in all—that is what seems to result from our inquiry into
the places of origin of Asian Christian social protest. True, in these territories are concentrated some 84 million Christians, making up well over half
of all Christians in Asia, and representing about a fifth of the territories'
total population. The fact remains that the total population of these territories is only about a tenth of the total Asian population.

Actually the implications go further than this. The timidity or intimida-
tion of Christianity among nine-tenths of all Asians must also have an effect
on Christians among the other tenth. The timid cannot fail to give pause to
the bold, even while being partly emboldened by them. The warning rum-
bles from the leaders of the Christians of India, which we have heard rever-
berating in the FABC and the CCA, are only the clearest of many illustrations of the limits of the possibilities of representative transnational Asian
Christian militancy.

All such transnational stances in fact are necessarily compromises. In
terms of prophetic militancy, as long as its minority Christian complex
holds it back, South Asian Christianity can never be expected to go more
than part of the way to meet the Christianity of other Asian regions in
which the Christian community feels less insecure. By the same token, as
long as it remains an overall minority of less than 5 percent, Asian Christianity as a whole can never be expected to go more than part of the way to
meet the Christianity of the non-Asian world, a world in which every second
person is at least nominally Christian.

This is necessarily the case, if not as regards pronouncements made, at
least as regards positions effectively maintained, and at fully representative
ecclesiastical levels. The same constraints will be felt much less consistently
at the level of the frontierspeople of the transnational avant-garde.

We have seen enough to show that there are areas in Asia where the pressures discouraging Christian militancy of any kind could be described as too
crushingly strong. Let us not fail to inquire whether there are any areas
where the pressures could be described as too enervatingly weak. There is
only one possible case: the Philippines, an island nation where the only
internal threat to Christianity as such comes from a (southern) Muslim
minority that is about as small in the country as a whole as the Christian
minority is in Asia as a whole.[6]

And in fact, with one important qualification, the case fits the description. It took the martial law regime of the 1970s to subject Philippine Christianity to its first real test in four centuries of whether there were any bones
at all within its soft and pliant body. The test proved, as expected, that

much of it had neither bone nor sinew—though it also proved what no one could have confidently said before: that a significant fraction of it was not second in fortitude to the Christianity of any other country.

We have already found, in the cases of Japan and Hong Kong, territories of which it could be said that in the postwar generation the Church was being killed by kindness. The same could have been said of the Church in the Philippines, before martial law cut through it like a knife through butter. It could still be said of that major part of Philippine Christianity that remains on easy terms with the wielders of power in the nation's New Society. As we have yet to see in further detail, the country that contributes most to radicalism in Asian Christianity is also the country that contributes most to its conservatism or inertia.

We are left with the conclusion that the overwhelming problem of Christianity everywhere in Asia has been to muster enough strength within itself to overcome a feeling of demoralization before the magnitude of the overall forces in Asia ranged against the realization of the vision of justice it is committed to promote. This being so, and the geographical distribution of Asian Christianity being so skewed towards the warm-water fringes, it should not be too difficult to get accustomed to the idea that there are only, at bottom, seven territories in Asia in which the Church has the minimum absolute and relative numerical strength it would need in order to be able to take a nonconformist stand and make it heard.

So much by way of a list of the possible places of origin of Asian Christian social protest. It will now be instructive to match it with our other list of actual locations of protest among some thirty relevant local events or event-clusters.

Six Key Locations of Christian Social Protest

There is in fact a correlation between the possible and the actual places of origin of social protest. About half the actual cases come from the two countries with about 40 percent of Asia's Christians: the Philippines and South Korea. These also happen to be the countries that lead the continent everywhere east of Lebanon in percentage of Christians (the percentages being in the range of 90 percent and 30 percent respectively). About another quarter of the cases come from four territories with about another 15 percent of Asia's Christians: Vietnam, Indonesia, Hong Kong, and Singapore. These also happen to be the territories next highest in Asia in percentage of Christians (of the order of 10 percent in each case).

This is about as much as we need to know in order to establish a certain fundamental correlation of territories of relative Christian strength with locations of relative Christian militancy. To put the point more precisely in our original terms, local cases of corporate protest are normally to be expected, and will normally be discovered, where the relations of force are not overwhelmingly unequal one way or the other, but remain balanced in a certain productive tension between the strength of a challenge and the strength of the Christian capacity to respond.

In this equation, relative Christian strength is one crucial factor. It creates the potential for social militancy in at least the seven territories we have singled out. At the same time, it is not the only factor. To turn potential into actual militancy, what seems to be required is a major but not overwhelming local provocation.

This condition has not been quite fulfilled in Hong Kong, in Singapore, or in Sri Lanka, with the result that protest there has involved, for the most part, only the avant-garde, as also in India and Thailand.[7] It was not being fulfilled in the other four territories either, prior to the provocations of emergency rule there. Finally, it has not been fulfilled in Vietnam when newly unequal force relations have supervened; when the same have prevailed in Indonesia (during the earlier years of Suharto's New Order); and when they have held temporary sway at various stages of the military regimes in South Korea.

It is in the interstices between all these inhibiting factors that the voice of corporate Christian militancy is heard. Among our seven territories, the cases that are most instructive are those of the Philippines, South Korea, Vietnam, and Indonesia. Outside the seven territories, there is much to be learned from the case of India (as we have seen, and as we might have expected from the sheer numbers and variety of Christians there). For reasons yet to be explored, there is also something to be learned from the case of Taiwan.

What has been said already must suffice as to the cases of India and Korea. What remains to be said must be confined to some notes in the cases of Indonesia, Vietnam, and Taiwan.

The essential ingredients for protest in Indonesia were provided in the 1970s: a Christian minority (mainly Protestant) possibly reaching, after rapid growth, 10 percent of the total population, and a military regime that had physically liquidated some hundreds of thousands of alleged Communists in 1965 and had kept in political detention some hundreds of thousands more.

The special inhibiting factor here was the dominance of Islam. If Islam had had anything like the dominance it claimed (95 percent according to its fundamentalists), Christian protest would have been as unthinkable here as in Bangladesh or Pakistan. But in fact Islam had a firm hold on no more than half the population, and was determinedly excluded from direct power by the Javan generals of the New Order. This gave minorities an interest in not carrying criticism to the point of overturning that order altogether; but at the same time it made room for some relatively daring contestation of its more corrupt and repressive features. The contestation was spearheaded by students; it occasionally involved the clergy; and on one occasion (the Sawito affair of 1976) it obscurely implicated the most representative figures of all the main religions of Indonesia.[8]

In the case of Vietnam, the essential ingredients for protest were present only in the early 1970s: a well-entrenched Christian minority (overwhelmingly Catholic) of at least 10 percent in the Republic of Vietnam; and a military regime comparable to its Indonesian counterpart in reputation for corruption and repressiveness.

The special inhibiting factor in this case was the imminent threat of communism, already dominant in North Vietnam, which was engaged in a bitter war with the South. A critical Catholic movement grew in South Vietnam from 1970 on, a time when it had no counterpart elsewhere in Asia except in South Korea. It was spearheaded by Young Christian Workers and their chaplains, and it did not shrink from including in its criticism official church privilege and complicity in abuses of power. It had become sufficiently broadly based by 1975 to bridge the traumatic transition for the Church from being a bastion of anticommunism to being a Church under communism. Two archbishops, because of it, were not treading a total vacuum when they called for a new beginning under the new regime. One of them, Archbishop Binh of Saigon, as we have seen, persevered in his new direction at least long enough to plead its case before the Synod of Bishops in Rome in 1977.

Obviously this experience would take on historic importance if it proved to be a breakthrough in Christian-communist relations. However, the signs on this were mixed at best by the end of the decade.[9]

The pattern of response to the challenge in Indonesia and South Vietnam was within the bounds of what might have been expected. It would have been less easy to anticipate the contribution of Taiwan. Its overall percentage of Christians is less than 8 percent; and the third of that minority represented by the Catholic Church is ranged massively and officially, with none of the qualms of conscience of its counterparts elsewhere, on the side of the powers that be. Indeed, the case of this largest denomination in Taiwan goes uniquely far to one extreme: we have here the most unreserved and longstanding official alignment anywhere in the world of a national Catholic community with a martial law regime.

That has been the situation as regards official alignment. At the grassroots level the attitudes could never have been so uniform; and at any rate the case of the second largest denomination goes uniquely far to the opposite extreme. With 1 percent of the population in the 1970s, the Presbyterian Church in Taiwan set itself against official national policy to a point that cost its national executive leader a seven-year jail sentence at the beginning of the 1980s.[10]

If the Presbyterian protest could be properly defined as social protest, it would invalidate our generalization that social protest is not to be expected from small minorities.

And in fact the case is at first sight persuasive. It is not as if the leaders had no mandate from their constituency; on the contrary, perhaps no leaders and no policies in the Republic of China on Taiwan were ever so democratically mandated. Nor is it as if a Christian case could not be made for the Presbyterian position; on the contrary, the Presbyterian leaders could claim that they spoke for a disfranchised majority (the non-mainlanders) as large as the non-white majority in South Africa (more than 80 percent in both cases).[11] By any definition the Presbyterian stand for Taiwanese self-determination and human rights has been an example of a church risking its own life for the sake of the people. It may seem like quibbling to point out that the solidarity here is ethnic rather than social.

The case may serve to clarify some concepts. Why, we may ask, should a church be drawn more easily into nationalist than into social solidarity?

The first reason is of general application: because it requires less altruistic motivation to struggle for an interest which, though broader than one's own, encompasses one's own. For what is the decisive difference, in this regard, between the Presbyterian and the Catholic Church in Taiwan? It is not as if one were sociologically a church of the poor to a decisively greater extent than the other. As far as that goes, while both have a substantial aboriginal community, both have their main roots, like most churches in Asia, in the urban middle class. What really distinguishes Presbyterians and Catholics in Taiwan is their ethnic background: the Presbyterians are overwhelmingly Taiwanese in membership and leadership, while half the Catholics and almost all the Catholic leaders are of mainlander extraction. Thus, on both sides the partisanship is only too understandable.

Another reason why the threshold of tolerance is higher for Christian social protest than for Christian nationalist protest particularly applies in a post-Marx world, a post-Lenin Asia, and a post-1949 Taiwan. It is all very well to call for opting out of the system of capitalist imperialism, as radical Christians might like to do in both Korea and Taiwan. But one has to think of the concrete alternative; and what if the available alternative has contrived to become equally unpopular, and moreover, as in the case of Taiwan, all too menacingly close at hand?

For the Catholic Church in Taiwan, the thought of that alternative has been enough to throw it without reservation into the linked arms of capitalism and its local client, the Kuomintang Party, which monopolizes power at the "national" or "Chinese" level in Taiwan. For the Presbyterian Church, the two options being equally repugnant, the only choice left is a generalized defense of human rights, set or not set in the framework of some sort of ideological third way.

At this point the problem in Taiwan becomes the same as that facing critical Christianity in South Korea. In both cases an element of nationalism becomes part of the third way, since both communities can see themselves as objects of military imperialism on one side and economic imperialism on the other. In the Taiwan (Presbyterian) case, the situation lends itself to more straightforward political nationalism, since the line of division there can be represented as running between the people (of Taiwan) and a foreign invader. And in fact, for Taiwan church history in the Presbyterian perspective, the period after 1949 is taken in stride as "the sixth colonial period on the Island."[12]

Nationalism and Christianity, however, though often in history found hand in hand, have never been comfortable for long in each other's company. A faith that can so easily serve the turn of conflicting tribalisms, as appears to have been the case in so many places and periods, cannot but feel embarrassed in its claim to stand for universal love. It knows that by playing the chameleon it feeds the suspicion that there is nothing constant, other than survival instinct, beneath its too frequently changing colors.

Because religion is used ideologically in many different ways, of course, it does not follow that all the uses are equally rationalizations of self-interest. A bias on the side of the underdog remains a perennial touchstone of the Judaeo-Christian ethos. If there is any credibility in the position of the Taiwan Catholic spokespersons, it can come only from their underdog status vis-à-vis the mainland colossus. If there is something more like Christian credibility in the homeland theology of some Taiwan Presbyterians, and in the *minjung* theology of some Korean Christians, it can be so only to the extent that in their case there is evidence of an identification with the underdog that is more immediate, more immediately costly, and more innocent of immediate consequences by way of making underdogs of others. A solidarity that lands people in jail carries more conviction than one that leaves them walking the corridors of power.

It has been necessary to review briefly these key locations of Christian militancy, even in this survey of the transnational dimension of the phenomenon, because of their repercussions there. All local experiences make their contribution to the transnational compromise, even at the level of the transnational avant-garde, but most especially at the level of the FABC and the CCA. One can imagine the constraints on an episcopal federation that has to take account of the views of the Taiwan bishops, and that actually held its first assembly as their guest.

By the same token one must suppose that a country embracing over a third of Asia's Christians and over two-thirds of Asia's Catholics must weigh particularly heavy in the balances of the FABC and the CCA. That is the case of the Philippines, and that is why we must single out the Philippines for some closer inspection.

Local Sources of Militancy: The Philippine Case

The place of the Philippines in the pattern of Asian poverty has been touched on under the heading Asia among the Continents; its place in the world market economy, under Asia in the Global Crisis of Change; its place in the history of Christianity in Asia, under Christianity among Asian Religions; its place in the confrontation of ideologies in Asia, under Christianity in the Asian National Security States; its place as regards the social role of religion in Asia, under The Critical Dimension in Catholicism; and its place in the pattern of post-colonial Asian Christian social protest, under the various heads covering the role of the transnational Christian organisms (most relevant here would be the PISA, the FABC, the OHD, the YCW, the IMCS, SELA, the ASC-AMOR, and EATWOT).

In all this the inevitable effect of concentrating on common features has been to obscure the singularity of the Philippine case.

In some ways, of course, the singularity has been impossible to obscure. We have already sufficiently reminded ourselves that the Philippines is the single Asian case where a country as a whole was won to Christianity during its expansion in the sixteenth century; and that the Spanish made Christianity in the Philippines take the form of Catholicism, thus making Christianity in Asia as a whole about one-third Filipino and about half Catholic. We have touched also on the singular extreme of paternalism that followed the Spanish flag, and on the passive and nominal character of the Catholicism that remained as its legacy until the martial law of President Marcos.

What happened then was bound to be portentous for Asian Christianity as a whole. The Church in the Philippines could not but be, for better or worse, the major influence on the Church in the rest of the continent, even if it had nothing new to offer it.

In fact, it proved to be the conduit between Latin America and Asia over which the social ferment in the Christianity of the New World found its way to the Christian fringes of the Old. At the same time, it proved to be a meeting place, and indeed about the only one of any consequence in the world, where there was some cross-fertilization between the Latin American form of liberation theology and the Maoist variety of Marxism-Leninism. No one could say how explosive the mixture might prove to be; but no one concerned with the future of Christianity and revolution in Asia could afford not to keep it under observation. "We are all watching to see how things go in the Philippines," said the chief theologian of the CCA in 1980.[13]

As an outline of how things were going, the local Philippine events listed in Appendix 3 are inadequate. Though there are twice as many local Korean events in the list, one should not conclude that Korean Christian social ferment was on a larger scale than its Philippine counterpart. One might rather say that Korea was a case of a smaller pot with a tighter lid, and that it blew off its lid in more spectacular eruptions in the 1970s—bolder trials of strength put on by workers and students; stronger support from the top Protestant and Catholic leadership; a bishop jailed; a famous poet brutalized in jail; alleged subversives executed; a president assassinated; another president violently dislodged from power; a popular insurrection bloodily suppressed; show trials dramatizing a ferocious purge of politics, education, media, and business.

Some of these convulsions did find parallels in the Philippines in the same decade: the Muslim war, for one thing, was immeasurably more devastating. But it could be speculated, nonetheless, that by the end of the 1970s the real trial of strength had not yet come for the Philippines.

One could also speculate as to why this was so—or at least why the Christian ferment in the Philippines was not observably, or not immediately, on the scale of the Christian population. The passive and nominal legacy of its Spanish colonial past is one part of the answer. Closely related to it, but ambivalent in its bearing on the question, is the low level of institutionalization of Philippine Catholicism.

A Case of Strength in Numbers?

A fundamental correction of perspective is needed here. It arises from the fact that the institutional Catholic Church in the Philippines is not on the same scale as the membership of the Church. This fact cuts the size of the Philippines down dramatically in the transnational institutional framework, where the institutional side of the churches is decisive.

On a per capita index of institutionalization based on the ratio of Catholics per pastoral agent, the Philippines is the last in the Asian league. Even in terms of total numbers of pastoral agents, the Philippines ranks far behind India and is not all that far ahead of Vietnam or Japan. If the non-Catholic contribution is counted in, the combined church personnel of India would rank as equal to three or four churches of the size of the aggregate in the Philippines, and the Philippines aggregate itself would barely exceed that of Indonesia. In terms of Christian periodicals, the Philippines ranks fifth after India, Japan, Indonesia, and Hong Kong.

What is the bearing of this low level of organization on the potential and actual contribution of Philippine Christianity to impetus for social change? We have already noticed the ambivalence of its implications. In trying to put the Philippine contribution in continental perspective, we cannot disregard either the Philippine strength in numbers or the Philippine weakness in institutionalization. The fact is that *both* indices are ambiguous in their significance for the course of developments.

On the one hand, take the equivocal notion of strength in numbers. On examination it proves to be partly strength and partly weakness.

The mere fact that most people in a country are Christian, as in the Philippines or Poland, does ensure that government policies cannot for long fly in the face of Christian sensibilities. However, the mere fact that most people in a country are Christian also ensures that these sensibilities will not deviate very notably from a certain sociological norm for similar conditions.

In other words, the more Christianity becomes common, the less it can be distinctively Christian. This fact makes it ultimately impossible to maintain that optimum church growth is the same thing as maximum church growth, even from the point of view of the Church's own objectives. The leaven role of the Church seems to require, ideally, not majority status or weak minority status, but something in the range of a healthy minority status.

On the other hand, take the equivocal notion of weakness in institutionalization. It too, in its own way, proves to be partly weakness and partly
(potential) strength.

A Case of Weakness in Institutionalization?

The weakness is all too evident in that vast area of world Christianity
where the Church has been traditionally understaffed—the area of the former Spanish and Portuguese empires, which includes Latin America and the
Philippines.

True, we may discount indices of weakness that presuppose the desirability of maximum institutionalization: priest-people ratio, church-controlled
schooling, church attendance. We may also discount the clerical disregard
of popular religion. All that being duly allowed for, the word "weakness"
still applies. "A tremendous force for social inertia"[14] was, we may recall,
Myrdal's verdict on religion-in-practice in South Asia, where religion was
lacking in any healthy corps of activists and energizers. Myrdal could have
said the same of religion in Latin America.

Where, then, is the potential strength in this institutional weakness?

Who, indeed, would have found signs of strength at the time when Myrdal wrote, whether in South Asia or in Latin America? In the latter region,
there was still no sign then of the militant gospel of Medellín and Puebla, or
of their vanguard, the theology of liberation. But few are now unaware that
it is precisely from this understaffed, underinstitutionalized backwater of
Christendom that there has come, for better or worse, the most revolutionary Christian historical force of our time.

It may be pointed out, of course, that the upsurge of revolutionary religion in Latin America is the product of a peculiar constellation of circumstances. Due credit must be given to North American economic rapacity for
providing a peculiar degree of provocation. Due credit must also be given to
nonreligious Marxism, inspired by the once-Christian Fidel Castro, for
spearheading the peculiar Latin American reaction. It must be recognized
that the pattern of Latin America as a protest-provoking periphery was a
secular reality before it became a religious one.

It remains true nonetheless that the subsequent shift in Christian weight
in the Latin American power balance remains in itself a momentous political development. On this point Castro can be our best witness, because
presumably our most reluctant one. "Times change," he said in 1980 in a
nationwide speech in Cuba, upon returning from the first anniversary cele-
bration of the Nicaraguan revolution, "and imperialism, the oligarchy, and
reaction are finding it more and more difficult to use the Church against the
revolution."[15]

Times change: such is the lesson of the 1970s in Latin America. More
specifically, we have learned from Latin America that times can change in

regard to the social role of religion in ways that are least expected. And now we observe the same kind of change in the Philippines, in the same sort of constellation of circumstances—essentially the same confrontation of transnational capitalism and social revolution in the setting of the same underinstitutionalized Catholicism.

Why did the change take a more significant form in that setting than in, say, the setting of India? Why has it become possible to find a change-oriented Church in the Philippines, not only among "the transconfessional groups of the tolerated and not excommunicated ministries"[16] (among whom it can be found also in India and indeed practically everywhere), and not only among the cadres of the national and international ecclesial avant-garde (URM, SELA, PISA, OHD, YCW, IMCS, WSCF, AMOR, EATWOT), but also at representative national levels, such as the national leadership of women and men religious, the national body responsible for official Catholic social concern, and even a significant segment of the Catholic episcopate itself?

We have dealt at length with one basic reason: the minority complex, the fact that only half a dozen territories in Asia contain Christian communities that are not too insecure for the sociological possibility of corporate social militancy. We could add several factors more specific to the India/Philippines comparison that also play major roles; for example, the inward-looking legacy of India and the fragmented character of Indian Christianity, geographically, linguistically, culturally, and denominationally. We could look for clues in the Marxist thesis about the "mode of production," which today would see different degrees of ripeness or unripeness for revolution in the varying conditions of "dependent capitalism," which are otherwise essentially common to India and the Philippines.[17]

However, insofar as one concentrates on the contrast in degree of institutionalization between Indian and Philippine Catholicism, and correlates it with the contrast in degree of social radicalization, one is forced to conclude that their inverse relationship is not entirely coincidental. In other words, just as optimum church growth is not to be defined as the highest possible growth, by the test of the Church's own objectives, so optimum church institutionalization is not to be defined as the highest (any more than as the lowest) degree of organizational development.

Once it is recognized that a prophetic or critical role in society is part of what the Church is for, and that for this purpose there can be such a thing as too extreme a degree of institutional entrenchment as well as too extreme a weakness in numbers, it can be speculated that the relative failure in India, in contrast to the relative success in the Philippines, is not unrelated to both factors.

The argument advanced long ago by Ivan Illich, that the problem of the institutional Church has not been understaffing but overstaffing, has come to look more plausible since it has come to be known that it is those so-called understaffed backwaters of the world Church, such as Latin America

and the Philippines, that have shown the most striking signs of new vitality
in the form of basic Christian communities, innovative ministries, and a
prophetic role in regard to society.

A Pattern of Protest from the Periphery

Let us look more closely at what we have just called the relative success in
the Philippines. The pattern of protest from the periphery does not apply
only to the Philippines as a whole within global Catholicism, or only to the
Philippines in a special way as compared with other former outposts of
empire, such as India. It applies in these ways, but it applies in a further way
also. The pattern of protest from the periphery is repeated within the Philippines itself.

First a word as to the reality of the radicalization in the Philippines. It is
beyond our scope to spell this out in much more detail than has already been
suggested. We can, however, speak in terms of several major indices: the
relative radicalization of a fifth to a third of the Catholic Bishops' Conference (CBCP); the relatively greater radicalization of its National Secretariat of Social Action (NASSA) and its regional Mindanao-Sulu Pastoral
Secretariat (MSPS); the spectacular radicalization of the Association of
Major Religious Superiors (AMRS), to the point of incurring the ire of both
the episcopal majority and the Roman Curia; and the rise of a massively
participatory and politically radical Church of the people in certain
dioceses, mostly remote rural ones.

To describe all this, an enormously complex story would need to be told,
on the basis of a vast proliferation of necessarily fugitive documentation.[18]
But it is necessary to call attention to this story for a couple of reasons.
First, it represents a reservoir of experiences unmatched in scale and social
significance in any of the other churches of Asia. Second, it reflects a pattern of interaction of church influences in the Philippines that can be seen as
paralleling the transnational pattern.

In this connection, we have the benefit of Robert Youngblood's research:
a detailed and copiously documented study attempting to quantify the data
in terms of Johan Galtung's center-periphery model of the international
system. The conclusion of Youngblood's study deserves to be cited at some
length.

> In conclusion, it appears that powerful forces in Rome and in Manila
> converge to maintain a harmony of interest between the center of the
> Center (cC) and the center of the Periphery (cP) within the church and
> between church and state in the Philippines, regardless of the nature of
> the regime. Yet the situation is by no means static, nor is it a foregone
> conclusion that the harmonies between Rome and Manila and between
> the CBCP leadership and [the President in] Malacañang will prevail in

the long run, for since Vatican II has thrust to the forefront the need to witness for greater social justice in the world, it is unlikely that the disharmony of interest between center and periphery represented by the progressive bishops will be overcome until the basic structures of Philippine society are changed. . . . The glacial shift of the Roman Church is clearly visible on the side of eradicating social injustice in the contemporary world, and even though many setbacks can be expected in the coming decades, the movement of the church in behalf of those on the economic and political margins of society will be inexorable. The crucial question for the Philippines is whether structural changes imperative in this shift can be brought about through peaceful or violent revolution.[19]

Unfortunately, there is no way to test the prediction about "the movement of the church" being "inexorable" except by living through the future. In the meantime all such predictions are likely to have an element of wishfulness in them.

As for the other assertions in this passage, they are all supported by some substantial evidence already available. In connection with them, the issue of violence is only one of several that deserve brief consideration here, because one and all have implications that go beyond the local or national context. We cannot speak of the issue of violence without bringing up the issue of communism; and we cannot speak of the local phenomenon of center-periphery relations without raising once again the issue of the relationship between the trend to transnationalism and the prospects for peace and justice in the world.

The Issue of Violence

The issue of violence in the Philippines was a particularly agonizing one by the end of the 1970s. President Marcos had ceased to have a normal constitutional mandate by the end of 1972. His continuation in power rested outwardly on an increasingly flimsy patchwork of constitutional pretexts. Meanwhile the effective basis of his rule was the iron hand of martial rule, partly hidden in a velvet glove, worn through at several points, and borne up on an arm of American economic and military reinforcement. This reinforcement had shown some disarray, especially when similar arrangements proved counterproductive in Iran, Nicaragua, and South Korea.

The issue was not whether violence could be prevented, but whether violent resistance to the manifold violence already endemic under martial rule would make things better or worse.

That question had become academic in some parts of the country. Even before the proclamation of the New Society, violent resistance to the political status quo had been a chosen option among one ethnic minority, the southern Muslims. The subsequent intensification of the hostilities on both sides created casualties by the tens of thousands and refugees by the hundreds of thousands. Earlier still, violent resistance to the social status quo had been the chosen option of a guerrilla group, the New People's Army (NPA), a Peking-oriented insurgency, which in 1969 seized the initiative from the older, Moscow-oriented, Hukbalahap. The martial law regime provided the provocation that turned this insurgency from a local irritant to a serious long-range contender for national power.

How serious a contender? Certainly more serious by the early 1980s than could have been anticipated in 1970. That is the measure of the contribution of the Marcos regime to the destruction of conventional politics and of the political middle ground in the Philippines. For nearly three decades the country had seen nothing like the "socialist upsurge in the countryside" that held sway behind the back of the Philippine Army in a string of provinces scattered the whole length of the archipelago from the Cagayan Valley in the north to Davao in the south.[20]

However, those who would agree that the Communist Party of the Philippines (CPP) had come a long way in a decade would also agree that it had a long way still to go. To have any important share in the picking up of the pieces after the inevitable demise of "the conjugal dictatorship," it would clearly have to come to terms in some way with that other power in the land, the Catholic Church. And before that church could even consider what kind of company it would want to keep in a violent struggle for justice, it would have to resolve the moral issue of violence itself.

That was one reason why Christian eyes elsewhere in Asia turned anxiously toward the Philippines as frustration built up there to the point where, by 1979, some small sparks of urban terrorism were struck even on the conservative wing of the opposition. The Cardinal Archbishop of Manila, never the first to confess discouragement about "critical collaboration" with the martial law regime, began to notice talk of revolution everywhere, and signed an "Exhortation against Violence" in the name of the Philippine hierarchy. The operative part of that pastoral letter read:

> In our country today, there is growing evidence that the call to violence is being sounded by the leaders of clearly identifiable ideological groups and by others who are collaborating with them. We must condemn as criminally irresponsible the inciting of the suffering poor to that revolutionary violence which promotes hatred, leads to useless bloodshed and the tragic loss of many lives, and seldom, if at all, achieves any good. Those whose first victims will be the poor masses must be answerable for what violence brings upon our people.[21]

Was this position as agreed upon and as representative as it professed to be? All that can safely be said is that its priorities would have been the priorities of the great majority of the bishops.

Skeptics noted that its only actual signatory was the Cardinal; that the pastoral itself recognized that "an absolute interdict on the use of violence is not part of the moral tradition of the Church" (and not part even of the 1967 encyclical, *Populorum Progressio*); and that the pastoral could be interpreted either simply and angrily as the Cardinal condemning the violence of the oppressed, or, at best, as an oblique way of urging on the oppressors the need, as the pastoral letter itself put it, "to prevent violations (or toleration of violations) of human rights which provoke counter-violence in turn."

And such skeptics were only the ones that troubled to read the document. There were others, including some in relatively responsible church positions, who no longer looked to such quarters for guidance on these matters.

As elsewhere in the world after Vatican II, this independent attitude toward magisterial utterances sometimes reflected loss of all faith and sometimes reflected simply a change of theology. In the Philippine case there was ample inducement for such a change. Any theology that relied heavily on the bishops to steer the Church through the shocks and shoals of the martial law period was bound to be found wanting.

As a body the bishops were quite unequipped for that experience. And as a body they proved incapable of learning from it, at least as far as can be judged from the record of the first seven years of the New Society. An analysis of more than a hundred documents emanating in that period from the hierarchy as a whole, from groups of bishops, or from individual bishops (there were over eighty of them by the end of the decade) shows that division emerged quickly, changed little, and fairly sharply separated a critical minority, who at the outset numbered seventeen, from a generally compliant or manipulable majority.[22] On crucial issues, such as violence, the net result was bound to be that such restraint as could be applied by the hierarchy as a whole would work more effectively on the powerless than on the powerful.

But was not that the tendency of history as a whole since the churches had first become pillars of their respective societies? From medieval crusades to twentieth-century wars, had they not lent themselves all too readily to the violence of the powerful, and blessed the revolutions only after they had triumphed? It would be simplistic to hold one cardinal responsible for a posture practically ensured by the ecclesiastical mind-set, and reproduced around him not only by most bishops but also by the local nuncio, the curial heads of bishops and religious, and the very latest popes. John Paul II had no different advice on this point when he visited the Philippines in 1981.

On the question of whether there was a *right* to violent resistance in the Philippine New Society situation, the minority of Christian consciences that would support it had grown by 1980 beyond the reach of magisterial restraint. On the issue of its general workability, the experience of Nicaragua in 1979 (but was not that victory much more dearly bought?) gave a lift to their hopes.

On the issue of timing, however, the pope and the cardinal would have had one authority on their side that was a professional in the matter. The

CPP-led National Democratic Front (NDF) was consistent in dissociating itself from the urban bombs and fires of the right-wing opposition, recognizing that it needed much more time to build up its base in the countryside. But that, of course, only shifted the Christian dilemma to new ground.

The Issue of Christian-Communist Collaboration

As already hinted in the passage from "Exhortation against Violence" quoted above, the problem of violent resistance was complicated for the Christians by the company they would have to keep to resort to it. Yet if there was no peaceful way to restore power to the people (a conclusion that had spread from left to right across the opposition by the end of the decade), still less was there any prospect of success for any violent revolution that was not a united front.

The most effective fighters already in the field were the NPA and the Bangsa Moro Army (BMA) of the Muslims. There were some uneasy links between them; and their political fronts, the NDF and the MNLF (Moro National Liberation Front), even managed to appear together before an international, self-proclaimed Permanent Peoples' Tribunal (PPT) in Antwerp in 1980. This panel claimed for them the status of legitimate belligerents against "the Marcos-U.S. neocolonial system," which it judged as amounting to "a continuing criminal enterprise" under "emerging international law."[23]

For the Antwerp participants, pronouncing this verdict was guaranteed to be much easier than making it stick. For one thing, it implied turning one country into two—an implication that PPT, NDF, and MNLF alike chose not to examine too closely. For another, it counted for less in international affairs than the two none-too-convergent movements to which it had to look for effective backing—those of the communist and of the Muslim worlds. For a third, its fate depended perhaps most concretely of all on the extent to which the Catholic Church in the Philippines could be neutralized, infiltrated, or honestly converted to its cause.

The prospects for any clear-cut outcome have looked more unlikely for the Philippines of the 1980s than they ever looked for the Nicaragua of the 1970s. Marcos was not Somoza; in particular, he would have to lose his gift for deflecting or defusing or confusing discontent before he could effectively unite the whole country against him. The southern Philippines corresponds to nothing in Nicaragua; and while that region of the Philippines boasted the most progressive church constituency in the country, it was far from ready to accept the Moro claim there to majority status and a mandate to secede and rule. As for the rest of the country, where were the ingredients for a Sandinista-style coalition?

On the Marxist side, there was a question as to the real strength of the NPA. All would agree that its support had grown rapidly in the late 1970s; but not all were certain that it had already shown itself to be the wave of the future. Those who were certain of that, given the security problem, were in no position to show why.[24]

On the Christian side, where were the priests or other leaders in the Church who could be the Filipino counterparts of the priest-ministers in the government of revolutionary Nicaragua? There were several who had been in jail or in the underground; there was Edicio de la Torre (see p. 92), who appeared to have grown with the movement; and by the end of the decade those who spoke for the NDF were less few, less circumspect, and less marginal in the Church.[25] But all that added up to something less than a conversion experience for the whole Church; quite the contrary in some quarters, as alarms periodically sounded, not always unjustifiably, about communist double-dealing, infiltration, and manipulation of the Church. By 1982 these had produced a dissociation between the bishops and the Secretariat of the Mindanao-Sulu Pastoral Conference.[26] Neither Church nor Party had come to this encounter with its heart on its sleeve.

Failing a clear-cut outcome, what prospect was likely? For a Church that was practically coextensive with the people, the only realistic prospect was for a splintering process in the Church corresponding to the splintering of Philippine society. More realistically, it could be said that the contribution of the Marcoses was to lay bare what was already there—in biblical terms, the secret thoughts of many hearts; in Marxist terms, the class struggle in society and in the Church.

For the New Society was nothing if not a sundering sword. We have spoken earlier of criteria of Philippine Christianity that cut it down to size. The sword of the New Society undoubtedly cut it down further.

The options of some church leaders there, whatever might be their subjective state of good or bad faith, put them firmly in the role assigned to church leaders by Marx and Lenin: the role of lackeys of the prevailing power. No clear-sighted analysis can leave any doubt that a struggle for a less unequal order in the Philippines must involve either the conversion of certain well-entrenched elements in the Church or a struggle against them.

In the case of a much larger segment of the Church, one can hardly speak meaningfully of any conscious option, in regard to the imbalance in public power, other than perhaps an option for inaction and inertia, which in practice also maintains the imbalance. If an option for the poor is a Christian duty, these are the elements that sin by omission. By failing to become part of the solution, they are part of the problem. Here again the analysis of Marx (and of Myrdal for a comparable situation) seems fairly applicable.

As for the remnant who have faced the issue and determined to opt for the poor in reality and not only in rhetoric, their troubles are only beginning. In the first place, they represent a church minority hardly greater in size and surely more marginal in the institution than the minority actively opposing them. In the second place, choosing sides does not settle the question of choosing allies. They have judged that national salvation is not to be expected from the New Society. Does it follow that it is to be expected from the Communist Party? For most of them that does not necessarily follow.

Are people-oriented church leaders to be blamed for holding back from this final plunge? On the contrary, it would be strange, in view of what they know or believe they know, if they did not think twice about it. Merely by being what they are, they have already broken the mold of the classic Marxist argument about the role of religion in relation to revolution. As Castro conceded, times change. Why then should times not change further? Why should there not be some special concern to ensure that this revolution will be a revolution with a difference?

Clearly, if there is ever to be a people's revolution that actually keeps faith with the people, it will have to be notably different from all the major specimens so far available for inspection. And Christians would scarcely be Christians if they were not convinced that they had something to contribute to the difference. Even granted an option for opposition to the New Society, even with acceptance of a need for violent resistance to its violence, even with openness to a need for some kind of rallying of opposition forces and hence of Marxists and Muslims among others, it never follows for Christians that any particular struggle must be victorious at all costs. It never follows for all of them, or even for most of them, or even for most of those thoroughly committed to the cause of the people.

Here is a political reality with which all calculations about church and revolution must reckon, whether they are calculations of Christians or of Marxists or of observers with no direct involvement. Radical Filipino Christians could see that times change for revolutions too. They could argue that China after 1949 had not been exactly like Russia after 1917, and that Nicaragua after 1979 had not been exactly like Cuba after 1959. They could contend that the Philippines in the 1980s, in turn, need not and must not merely repeat any set pattern of the past, including the pattern in which Christians learn nothing from Marxists and Marxists learn nothing from Christians and both get defeated because of their inability to come to terms with each other.

Delusion, of course, was sure to stalk such calculations; some delusion was inevitable for Christians in the New Society Philippines who had resolved to follow the option for the poor and powerless wherever it might lead them. But the option confronted them none the less. Thrown together by history on the same field of struggle with Marxists, they were faced with the opportunity and responsibility before their people, and before the Christians and people of Asia, to make their inevitable contribution to the record a constructively different one in terms of matching Christian deeds to Christian words in the domain of social concern.

The Issue of Organization and Dependency

A further major issue illustrated in the Philippine case is the issue of the relationship between organization and dependency. This cannot be ignored because of its relevance to arguments about center-periphery relations put forward by writers like Galtung and Prebisch.

We have cited a source which demonstrates in some detail that the transnational organization of the Roman Catholic Church lent itself to a reinforcement of the "center of the Periphery" by the "center of the Center" against the "periphery of the Periphery" in the context of the Church and of the state in the Philippines (pp. 111-12).

This argument by Youngblood, adapting the "harmony of interest" criteria of Galtung, purports to establish (1) a general harmony of interest between the Vatican and the CBCP (in favor of martial law or at least in disapproval of substantive church resistance to it); (2) a general disharmony of interest between the CBCP "center of the Periphery" and the CBCP "periphery of the Periphery" (reflected in their open conflict over martial law and the role of the Church in society); and (3) a correlation, explained as a circular cause-and-effect relation, between degree of marginality and degree of disharmony (in that the bishops most critical of the authoritarian regime regularly hold the least powerful positions in the hierarchy, control fewer of the Church's resources, and are located frequently in the most geographically peripheral areas of the country).[27]

As key examples of how the harmonies and disharmonies have worked out, Youngblood cites, besides the original disagreement among the bishops over the declaration of martial law, the further discord among them over the use of the ballot in the New Society, the inaction of the hierarchy regarding deportations of militant foreign clergy, and the interventions of the Vatican against the militancy of the AMRS.

There is no question that the Vatican and the AMRS were on opposite sides of this argument, nor that some of the measures resorted to by the episcopal conservatives, the nuncio, and the Roman Curia savored more of Macchiavellian power politics than of evangelical dialogue. But the entire experience showed the fragility of the gentler conventions on both sides, once the substantive power issues had been forced out in the open.[28]

The argument of Galtung is that the term "structural imperialism" is fairly applicable to a world in which harmonies and disharmonies operate in the manner indicated. The argument of Youngblood is that the case of the CBCP fulfills the essential conditions of structural imperialism both within the Philippines and in Vatican-Philippine church relations.

Both arguments appear to hold good within the limits of the definition. In other words, that is the way things are; and, as further reflection suggests, that is the way things inherently tend to be. As structuralists like Claude Levi-Strauss have argued, a certain degree of correspondence is simply inevitable between the systems of a society, as long as that society is functioning. When the society itself is unequal and divided, institutional religion, for the sake of peaceful coexistence with the political system, can only tend to reinforce the inequality and the divisions. It must do so all the more in the measure that it is highly institutionalized; and this tendency is not overcome merely by resolutions to overcome it, since it is not in itself a matter of good or bad will.

These considerations recall us to a recurring theme in these pages—that of the ambivalence of institutionalized agencies, even institutionalized agencies of change. In this unequal world it is not at all to be assumed that communication and contact on an ever larger scale lead of themselves to a strengthening of the church periphery, unless they are in some way coupled with a weakening of the gravitational force of the center, which tends to make the periphery serve the interests of the center and to make the religious center in turn serve the interests of some center of gravity in world society as a whole. In global politics, as in planetary physics, the existence of centripetal forces creates the counter-necessity of centrifugal ones if the system as a whole is to remain in being and in equilibrium.

That is perhaps the most constructive lesson of the Philippine experience.

The Philippine experience does not settle the question of the rightfulness or usefulness of Christian participation in violent resistance to state violence, except to the extent of showing the credibility problem involved in attempts to settle it by high ecclesiastical fiat.

Neither does it settle the question of the rightfulness or wisdom of Christian-Communist collaboration in extra-legal resistance to state repression, except to the extent of suggesting that such collaboration need not and indeed must not occur according to any fixed formula from the past.

The Philippine experience does, however, have something categorical to say about the relationship between transnational interactions and center-periphery asymmetries. On the one hand, it shows existing interactions actually exacerbating the asymmetries both nationally and transnationally. On the other hand, in practice a certain amount of such unintentionally creative "imperialism" is perhaps part of the price that must be paid on the periphery for the emergence of a Church of the people and for the people there.

As with the experience of Latin America, the Philippine experience suggests that there would have been no Christian ferment on the fringes had there been no heat applied by national security ideology from one direction and by Roman curial centralism or Protestant mission-board possessiveness from another.

7

AN OVERALL
TRANSNATIONAL PERSPECTIVE

Today the principal fact that we must all recognize is that the social question has become worldwide [*Populorum Progressio*].

All the major issues—political, economic, social, racial, or sexual—are global in character and interrelated. They demand global solutions [Report to Fifth Assembly, World Council of Churches].

Beyond the transnational perspective proclaimed in these words, what is significant for our inquiry is their sources. The first statement was made by Pope Paul VI in 1967 in his major social encyclical, *Populorum Progressio*; the second by Philip Potter in 1975 in his report as General Secretary to the Fifth Assembly of the World Council of Churches in Nairobi. The two quotations represent a central insight of the churches in the third quarter of the twentieth century.[1]

Even if this insight were not valid, or not entirely valid, it would still suffice to show why we need to relocate our Asian findings in a larger perspective. That larger perspective is necessary simply in virtue of the fact that the churches have come to see it so.

We would be still far from a complete appreciation of Asian Christian social protest if we confined our attention either to Asia alone or to Christian protest alone. Just as it has not been possible to learn all that can be learned about Christian protest at its transnational Asian level without considering the underlying local contexts and the very particular distribution of the local sources of militancy, so it would not be possible to learn all that can be learned about it without reference to other international contexts that are perceived as intersecting or overarching it.

Some of these other contexts have forced themselves on our attention repeatedly. We could not consider these matters at any length without observing a transformation of international consciousness promoted in very different ways by the capitalisms, the socialisms, the humanisms, and a multitude of other forces of our day.

We have not needed to enlarge on the influence of the humanisms, diffuse as it is and not given to appearing as a distinguishable actor on the contemporary international political stage. But these pages would be remote indeed from reality if they failed to suggest that the part of Christian protest on that stage is a part in a drama largely dominated today by the transnational actors called capitalism and socialism.

Nor is it inadvisedly that we have referred to these actors in the plural.

A monolithic capitalist bloc, facing a monolithic socialist one, would present one kind of context for Christian social concern. There was a time when the confrontation was perceived largely in these terms, when the situation was seen as one of East confronting West. In Stalinist or Maoist terms, it was seen as revolution confronting imperialism; in terms of the Western alliance, as one of godless communism confronting the free world.

This rhetoric survives, and so does some of the conviction behind it and some of the basis for it. No analysis can dismiss these black-and-white or rather red-and-white perceptions as long as their influence is reflected in the course of events. For the same reason, however, no analysis can neglect to look at the drastically changing realities underlying the stereotypes.

To try to do justice both to the realities and to the perceptions, we must once more broaden our focus beyond the Asian horizon we have been exploring throughout the five central parts of this study. Returning to the place we began, taking our distance from contemporary Asia in space and in time, but now taking account of what we have been able to observe of it at closer range, we must try to set it in the context of (1) an overall perspective on modern history, (2) an overall perspective on contemporary options, and (3) an overall perspective on the options involved specifically in Asian Christian social protest.

A Perspective on Modern History

Any overall perspective on any historical period must take account of the dominating realities and issues of the period and take a position among the actual and possible ways of interpreting them.

Any overall perspective on the historical period called modern during the second half of the second Christian millennium must take account of the reality and the issue of the haves and the have-nots. That concern is never far from the consciousness of any organized society. However, it was thrust to the fore by Marx and others with unprecedented vigor in Europe in the middle of the nineteenth century; it was forced onto the agenda of non-Marxists as well as Marxists around the world by the revolutions of the early and middle twentieth century; and it dominated and determined the East-West and North-South divisions of the world in the later decades of the same century.

Any overall perspective on modern history, all the more if it takes particular account of divisive and explosive issues of that history, must search for a certain bedrock of acknowledged fact that is common ground to the diverging interpretations, and seek to base on that bedrock its own choice among the interpretations.

We take it as being part of this bedrock of acknowledged fact that modern history, by comparison with medieval, has been revolutionary in its impact on the distribution of haves and have-nots in society; that in its revolutionary development the broadest and most basic distinction is to be found between an older stream called capitalist and a later stream called communist, or, more broadly, socialist; that in the period when capitalism had the field to itself its revolution was by far the most successful the world had yet seen; and that since the time when the world has been divided between capitalism and communism there has been no consensus about their competing claims.

It is well to be clear at the outset about the fact that the quarrel between capitalism and communism does not involve any basic disagreement as to the scale of the original success of the capitalist revolution. We do not need to leave it to capitalism alone to sing the praises of its revolution of productivity, of the horn of plenty it produced out of the midst of the indigence and indolence of feudalism. The fact is that its praises have never been sung more magisterially, precisely for this achievement, than in the *Communist Manifesto*. The backhanded compliments of this document show the extent as well as the limits of agreement on the question of the success of capitalism.

> The bourgeoisie, historically, has played a most revolutionary part. . . .
> It has been the first to show what man's activity can bring about. . . .
> The bourgeoisie . . . has created more massive and more colossal productive forces than have all preceding generations together.[2]

Needless to say, the bourgeoisie has never had any quarrel with any part of this argument, except possibly with the actual term *bourgeoisie*. In the measure that this term has been appropriated for unfriendly use, the people it is applied to naturally dislike and disown it. That is their privilege; and inasmuch as our interest is not in generating heat but in shedding light, we can make do with a term in which they more willingly recognize themselves: we can call their revolution the *middle-class* revolution. This term, apart from being less emotionally loaded, has the advantage of implying rather clearly not only how far this revolution has gone but also how far it has yet to go.

How far, then, has it gone? In feudal terms, one would have to say that it has let more of the people into the manor, that it has broadened the scope of the demesne to enable multitudes to enjoy an abundance and a freedom formerly beyond the dreams even of the feudal aristocracy. It has certainly changed the shape that society had in the days of the seigneur, his suzerain, and his serfs. It has drastically altered the proportions of the haves and the have-nots.

To be able to say that much is no mean claim, especially when, as we have seen, the soundness of the claim is conceded by friend and foe alike. But we must not leave it at that, since we need to explain why there are still foes. How far, more precisely, has the revolution gone? Has it replaced a tiny minority of haves, a feudal minority, simply with a less tiny minority, or with a large minority, or with an actual majority?

The *Communist Manifesto* had a judgment on that too: it was here that it parted company with the champions of capitalism. "All previous historical movements," it said (meaning movements previous to communism), "were movements of minorities, or in the interest of minorities."[3]

This was no doubt a defensible assertion in 1848, even in the context of the homelands of capitalism. During the following century and a third, contrary to the predictions of the *Manifesto*, it ceased to be defensible within the limits of those homelands. In the industrialized countries the beneficiaries of the middle-class revolution actually became a majority, even a large majority.

The revolution could certainly be faulted with failing to extend its benefits to everyone. It could even be plausibly accused of being actually incapable of reaching everyone, despite all its later inventiveness, given the persistence of intractable deprivation for a sizable minority of the home populations. But obviously that alone would not justify Marx and Engels in denying it the merit of being the first social revolution in history to benefit a majority.

There is a more serious reason why the middle-class revolution can still be accused of being the movement of a minority, in the interests of a minority. It can be so accused because the middle class not only remains a numerical minority in the world as a whole, but does so in a situation where, much more manifestly than in Marx's day, the world's majority is integrated into the system by which the middle class benefits.

Have we now strayed beyond the bedrock of acknowledged fact that is common ground on to more contentious ground? Cannot one find informed commentaries, more than a century after the *Manifesto*, dismissing its claims on this very point as sweepingly as it had made them? The historian A.J.P. Taylor, introducing the *Manifesto* in 1967, could speak confidently not only of "the failure of the law of increasing misery" (a law propounded explicitly in the first chapter of the *Manifesto*), but also of the failure of the revised version of that law later formulated in terms of "imperialist super-profit."[4]

Well, the law may have been prematurely formulated and reformulated, but so was this particular postmortem on it. Even in 1967 it was still too soon to be sure the bourgeoisie was not producing, as Marx asserted, "above all, its own grave-diggers," not indeed in the short term and on the home front, but in the longer term and on a more distant front. At any rate, what gave a new lease on life to the Marxist thesis was the growing awareness (nowhere adverted to in the sophisticated 1967 liberal commentary) that the majority of people affected by the middle-class revolution were outside the Western world altogether—enduring in the 1960s the Asian drama of which Myrdal wrote, and causing in the 1970s even the president of the World Bank to question whether a global society that had "such an enormous mass of misery piling up around its base" could survive.[5]

As to the more precise facts of the situation, let us make do with one of the more authoritative of the current formulations of the rich-poor division of the world of the 1970s. The UN "Declaration on the Establishment of a New International Economic Order," which was approved without a vote by the General Assembly in 1974, puts it in these terms:

> The developing countries, which constitute 70% of the world population, account for only 30% of the world's income. . . . The gap . . . continues to widen in a system which . . . perpetuates inequality.[6]

If this version of things could command a grudging consensus in the mid-1970s, it had no need to fear being shaken by the main events of the remainder of that decade: the energy crisis, the continued deterioration of the North-South imbalance, and the continued spread of the reach of transnational capital into the socialist economies, notably with its post-Mao breakthrough into China.

The notion of global interdependence had by then become a truism accepted, though equivocally, both by the rich nations of the Club of Ten and by the poor nations of the Group of 77, which had not taken long to become a group of more than a hundred. Global interdependence had become a postulate uniting the more disinterested from North and South and West and East, such as those eventually represented in the Brandt Report of 1980, itself the inspiration of the Cancún Summit of 1981.[7]

What we have to do with, then, is a theme that has maintained a certain constancy for a century and a third despite disconcerting transpositions of context and definition. In the *Communist Manifesto* it was a rallying cry to "working men of all countries." After Lenin and Stalin the battle lines seemed to be drawn between East and West. After Nehru, Nasser, the Cuban Revolution, and the Chinese-Soviet split, it bore signs of developing into a confrontation between North and South. To situate the theme in the closing decades of the twentieth century, we must keep in mind both how much has changed and how much has remained constant through thirteen decades of verbal battle and bloodshed without precedent in this conflict which continues to be, in the words of the Brandt Report, "the great social challenge of our time."[8]

A Perspective on Contemporary Options

The last wave of middle-class revolutions, or of high points in the overall social revolution, after it had been secured politically by the English, the French, and the American revolutions, came in the decade after 1860.

One thinks of the American Civil War, categorized by one historian as "the last capitalist revolution."[9] It liquidated the slave-and-feudal society of the American South and set Yankee America on the road to becoming the world's leading superpower in the following century.

One thinks of the Meiji Restoration in Japan, which liquidated the feudal Tokugawa society and set Japan on the road (a more authoritarian road in its earlier stages) to becoming another of the world's economic superpowers.

One might think of the Risorgimento in Italy, not only because of the way it transformed Italy into one nation under middle-class hegemony, but also because of the way it incidentally liquidated an internationally important symbol of the feudal past, the Papal States. The digestion of this defeat by the papacy marked an essential change in its social outlook between the First and the Second Vatican Councils. Though once again it took a century to make the transition definitive, by the end of Vatican II the Catholic Church had pronounced itself reconciled to the world the middle-class revolution had made.

By that time, however, that world was not the only world, nor was that revolution the only revolution, or even the one with the freshest claim to being the wave of the future. While producing its capitalist revolution by its willed activity, the middle class had also been unwittingly producing by reaction the makings of a whole new series of revolutions in the name of that other class, the proletariat, which capitalism could not help setting apart, thus causing it to become conscious of itself.

"A specter is haunting Europe," proclaimed the *Manifesto*; and indeed the specter went on to haunt the world. For the working-class revolution spelled doom for the hegemony of the middle class as surely as the middle-class revolution had spelled doom for the absolutism of the monarchs and the nobles. What was merely a threatening blueprint in the hands of Marx and Engels was translated eventually—too late, however, for the designers to pronounce on the faithfulness of the translation—into still more threatening realities in the hands of Lenin, Stalin, Tito, Mao, Ho, Castro, and Kim Il Sung.

The more general effect of this, and the one that here concerns us most directly, was to make a battlefield of those areas of contemporary society formerly considered most sheltered from the dust of the arena—the fields of research and reflection, especially of all that is known as ideological superstructure to Marxists and as the cultural sphere to others, and most particularly of social sciences such as history and politics. If Marxism is right in its inverted Hegelianism, then ideas, far from being above the conflict, are at once its echoes and its instruments. The pretension of scholarship to stand on the sidelines, playing the impartial scorekeeper, can only be a bourgeois delusion.

"He who is not with me is against me." Such is the absolutism that Marxism in its purest tendency shares with all the absolutisms it claims to dethrone and discredit. When one takes a position—and one takes a position, whether one knows it or wants it, the moment one forms an opinion about human affairs—one takes it in the face of this all-or-nothing Marxist tendency.

What, then, are the options of the contemporary researcher on social issues, landed as he or she is in the middle of this contemporary battlefield of ideas? In the most general sense there appear at first sight to be only two options; but for reasons to be indicated later we shall venture to distinguish a third and a fourth.

First, there is the option of thoroughgoing rejection of the claims of Marxism to be a serious contribution to social thought.

In this perspective, "scientific" and "scholarly" analysis of contemporary problems means analysis in the light of "orthodox" (that is, non-Marxist) economics, sociology, and politics. A "universal" approach means an approach on the basis of economic liberalism—an approach definable broadly enough to encompass a multiplicity of revisionist theses, but not broadly enough to admit the possibility that the free market could end up by being self-defeating. On this premise, Marxism is deluded as a theory and disastrous as a practice. An important part of any sound strategy for coping with the world's ills must be to ensure the frustration of the designs of the movements operating under its banner.

This kind of thinking is still alive and strong. It was strengthened in the West in the measure that the West was polarized against the East in the Cold War. It was enjoying a revival in America and Britain in the early 1980s. It has been nowhere stronger than in the churches, and has remained the instinctive reaction in Western pews and pulpits in the measure that more nuanced approaches at the top have been slow to filter down. It remains the dominant mentality among the rank and file of Asian Christians.

This way of looking at things, left open at the beginning of this inquiry, is closed now at the end. The essential reason for setting it aside is the greater plausibility of the alternatives considered below. In itself, a merely negative appraisal of Marx and Marxism requires a resolute myopia in considering modern history, in the world as a whole and in Asia in particular.

Even apart from the question of its truth or falsity, it would be as unscientific today to disregard Marxism as to disregard Christianity, since both have become and remain part of at least the mental makeup of so much of our world. But there is also the fact that, as noted by a major contemporary non-Marxist economist, "had Marx been mostly wrong, his influence would quickly have evaporated."[10] And there is the corresponding fact that, had simple economic liberalism been entirely right, and had its preventive or cure for Marxism been effective, the results might be expected to be less catastrophic and apocalyptic than the situation of the world in the early 1980s.

Let a non-Marxist say it for us, though in fact he says a bit more here than we could confidently vouch for. Having established his non-Marxist credentials in the first part of his essay, A.J.P. Taylor writes: "Anti-Communism causes more trouble in the world than ever Communism does or did."[11]

A second option, at the opposite pole from the first, is that of thorough-going rejection of Marxism's rival or rivals as a framework of interpretation for the problems of our time.

In this perspective Marx is a point of departure, a first principle, whether in the state ideology as in Marxist-Leninist states, or in the discourse of the group or individual engaged in social theorizing. This perspective exists in any discourse in which it is presumed to be beyond question that Marxism is the right and necessary point of departure. Its strength is to cover the theoretical possibility that all other points of departure have been definitively superseded. It enables research and reflection to be carried very far along one line.

This second option, like the first, can never be fairly tested except by those who are open to the possibility that it is the correct one. For this inquiry, however, the parallel with the first option does not end there. In the final analysis the second too has to be set aside as an inadequate approach to the problems considered in this study. It requires a myopia that would be the mirror image of the liberalist myopia. The world this study has encountered, inside and outside Asia, is simply too complex—and that means, among other things, too rich in mutations and cross-fertilizations of liberalism and Marxism—to be capable of being fitted on to one or the other Procrustean bed.

But let us allow a Marxist to pronounce on the inadequacy of doctrinaire Marxism, as we have allowed a non-Marxist to pronounce on doctrinaire anticommunism.

But has the value of his general *model* of society and of history been destroyed by the run of historical events that have overturned specific theories and expectations? My answer to this question is substantively, yes. The model as Marx left it is inadequate. One can use it only with great intellectual clumsiness and wasted sophistication, and often only with doubletalk. For us today, the work of Marx is a beginning point, not a finished view of the social worlds we are trying to understand. So far as our own orienting philosophy and our own social theories are concerned, we may not know just where we stand, but there is little doubt that we are somewhere "beyond Marx."[12]

Once, then, we have eliminated the pure positions at both extremes, what options are left to us? While reopening all the questions, we have not greatly simplified the choice of answers. But within the remaining range of possible approaches, it may be useful to draw a further distinction on the basis of attitude toward the excluded options, in such a way as to distinguish a third and a fourth overall orientation.

The third option is the attitude "a plague on both your houses" toward the other two options. This option takes cognizance of the catastrophic impasse to which the clash of two irreconcilable dogmatisms has brought the world. It concludes, with Solzhenitsyn, that it is precisely ideology that has been the great mass murderer of the twentieth century. It looks, with Peter Berger, on capitalism and communism, and their "myths of growth and revolution," as "pyramids of sacrifice," like those of Aztec Mexico, on which countless human beings have been sacrificed to abstractions. And in its revulsion it may incline, with Emerson, to "leave theory, as Joseph left his coat in the hand of the harlot, and flee."[13]

This option too must be weighed before it is set aside. Any attitude that would dismiss its moral indignation as irrelevant would be itself a moral obscenity. It is the merest sanity to recognize that something has gone grievously wrong with the whole revolution of modernization, and that any attempt to grasp it as a whole without recognizing something pathological about it as a whole can only make it more pathological. To explain a world that is spending over half a trillion dollars a year on arms, while over three-quarters of a billion people live in the condition defined by the World Bank as absolute poverty, requires something more radically wrong than any mere wrongness in one or other of the rival systems. The least one can say is that both must have a share in the blame.

That is the least, then; but it is not enough by itself. To acknowledge that multitudes have been seduced from sanity by theory is an argument against seduction, not an argument against theory. To find the enemy of humanity in the exclusiveness of the rival claims, in their refusal to see anything good beyond their borders, is an argument for less exclusivism, not an argument for more. A new approach to the world's problems that would be primarily negative in relation to other approaches, or that would appear as such, would only compound the tendency to mutual extirpation that is at the heart of the trouble. A theoretical approach to social questions that is to be consistent in rejecting only the spirit of rejection—the liberal rejection of any Marxist contribution, the Marxist rejection of any bourgeois contribution—must a fortiori reject the temptation to base itself on rejection of both.

And so, by elimination, we are led to a fourth option.

In our task of making some overall sense of the contemporary phenomenon of Asian social protest, we have tried at the fact-finding stage to make do with as little as possible by way of choice among explicative theories. Even at the fact-finding stage, however, we find it difficult to resolve questions of fact without first coming to terms with some larger questions of theory and value. Now that we face the task of putting our Asian findings in a global perspective, this coming to terms with larger questions of theory has to be made more explicit.

Confronted with a spectrum of ready-made interpretive frameworks that are mutually exclusive at their extremes, and failing to be persuaded by the attitudes "either-or" and "neither-nor," we are left with some sort of "both-and" attitude.

This is the time to recapitulate some generalizations made tentatively in the course of this study, and to give them as much more definiteness as the evidence accumulated may warrant.

1. Historical reality will always be more complex than the abstractions captured in our dichotomies between "material" and "spiritual" factors and between causes and effects. The essential idea here is scarcely disputed by anyone; but insofar as it involves a choice of approaches, it is Weberian rather than Marxian.[14]

2. The world this study has encountered, inside and outside Asia, is too complex to admit of adequate interpretation in terms of any approach that could be accurately labelled classically liberal or classically Marxist. We are beyond Adam Smith, beyond Karl Marx, and for that matter beyond Max Weber, if only in virtue of the principle of "historic specificity," insisted on by Marx himself,[15] which limits the applicability of historical generalizations to specific historical spans.

3. Fundamental to the complexity of today's world are the mutations and cross-fertilizations of Marxian and liberalist thinking since the time of Marx. These have made it increasingly unreal to speak of either socialism or capitalism in the singular, or even to imply that the boundary between them is still distinguishable to an extent that would be beyond dispute.

Marx himself insisted that he was not a Marxist. The contemporary sociologist who affirms that we are "beyond Marx" proclaims himself "a plain Marxist" (after defining what he means) elsewhere in the same work.[16] Within the socialist world, no student of contemporary China can fail to be struck by the range of ideological positions, from "Maoist" and "Linist" to "Liuist" and "Dengist," that have claimed to represent authentic Marxism and socialism in the name of hundreds of millions of people. Meanwhile, back in the capitalist world, the contemporary economist who wrote the landmark work *The Affluent Society*, in what he called "the central tradition in economics" (that is, capitalism), was not being entirely facetious in saying that his work might be categorized as "semi-socialist."[17]

In short, on the one hand there is no such thing anywhere as *the* Marxism (and apparently there never was such a thing), and on the other hand there also is no such thing anywhere as serious social thinking without an acknowledged or unacknowledged debt to Marx.

The least we can conclude from this ideological miscegenation is that we now have a sizable overlap in territory claimed by some for Marxism and by others for liberalism. At this point it becomes of secondary importance to judge between preferences in nomenclature. What is more important is not to be deterred or detoured or seduced by labels in the task of applying to today's realities the insights available today.

4. Also basic to the complexity of today's world are the mutations and cross-fertilizations underlying not only the theories but also the realities confronting us today. We cannot do justice to the complexity without taking account of the master-ideas that had so much to do with the making of it. We cannot do justice to it without also taking account of the hybrid historical forms that have resulted from the entry of these master-ideas into the historical process. We cannot do justice to it without taking account, still further, of those novelties on the historical horizon to which the original master-ideas have nothing to say.

The world we now confront has too much in common with the world analyzed by the classic liberalist and Marxian traditions to permit us the luxury of supposing that we have nothing more to learn from them. At the same time, their original world has grown and changed too much—in evolutionary and revolutionary ways, in ways beyond anything programmed or predicted by them, in ways resulting from interaction between them or reaction against one or other or both of them, and in ways that have been quite unforeseen—to permit us the luxury of supposing that their help can be more than partial and transitional. The resources of the past need to be used with a freedom that permits them to be progressively let go as they inevitably become less a help and more a hindrance to the grasping of the present and the making of the future.

To settle for this way of looking at things is to be open to all perspectives and prisoner of none. Clearly that is more easily said than done. By capitalist criteria it risks playing the communist game. By communist criteria it risks playing the capitalist game. By any criterion it is liable to land somewhere on the middle ground of social democracy or democratic socialism, or of some humanist form of neo-Marxism, which may or may not be the best point of departure in the search for a future that will fulfill and transcend the legitimate goals of liberalism and Marxism.

All things considered, this choice among the perspectives discussed above has to be the preferred one. Despite assiduous search, this study has not encountered the kind of data that would seem to justify a more categorical choice. To the task of situating Asian Christian social protest in relation to the intersecting transnationalisms of capitalism and communism it brings the following conscious premises:

- what we call capitalism today is the contemporary heir of a middle-class revolution that has been the most fruitful in human benefits of any revolution that has yet come to the full light of history, though at an enormous human cost still being added to;
- what we call communism today is the contemporary heir of a working-class revolution, also enormous in its human cost, which has been successful in exposing inherent and still unresolved short-

comings at the heart of the revolution of the middle class;

- both revolutions, through their encounter with each other and with the refractoriness of their historical material, have changed in the course of time, not beyond recognition, but beyond the possibility of useful application of their classical stereotypes;
- neither in isolation, even with all its mutations and adaptations, looks sufficiently like the wave of the future today to have serious hope of breaking the present deadlock decisively in its own favor within this century; and
- if anything can be confidently predicted, it is that the historical pattern of the twenty-first century will not fit, except remotely, any blueprints drawn in the nineteenth or the twentieth.

Asian Christian Options in Contemporary Transnational Perspective

Where is Asian Christian social protest going? Where, when the terrain around it has been taken into consideration, does it have to go? Does it have anywhere to go?

We have had ample occasion to get the impression that, humanly speaking, Asian Christian social protest would have nowhere to go if Asia had to be considered in isolation from the rest of the world. If it were, there would never be a better example of a David taking on a Goliath.

But there can be no question of considering Asia in isolation from the rest of the world. This fact transforms the whole problem. In a global perspective, the Goliath of entrenched social inequity looms larger than ever, but the David of a Christian disposition to join the battle against it no longer looks so helpless. A 33 percent minority in the world as a whole need not feel as overwhelmed as a 5 percent minority in Asia; and a historic new direction deliberately given to both minorities by its most representative leaders, under powerful pressures from within and from without, will not be so easily repudiated or neutralized.

If we take Christian social protest in the broadest sense we have been assigning to the term, then the least that can be expected during the remainder of the present millennium is that, in the scales of history, Christianity as a whole will weigh significantly more heavily than before on the side of social change, and significantly less heavily than before on the side of the social status quo.

That is not to say that Christianity, either in the world as a whole or in Asia in particular, can now be regarded as more a force for social change than a force for inertia or stability. On such a large question opinions could honestly differ, not only in regard to influences too close to us for full assessment, but also in regard to eras that have already receded into historical perspective.

Categorical conclusions on this point, therefore, are not to be expected here. What may be more realistically attempted, by way of a summing up of the findings of this inquiry, is to locate the phenomenon of Asian Christian social protest more precisely and systematically in relation to some of the historical coordinates that have been drawn at the beginning of this study.

These coordinates may be reduced to three. In connection with Asian Christian social protest, we have posed the problems of nationalism and transnationalism in general, of capitalist and communist transnationalisms in particular, and of the possibility of a post-Constantinian era in terms of the corporate relations of Christianity with the powers that be in state and society. We ask, then, where Asian Christian social protest is going, in terms of its transnational trend in general, in terms of its apparent dilemma between capitalism and communism in particular, and in terms of its still more ancient dilemma between the powers that be and the cry of the people.

Between Nationalism and Transnationalism

The word *transnational* has reechoed throughout this inquiry. If we turn to recent academic writing on international relations (as is done more in detail in Appendix 7), we observe that the phenomenon of Asian Christian social protest needs to be related to the alleged rise of a transnational society, involving on the one hand a diminution of the tendency to reify nations in favor of various forms of transnational consciousness, and on the other hand an increase in humankind's capacity for organization in a way that is outrunning the nation-state system.

We find ourselves in the presence of masses of information from a particular sector of human activity that lend credence to these academic assertions. They also give us pause before we endorse them completely. There certainly is a transnational trend, and it is a powerful trend, but there are also powerful currents in the opposite direction.

The evidence is persuasive in regard to the growth of transnational consciousness; but we are still far from McLuhan's "global village" or Teilhard's "noosphere."

There is also evidence suggesting an increasing incapacity of the nation state to exercise fully its accustomed sovereignty. But we have seen the nation-state system and the nationalist spirit actually showing new strength—not only in capitalist countries where a Marxist would expect it (the state being "the committee of the ruling class") and not only in communist countries where the socialist transition should be bringing about "the withering away of the state"; but also, and most significantly for our purpose, in nonaligned Third World countries in reaction at least partly to some aspects of the transnational trend that are unacceptable there.

Theories devised to explain and predict the development of a world in which either capitalism or communism will have won out have definite drawbacks. They fail to do much about explaining and predicting what happens in a world characterized by prolonged antagonistic coexistence of the two.

Making too clear-cut a distinction between national, interstate, and transnational political influences has its drawbacks too. As Keohane and Nye have noted,[18] there is such a thing as "the 'domesticization' of international politics," which from another angle can be seen as "the 'internationalization' of domestic politics." They could also have said that there is more than one kind of trend that can be called a transnational trend.

Some of these trends are one in their ambition to create a global transnational society, and differ only in their vision of what that society should be like. Such is the case of the transnational trends called capitalism and communism. Other trends may be at cross-purposes with each other because their transnationalisms are not equally far-reaching. Thus it is that one can speak of international solidarities such as those of the Association of Southeast Asian Nations, or of Asia as a whole, or of the Third World as a whole—solidarities that take their shape as much from their resistance to more enveloping transnationalisms as from their efforts to transcend merely national horizons.

Let us give full weight to the purely national component of Asian Christian social protest. Let us say frankly that, if we consider where the bulk of it comes from, it is not so much Asian as it is Philippine and Korean. If these two national experiences did not exist, Asian Christian social protest would be transformed (and shrunken) almost beyond recognition. Or rather we should say that the muted condition of social protest in Asia would show just how impotent minorities of 5 percent or less are doomed to be in the hands of state autocracies solidified by confrontation across a continent-wide ideological divide.

In its local sources we have found Asian Christian social protest practically confined to half a dozen political jurisdictions holding about a tenth of Asia's people on the warm-water fringes of Asia, where three-fifths of Asia's Christians constitute about a fifth of the overall local population.

Geographically considered, Christian social protest is almost entirely a phenomenon of maritime Asia; and indeed, apart from Korea, it is now overwhelmingly a phenomenon of insular Asia. Politically it has been almost entirely a phenomenon of the national security regimes produced by reaction to "the communist threat" in Taiwan, in South Korea, in South Vietnam, in Indonesia, in the Philippines, and, less directly and lastingly, in India.

It has been, in short, a reaction to a reaction; and the articulation between the reactions has been so close that without the national security trend the Christian social protest trend might never have materialized. It is as if both trends are triggered by extreme swings of one pendulum.

Closer examination of these local particularities brings us back to our point about the difficulty of disentangling the strands of national, interstate, and transnational political influences.

In both Latin America and Asia, several conditions have been required for the emergence of corporate Christian social protest: first, on the part of the churches, minimal local numerical strength combined with institutional flexibility; then, on the part of individual national political regimes, provocation typically taking the form of exacerbation of class war in the name of mobilization against communism; and third, the reinvestment of this experience in the international arena through old and new channels of transnational Christian linkage. It is a good example of a phenomenon that from some angles can be seen as a domesticization of international politics and from other angles as an internationalization of domestic politics.

We cannot say absolutely which comes first. The chain of reactions is in fact a circle, perhaps better a spiral: communism was a reaction to capitalism before the reaction to embattled communism took the form of embattled capitalism. What seems clear is that the spiral had to touch the extreme of what we now call the national security regimes before it could touch off the reaction we now call Christian social protest.

There is a bias in historic Christianity, arising partly out of its pacific ethos and partly out of its institutional entrenchment, which gives the benefit of any doubt to the social status quo, preferring the devil it knows to the devil it doesn't know. That is why there is an element of truth in the Marxist stigmatization of Christianity as "the opiate of the people"; and that is why the first effective stirrings of moral revulsion from modern social exploitation had to take the form of a revulsion from religion.

One could put this sociotheologically by saying that, while religion may be God's right arm in the world, the world needs and gets periodic reminders that it is not God's only arm; that there is something in the nature of God or of religion, or more exactly perhaps in the difference between the two, which ensures that history shall not be moved forward by religion exclusively. There are historical circumstances, such as those involved in the first century or so of the development of the contemporary social conscience, where a believer can only conclude that God's right hand has left much of the initiative to his left.

Be that as it may, what concerns us directly is that a new development of social conscience is now a transnational and (in some degree) transideological fait accompli. Just as the churches finally reconciled themselves to the ideal of bourgeois liberation rudely thrust upon them by the middle-class revolution, so they have been reconciling themselves to the ideal of proletarian and peasant liberation even more rudely thrust upon them by the working-class revolution.

A century after the French Revolution, Pope Leo XIII could tell workers that democracy was now acceptable, provided it went with a religious resignation to the necessity of class distinctions. Eight decades after Leo's encyclical on the working class, the preoccupation of that encyclical with keeping workers' welfare within the limits of the existing (capitalist) system was conspicuous by its absence in Paul VI's updating of Leo XIII's teaching.[19] That is one measure of the fait accompli referred to. It was brought about, not by mere magisterial reflection on gospel principles (otherwise it should have happened earlier), but only after a situation of extremity had developed and been certified to by forces outside the Church as well as by forces on the Latin American fringes of Christendom.

As a phenomenon with official ecclesiastical sanction, Christian social protest clearly has a very mixed parentage. It could not have developed in the first place without authentic roots in the Judaeo-Christian tradition; it could not have developed into what it is today without drawing some of its insights from the liberal humanist and the radical Marxist traditions of recent times. It could not have gained a broad base in the Third World churches without sanction at the level of the Church Universal; and it could not have been galvanized into becoming preeminently a Third World phenomenon without some extra measure of provocation in the Third World. Neither the provocation nor the reaction could have been what it has been without the very specific national experiences associated with names like Pinochet, Somoza, Marcos, and Park. Neither would it have been what it has been without the transnational reach of the influences and ideologies of multinational capitalism, national security ideology, Marxism-Leninism, and other models of socialism.

Let us pause for a moment on the paradox involved in Christian social protest becoming preeminently a Third World phenomenon under the spur of that extra measure of provocation in the Third World. There is a paradox here both from the standpoint of classical Marxism and from the standpoint of a "classical" version of transnational theory.

For Marx, Engels, Lenin, and Stalin, what we now call the Third World was a backwater, a residue not yet "rescued" by the industrial revolution from "the idiocy of rural life." Precisely because their theory required the feudal world first to produce the bourgeoisie and the bourgeoisie then to produce the proletariat and the proletariat to be "the main force" of the socialist revolution, the only role they could envisage for the "toiling masses" of Asia, Africa, and Latin America was that of anti-imperialist auxiliaries harassing the flanks of capitalism while the industrial workers of the West bore the brunt of the attack upon it.

This scenario became questionable with the arrival of the Soviet revolution and was explicitly discarded in the course of the Chinese one. For Mao and his lieutenants of the 1960s, the rear in the global battlefield had become the front, the global countryside was encircling the cities, and the preindustrial continents were now the storm centers of world revolution. This rhetoric abated after Mao's death and downgrading, but the fact remained that the proletariat had won no revolution in classic Marxist conditions, while peasant armies had marched to lasting victories in China, Cuba, and Vietnam.[20]

Mao Tse-tung Thought thus provided one controversial adaptation of Marxist theory to Third World reality. It had no particular explanation to offer for distinctive forms of *resistance* to communism in Third World conditions; nor could it do much more than repeat some clichés about the role to be expected from Christian churches in such circumstances. For both these questions, more particular interest has attached to the reflections produced in the jails of Mussolini by the Italian Communist leader of the 1920s, Antonio Gramsci.

Gramsci's context was closer to the contemporary Third World context than Marx's was in several respects. Italy in Gramsci's time, in its relative poverty, its dual economy, its frontier status in the capitalist world, and its nominal Catholicism, was not too unlike a typical Latin American outpost of dependent capitalism today. The process of modernization was creating a minority of beneficiaries who were not yet secure in their hegemony over the rest of the population. The most threatened among them found a champion of their interests in a Fascist dictator, who proceeded to link their destinies with an international axis of military-industrial regimes.

Gramsci could not foresee the full complexity of the next half-century's global experience of capitalism and communism. Still, he appears today as a bridge between Marx and Medellín with his application of "the philosophy of praxis" (Marxism as he understood it) to "superstructure" in general and to the role of the Church in particular, in unstable conditions on the expanding front of capitalism, where a new elite riding the wave of the world market needed and found Caesars and their international allies to hold down the marginalized masses.[21]

A true political scientist, Gramsci drew a profile that could fit many a reactionary Caesar of our time. A true atheist, he failed to anticipate the emergence of a Church that would resist them. There is irony in the fact that his line of analysis is most vigorously and prolifically carried on, especially in the Asian context, by a Catholic canon from a pontifical university.[22]

So much for the paradox involved for classical Marxist theory in Third World provocation and protest. Let us observe also the paradox involved for any "straightforward" version of transnational theory.

A "straightforward" vision of transnationalism assumes that the transnational trend, by helping the overcoming of nationalism and parochialism, marks a step in the direction of a unified, peaceful, and fraternal world. Unfortunately, this vision overlooks the unequal terms on which the process is based.

Just as the parade of "sovereign" nations in the United Nations disguises the fact that some are very much more sovereign than others, so also, in the multiplication of transnational contacts, the haves are once more strengthened at the expense of the have-nots. In a world in which nine-tenths of the headquarters of all international organizations have been concentrated in the developed Western world, and in which 98.5 percent of the managers of U.S.-based multinational corporations have been U.S. nationals, it need not surprise us if what the rich rejoice in under the name of transnationalism comes to be seen by the poor as no more than imperialism in a more insidious form.[23] The trouble with the "free" domain of transnational interactions, as with the "free" market and the "free world," is that "free" holds meaning only for the masterful few who have preempted the freedom of all the others.

The most conspicuous instance of this ambivalence in the effective role of transnational interactions is the multinational corporation. There could hardly be a greater contrast between the way this phenomenon is perceived from the vantage point of the Manhattan boardroom and the way it is perceived by the mass of the populations affected by its Third World subsidiaries.[24] In the 1970s the association of the word *transnational* with transnational corporations was a key factor in giving them, even in ecclesiastical circles, the status of a Third World dirty word. If a true transnationalism is to arise, contributing to true world development through true transnational capital interactions, it will first have to live down the image of the multinationals as they have been experienced in the developing nations.

Since this image may be too easily explained away as a case of Marxist mud thrown at the corporations just managing to stick, it may be well to see the main point reformulated in the terms of a liberal exposition of transnational theory:

If transnationalism has become the ideology of some of the rich, nationalism remains the ideology of many of the poor. . . . The trouble lies in the gap between elites and masses in less developed countries. The increased mutual sensitivity of societies that is created by transnational relations touches only a tiny proportion of the population. As elites are absorbed into a transnational network, the gap between elites and masses is increased and intolerable political tensions may be created. . . . The creation of a single global economy is rational, perhaps, to achieve optimal allocation of global resources, but it is also a severe limitation on national autonomy. The transnationally mobile are rewarded at the expense of the nationally immobile.[25]

This passage focuses on the polarity between nationalism and transnationalism. With a few adjustments it could also serve to call attention to intermediate solidarities that are nationalistic in relation to the super-transnationalisms, but transnational in relation to perspectives and loyalties confined within state boundaries.

The Third World itself is a concept, and a more or less nebulous reality, in this category. Slogans like "Asia for the Asians" reflect a common consciousness forged in reaction to extra-Asian pressures too strong for isolated nationalisms to resist. The drive for indigenization in the churches gains much of its force—and, at least in the case of Roman Catholicism, most of its hopes of balancing the domination of the Center—from this source. In the Ecumenical Association of Third World Theologians we met a new movement in the world of theology that illustrates the same trend.

The transnational trend in Asian Christianity as a whole also turns out to be a Janus-faced phenomenon.

Within its own context it is unequivocally transnational, not only in the literal sense of crossing state boundaries, but also in its aspiration toward mutual enrichment and reinforcement, expressed in its very origins in the classic transnational rationale that "national boundaries could no longer be the only basis for effective work in Asia."[26]

Meanwhile the face it turns toward the wider world is distinctly more ambivalent. Only the social protest part of it can look to its extra-Asian counterpart (Christian social protest movements elsewhere) with assurance of being reinforced in resistance to the status quo in church and society; for such resistance is the raison d'être of both. In all other respects it can greet extra-Asian Christianity (or rather, the First World part of it) at best with an arm's-length embrace, like the embrace of a younger and weaker sister more accustomed to domination by than partnership with her powerful sibling.

This sense of a need to assert Asian identity over against Western Christian identity is open and aggressive, as we have had occasion to see repeatedly, in the Christian Conference of Asia. It is more muted in the Federation of Asian Bishops' Conferences. A centralizing agency like the Vatican can only look on structures like the FABC and the CELAM with much the same uneasiness that the Soviet Communist Party shows in looking at the growth of horizontal structures in a Warsaw Pact country such as Poland. It would be justified in suspecting that the imperial-curial concept of Catholic transnationalism (the parental Center, the filial peripheries) has no future if a genuine regional Catholic transnationalism succeeds in establishing itself.

Paradoxically, the Center might bring this regional transnationalism to earlier maturity more quickly by mistrusting and repressing it than by gracefully abandoning the more provocative aspects of its "imperialism" while saving the substance. What we have found in the Philippine case (pp. 117-19) appears in retrospect to be the most pragmatic lesson of the entire transnational trend in Third World Christianity.

Between Capitalism and Communism

Christian social protest, this child of our time, is not the child of any virgin womb. One parent was misery, the other the not-so-common idea that misery does not have to be endured. This idea came into the making of Christian social protest, as we have seen, not through historical Christianity alone, and not through any extra-Christian influence alone, but through another not-so-common marriage of influences, a cross-fertilization of the ancient Judaeo-Christian tradition with recent liberalist and Marxian humanisms. The final phase of the gestation took over a century. The midwife was the national-security states of the Cold War in the Third World, not without positive and negative stimulation from the institutional churches of "the center of the Center" and the "center of the Periphery."

In the 1960s and 1970s it was common to dismiss the phenomenon of

Christian social protest with much the same contempt expressed by Marx for the Christian socialism of his day. Indeed, its enemies have always been as plentiful inside the fold as outside it. A historical perspective on Church and State and social issues from a conservative Christian standpoint could maintain as recently as 1980 that the theology of liberation represented essentially a surrender of Christian to Marxist thinking in which "theological rationalizations have followed the absorption of political ideologies."[27]

Contempt was never the only attitude. In Britain, for example, there has always been a school of thought maintaining that whatever was gained for socialism there was gained more by Christian than by Marxian socialists. In Anglo-America, insofar as any socialism has surfaced at all, it has tended to acknowledge Christian more readily than Marxian inspiration.

As for contempt for Christian socialism in the context of Latin America, it might have seemed realistic before the 1970s. By that time, after the milestones associated with the Puebla CELAM Assembly, the Nicaraguan revolution, and the sanctuary slaying of Archbishop Romero of San Salvador, it was beginning to be plausibly claimed that church-based social activism had shown itself to be a more broadly based and effective force than the activism based on communism and its Cuban sponsors.[28] History would have to be the judge of that; but there was no denying that in Latin America Christian social protest had become a political force to reckon with in the 1980s.

Could the same be said of its Asian counterpart? Before answering, one should take account of all the qualifications we have formulated in the course of this inquiry.

As a local manifestation of a global phenomenon, Asian Christian social protest carried with it all the weight of the most conspicuously transnational religion in the world. As an *extremely* local and indeed marginal phenomenon in Asia—marginal within the churches, which themselves were marginal within the continent—it faded into local irrelevance over all but half a dozen political jurisdictions on the warm-water fringes of Asia.

Even there, in the one country that belonged more to the Latin American than to any Asian pattern, Christian social protest fell short of the average Latin American degree of vigor. At the same time, even in that country (the Philippines), insofar as "church" and "communist" protest could be weighed against each other there, it is premature to think that the balance of influence would ultimately go to the communists as compared with that fraction of the nominally Christian mass base that was partly or thoroughly energized by the rise of the Church of the people.[29]

In general the problem of the Church in respect to social protest was no longer a problem as far as mere words were concerned. At a certain level of generality, the positions taken in the name of all the mainstream churches were more or less equally forthright by the end of the 1970s, in the First World as well as the Third, and in Asia as well as Latin America. These churches committed their constituencies to a struggle for justice and peace, involving in practice a preferential option for the poor, as the Catholics tended to put it. Or, what came to the same thing, they took a stand, in the favored World Council of Churches formulation, for "a just, participatory, and sustainable global society."

It was when it came to matching deeds to words that this solid front generally ceased to exist.

At "the center of the Center," the weight of the Holy See was regularly thrown into holding back the avant-garde contestants of the capitalist regimes, while the weight of the Russian Orthodox in the WCC was regularly thrown into preventing any criticism of the Warsaw Pact regimes.

At various "centers of the Periphery" a similar political fault line opened up within the churches. The official CELAM spokespersons after Puebla took on the same braking role as the Vatican. Indian church leaders of all stripes during the Emergency protested mainly against the protests. The official church spokespersons of China and Taiwan (Taiwan Presbyterians excepted) sternly repudiated all calling in question of their respective political authorities. The episcopal majority in the Philippines prevented or diluted all but the mildest remonstrances against the direction of their New Society. Conflicts in Singapore in 1976 over sterilization, and in Hong Kong in 1978 over the Golden Jubilee School affair, found the Catholic Church authorities taking the side of power rather than the side of protest.[30]

What are the implications of the opening up of this political fault line in the churches? We have yet to make a final assessment of them in relation to the question of the possibility of a post-Constantinian Church. We have first to assess them in relation to that other political fault line in global society as a whole—the line between capitalism and communism.

As we have repeatedly had occasion to note, there is clearly a connection between the two fault lines. The way lofty generalities have been translated or not translated into concrete options has obviously depended on the concrete options that have been available.

Capitalism or communism? If the choice for Christians depended on the formula of each for relations among human beings in society, it ought to be easy. As Tawney pointed out, the idolatry of wealth is as irreconcilable with the gospel as is emperor worship. As Headlam remarked, people who go to Holy Communion should be holy communists.[31]

Capitalism as Christians had grown accustomed to it, or communism as Christians were learning to fear it? For better or worse, that was the way the question was posed in its modern form; and once again, as long as it was posed in these stark terms, there could be no contest.

Christianity in its day had indeed done battle with capitalism, first when capitalism was encountered in the guise of usury, then when it was perceived as a middle-class revolt against feudal Christendom. Christianity had lost the battle by the nineteenth century, and had made its peace with the winner by the twentieth.

Marxism, for its part, caught the churches on the anti-Marxist side of the argument about property versus people. It left them little choice but to stay there when it identified its own side with atheism. The rise of the Marxist-Leninist bloc effectively locked the churches into the Western liberal-capitalist bloc. At the same time it effectively convinced them, for a while, of the truth of its own contention that they had nowhere else to go.

Had capitalism proved quickly to be the decisive failure, and had socialism proved quickly to be the resounding success, that had been envisaged from the time of the *Communist Manifesto*, Christians might have been presented earlier with a second serious chance to take a fresh look at both, with no greater prejudice against one than against the other.

History, however, failed to unfold in any such straightforward fashion. By the 1980s both blocs had registered enormous successes and enormous failures, in ways that corresponded to their original strengths and weaknesses, and in ways related to the fact that they had been interacting—paralyzing or galvanizing, contaminating or fecundating each other. Already in the 1970s the choice for the churches was not so much between capitalism and socialism as between several capitalisms and several socialisms, with more than a little overlap between the two.

Meanwhile a contribution of decisive importance was being made by the continent of Latin America. That continent belonged to the Third World, the underdeveloped world, which was by then the battlefield par excellence of social change. By a crucial coincidence, it was at the same time the one Third World continent that was overwhelmingly a Christian continent, and the one continent where the threat of imperialist domination was overwhelmingly experienced not from the Soviet Union but from the United States.

For the churches of Latin America, from Medellín through Puebla, the rejection of capitalism became not just a generalized gospel rejection of Mammon, and not just a generalized papal rejection of unbridled economic liberalism. It became a visceral rejection of a concrete capitalist system, typified above all by the leader of the "free world," the United States.

Thus it was that Latin America became the pivot on which Christian social thinking began to make a decisive historical turn. It was Latin America that supplied the Christian world for the first time with an experience of the unacceptable face of capitalism on a scale sufficient to balance its Eurasian experience of the unacceptable face of socialism. Through Latin America the perception became part of the Christian awareness that capitalism in the raw could be as heartless, as oppressive, as ruthless, as unscrupulous, as demonic, as communism in the raw was perceived to be. Through Latin America the Christian world discovered that capitalism had not after all left the days of Dickens and Marx behind it: instead, while its victims at home might now be a minority, they were more than made up for by a majority of victims abroad. At the receiving end of this treatment, the hope that the benefits would eventually trickle down to the masses appeared increasingly derisory.

This turn in Christian social thinking was of course not a simple 180-

degree turn, or even a simple 90-degree one. It did not replace an implicit trust in capitalism-in-the-concrete with any comparable trust in socialism-in-the-concrete. It did not even amount to anything like a wholesale break in the links that bound the churches to the power centers of capitalism. Its effect was no more than to shatter the easy conscience with which Christianity had hitherto cohabited with capitalism.

Insofar as it really was a decisive historical turn, that was what was decisive and historic about it. For the foreseeable future, the pull of some elements in the churches back toward capitalist versions of socioeconomic orthodoxy would be balanced by the pull of others toward socialist ones. In other words, there was no longer any version of socioeconomic orthodoxy that could impose itself on the churches implicitly or explicitly with the authority of Christian faith.

Such, roughly, are the latest terms of the contribution of Christian social thinking outside Asia to Christian social thinking inside it. Such are the terms into which the options of Asian Christian social protest translate themselves, when considered in global perspective along the axis of capitalism versus communism. These options could not be expected to be any wider in Asia. In the Asian context the room for maneuver could only be much more limited.

In particular, the dice would be heavily loaded in Asia against any pure form of the socialist option. This can be said on at least three grounds: because of Christian marginality and insecurity, because of communist power and proximity, and because the Marxist-Leninist front itself was split in Asia, after 1978, between a Chinese version and a Soviet-and-Vietnamese version, each of which would regard any rapprochement with the other as the most hostile possible act toward itself.

In this connection the only extreme scenario that had any remote plausibility was the notion of a radicalized Philippine Catholic Church constituting a Trojan horse for communism in the Association of Southeast Asian Nations.

This speculation had some facts in its favor. The Philippines was the only country in the region where communist insurgency had actually gained ground in the late 1970s and the early 1980s. It was also the only country where significant links existed between the Communist Party and the left in the institutional church. The Communist Party of the Philippines (CPP) had been China-oriented since 1969; and Christians for National Liberation, its partner in the National Democratic Front (NDF), was the only activist Christian group known to have dabbled much in Maoism.

In the post-Mao era the Chinese connection in the CPP had been wound down or played down. The CPP appeared to be outgrowing its Maoism as it had outgrown its Stalinism; it appeared to be putting its nationalist foot forward rather than its communist one. Meanwhile the NDF was reaping the fruits of polarization and demoralization in the country. The Marcos regime had more or less completed the destruction of the political middle ground; in the midst of political and economic malaise, Marcos continued to entrench himself in power; a vice-president of the United States had said to him in public: "We love your adherence to democratic principles and democratic processes."[32]

In short, the moderate opposition now had nowhere to turn but to the radicals; and the slide to the left accordingly seemed set to continue in the early 1980s. A map of guerrilla activity in late 1981 covered most of the territory of most major islands in the archipelago.[33]

The Trojan horse scenario nevertheless still seemed a remote one even in 1982. No one believed the New People's Army was ready for a direct trial of strength with the Philippine Armed Forces—least of all the NPA itself. Even with one hand busy holding the southern Muslim insurgency at bay, the military establishment could still pretend to wave away the NPA threat with the other.

Outside observers of the Philippines continued throughout the 1970s to discount the potential of popular unrest there. There was always a possibility, of course, that they would be proved as wrong about the Philippines as others had been about Iran or Nicaragua; but the signs of that eventuality would have to become much clearer than they were in 1982. The repression would have to get much worse, and the situation generally would have to deteriorate much further, before the NDF would begin to look like the Sandinistas, or Cardinal Sin like the Ayatollah Khomeini. And even if the Marcos regime should eventually meet its end at the hands of a Marxist revolution, realpolitik would surely dictate that the victor stand aloof from alignment with either China or the Soviet-Vietnam axis—at least as aloof as, say, North Korea.

Such, in brief, are the reasons why we conclude that for Asian Christian social protest, by the turn of the 1980s, the dice were loaded, not only against any Trojan horse scenario, but against any "pure" form of the socialist option. For as long as such an option was not a plausible prospect for church bodies in the Philippines, there were surely no church bodies elsewhere in Asia for which it was a plausible prospect.

We must now go further and say that some of the same reasons also militate in Asia against any "pure" form of the capitalist option. If by 1980, after the downgrading of Mao in China and after the intersocialist wars in Indochina, it had become harder to sell Marxism to Christians in Asia, then by 1982, especially after the Christian militants had digested the American role in post-Park Korea and in the "normalized" New Society Philippines, it had also become harder to sell capitalism to Asian Christians.[34]

With or without a Marxist revolution, in the Philippines or elsewhere in Asia, the options pragmatically open for the churches fell clearly short of any corporate endorsement of any of the conflicting blocs or systems. Like their Latin American counterparts, the representative Asian church leaders had learned a measure of anticapitalism without unlearning anticommunism.

Perhaps more to the point, they had been at least partly inoculated against the ecclesiastical tendency to assume some divine sanction for existing political powers and superpowers. They were at a juncture in history and geography from which they could see all the major actors along the great ideological divide in dismal and disillusioning parallel. Their view was a view from the underside of history; and at this juncture it looked particularly like the underside of marching jackboots. They were finding that the underside of jackboots look and feel alike whether the brand they bear is linked with the Soviet Union or with the United States.

What, then, can be expected, nationally and transnationally, from Asian churches that unite in affirming a new solidarity with the Asian masses while refusing to choose between either the slogans or the blocs that claim to represent the alternatives? Must they be seen as neutralized somewhere in the middle, or as immobilized by their own internal divisions, or as offering a third way out of an impasse, or as still searching for a role?

These possible answers are perhaps best seen as ranging in an ascending scale of plausibility.

It is least plausible to say the churches are neutralized in the middle. What middle? A midpoint between two false alternatives is all that could be in question, once one has ceased to regard either old-fashioned capitalism or old-fashioned communism as the wave of the future.

It would seem closer to the truth to represent the churches as immobilized by internal divisions. We have repeatedly been faced with the fact that elements in them pull in different directions—the standardbearers and the scouts, the center and the periphery, and the complex range of orientations of nationalism and transnationalism. Yet to say "immobilized" is to say more than the evidence warrants. The social scene in the Asian churches is nothing if not a scene of creative ferment.

At the same time, it is certainly saying too much to suggest that a hundred million Asian Christians have a sociopolitical way of their own to show to the other two billion of their fellow Asians. Undoubtedly, like Asia as a whole, they are still searching, though not without having found at least a new orientation for their search.

A minority like the Asian Christian one, newly conscious of its solidarity with its two gigantic reference groups (more than a billion non-Asian Christians, more than two billion non-Christian Asians), has a bridging role to play that should tend to focus its attention on points of proximity between Christian and Asian problems and solutions.

As an Asian group, it cannot but tend more and more to see its future in terms of the South, the Third World, the nonaligned nations, the struggle against neocolonialism and neoimperialism, the New (or at any rate some new) International Economic Order.

As a Christian group, and given its own weakness, marginality, and heterogeneity in Asia, it cannot but prove more receptive and cooperative toward proposals that are representative, inclusive, pragmatic, pacific, and conciliatory, even at the price of seeming tame, gradualistic, and middle-of-the-road. It will talk more of human rights than of systems claiming to guarantee individual or social rights, even if that makes it seem an inveterate fence-straddler, as if it could not differentiate between a human-rights approach and a liberal-capitalist one.[35] It will no longer preach peace without regard to justice, but its new thrust towards justice will continue to be balanced, if not blunted, by its bias towards peace.

And who is to say that, on the whole, if Asian Christianity were to succeed in its search for this precarious balance, it would not thereby be proving faithful, for better or worse, to the deepest imperatives of the gospel it professes to live by?

We have noted already that the institutional churches have too long a record of acquiescence in the violence of the powerful to be altogether credible in the reprobation of the violence of the oppressed. But not all those church leaders who have shrunk from the idea of armed revolution have done so because of weakness or double standards. There is an authentically Christian (as well as authentically Hindu and Buddhist) tradition of pure pacifism that is as much a factor in the political role of the religions as revolutionary violence or complicity in repression. It appears as regularly as these other phenomena wherever in the Asian crucible Christianity is put to the test.

If we may take the following 1981 testimony at face value, such pure pacifism can represent the united stand of a whole diocese, small and rural and peripheral indeed, and not even representative within the southern Philippine ecclesiastical ferment, but outstanding in its claim to be one of the rare examples of an Asian church of the people on the scale of a diocese:

> Consensus . . . arose from our last general Prelature meeting in February of priests and religious, lay leaders and church workers. At that meeting we faced up to the problem of armed power in Bukidnon and its consequences for ourselves and our people. The consensus was an option for, to put it in a formula, *total vulnerability*. In effect, it was a rejection of violence as a way of righting wrongs and an affirmation of the Prelature's thrust for justice. We said *no* to the "salvaging" of the military, to the "liquidation" of the NPA; *yes* to the continued striving for justice and the peace that comes through justice.
>
> From a sheerly human—intellectual, political, ideological—point of view, we know the option made no sense. We saw clearly that by our open disavowal of the violence of both the military and the NPA and all other armed powers, we were putting ourselves completely at their mercy; worse, we were inviting, even provoking, the very violence we were rejecting by our insistence on the forceful doing of justice; and possibly, worst of all, we arrived at the option in the clear-eyed conviction that we would never be able to bring about full justice in society, but for all that we would have to keep striving mightily for it—even unto death.
>
> It does not make sense. Except in the context of a faith . . .[36]

Between "the Powers That Be" and "the Cry of the People"

It is worth recalling that both of the above phrases are of biblical origin. They come from the two biblical passages most representative of the two political poles of attraction in any community in the Judaeo-Christian tradition—the pole of submission to authority (Romans 13:1ff.) and the pole of liberation from oppression (Exodus 3:7). Thus, the roots of the dilemma these phrases express go back to the sources of the Christian faith itself.

We must dispense ourselves here from discussing the respective biblical contexts of the two emphases, except to note that neither was left long without being balanced by a contrary emphasis. In the New Testament case this can be found especially in the rage of the Apocalypse against Caesar; in the Old Testament case it runs through the long drawn out struggle of the monarchical and the priestly principles against the prophetic one.

We must dispense ourselves also from repeating what we have said (pp. 9-16) about the contexts of the two emphases in Christian history—except to pose once more, and more specifically, the questions they put to Christians on the social front today about the desirability and the possibility of a post-Constantinian Church.

We must dispense ourselves further from repeating the general considerations that have suggested themselves in connection with particular aspects of our inquiry—except, once again, to recall that insofar as they are valid at all they are relevant to any general understanding.

Thus, it is still relevant to recall, from our discussion of the transnational avant-garde in Asia (pp. 69-70), that for empirical study it is simply not useful to think of the Church as a fixed point in the firmament, but that what we have under observation is more like a rather scattered moving pilgrimage in the midst of a larger mass of people also on the move. When we speak empirically of the Church or the churches, we are generalizing about an entity that undoubtedly has a certain unity, or at the worst a certain aspiration toward unity, but only within the limits of a permanently precarious distance between the head and the tail of the procession, and between the standardbearers and the scouts.

As long as we bear this aspect of things in mind, and as long as we recognize its inevitability and normality, we need never make the mistake of expecting the overall reality of "the Church" to be reflected either exclusively in the pronouncements of the standardbearers or exclusively in the manifestos of the scouts. It will be more realistic, where social questions are concerned, to take the former as likely to be more indicative of where the tail of the procession is, and the latter as likely to be more indicative of where its head is.

Any talk of an overall position or orientation of the Church will then be, at its crudest, little more than the result of adding the extremes together and dividing by two. And any proposition to the effect that the Church is now more a force for change than a force for inertia will imply, not that the rearguard is no longer dragging its feet, but that it is no longer doing so sufficiently to nullify entirely the forward thrust of the advance guard, or to dissociate itself entirely from it.

Similarly, it is relevant to recall from our discussion of frontiers in ministry (pp. 85–88) the ambivalence of institutionalized agencies, even institutionalized agencies of change, with the corollary that even in these latter we must look somewhere between the extremes of top-heavy structures and bottom-heavy bodies for an always fluctuating area of leverage for change.

If change must begin, when it does begin, from circles outside but not too far outside the centers of power; if it must begin from nonruling groups within striking or destabilizing distance of rule, from nonhierarchical groups in orbit between the hierarchical centers and the marginalized masses, from groups not too near either the gravitational force of the center or the tangential force of the fringes; then it is not in itself a sign that change is effectively blocked when ruling groups, hierarchical centers, and even institutionalized change agencies seem to relapse, as we have seen repeatedly in Asia, into postures of intransigence and resistance to change.

Plus ça change, plus c'est la même chose. "The more things change the more they stay the same." That is true of society whether it is a question of Marxist class domination or Weberian routinization or the structural correspondence proper to social systems according to Levi-Strauss or the structural-functional pattern perceived by Talcott Parsons. These are explanations of the forces that keep society the way it is.

E pur si muove! "But it does move."* Change also is a reality! Change eventually overtakes all human creations, including all theories that have no place for change.

Nonruling groups sometimes do prove themselves to be within striking or destabilizing distance of rule—even in strategic bastions of one or the other superpower bloc. Iran and Poland are among the most recent illustrations of that.

Nonhierarchical groups, especially in the Third World, sometimes do capture the initiative in the life of the Catholic Church as a whole—provoking the Vatican and the hierarchies into strenuous efforts to recover control. Such has been the case with movements of Third World theology, of women and men religious, and of basic Christian communities.

Groups as far from the gravitational force of the center as are the radicalized margins of the churches in Asia sometimes do exercise crucial leverage on policies at the center. So it has been with URM in the CCA, with the CCA in the WCC, with the AMRS and the NASSA in the CBCP, with the OHD and the BISAs in the FABC, and with the FABC itself, as with

---

*Remark attributed to Galileo after he was forced to recant his views on the motion of the earth before the Inquisition in 1633.

CELAM, by its mere survival as a transnational novelty and potential locus of power in the global organization of Catholicism.

A third consideration that is relevant to recall from our discussion of local sources of militancy in Asia is the notion of unintentionally creative consequences of political and ecclesiastical "imperialism" (pp. 117-19), within the limits of a certain productive tension between the strength of a challenge and the strength of the Christian capacity to respond (p. 103).

We have said enough about how narrow these limits are in Asia, and how it is not surprising to find that only in half a dozen local situations have the relations of force not been too unequal to permit the tension to be productive.

We have also sufficiently highlighted the paradoxical reality of creative repression within these limits, and the vital contribution such repression is capable of making, unwittingly, to the emergence of a people-oriented Church. For at a certain stage, when such a Church is emerging, even when the process seems entirely and inescapably in continuity with the original trajectory of the Christian ideal, this continuity is not enough to give the forces in favor of a people-oriented Church the power to prevail. At such a stage, a certain provocation, by way of ill-judged obstructiveness, can serve to rally the decisive degree of further support. It is thus that attempts to dam the undammable have often proved in the end to be the most far-reaching forces of change.

All these considerations still do not suffice to permit a categorical answer to our question as to the possibility of a post-Constantinian Church. They merely permit us to define more narrowly what is in question, and thereby to distinguish some possibilities that may be plausibly entertained from others that may not.

On the one hand, it seems clear that, short of a social miracle, there will never be anything like complete emancipation of large ecclesiastical bodies from the pull of the social status quo. In this sense, what the Asian bishops said in 1970 must be considered as promising more than mere bishops can deliver: "We will not tie our hands by compromising entanglements with the rich and powerful in our respective countries." The truth is that their hands are already tied, and that their entanglements must remain in varying degrees compromising. All that can be done—but this badly needs doing—is to distinguish more clearly between the degree of entanglement that is sociologically inevitable and the degree that is a proper subject for moral suasion or censure.

We have put ourselves this question at the outset of our inquiry: Is there any exception to the rule by which large institutions, such as churches, tend to privilege the status quo in society precisely in the measure that they are rooted there?

For reasons first hinted at then, and made more fully apparent in various connections (the Christian experience in the world and in Asia, in colonial times and today, in positions of internal or external strength or weakness), we are led to affirm that no true exception can be found in that experience. Similarly, for reasons outlined in our discussion of standardbearers and scouts within church institutions, we are led to affirm that a change in this pattern would be not merely historically improbable but sociologically impossible, insofar as it would involve a systematic rupture between a large social body and the social power center on which its survival depends.

We say, *insofar as*. The root of the impossibility is found in the extreme case, where rupture would be suicide. Self-preservation, that first law of nature, admits exceptions at the level of individual human beings, and even at the level of organizations small enough to be wholly subject to one or a few human wills. It ceases to admit exceptions at the level of true social institutions, which are characterized by the fact that human volition is only one of the forces at work in them.

Among these forces at work in human institutions, sociology insists that some at least are irreducible to the forces of human volition. One view, which seems most easily reconcilable with the facts of experience, is that there are three fundamental forces, or sources of social and historical dynamism, which are irreducible to one another: the force of human volition (the human actor), the force of the cultural complex (language, for instance, though originally a mental product, cannot be bent entirely to the actor's will), and the force of social structures and systems.[37]

Even if human volition could be decisive in social institutions, the human wills involved are too numerous and too exposed to varieties of conditioning to be capable of uniting in favor of such an extreme option as liquidation of the institution itself or of something perceived as a vital part of itself. But in any case those wills are faced with the other irreducibly separate factor, the social factor, whose tendency, whether interpreted according to Marx or Durkheim or Weber or Parsons or Levi-Strauss, is to make the social institution cast its lot in with the lot of the prevailing social formation.

This may seem a hard saying from the standpoint of Christian idealism. Other institutions may be self-interested, but is not the Church the institution whose essence is to be *dis*interested? Does it not claim to believe (Matt. 10:39) that only through dying to self is true life to be found? Does it not take its cue from a Master who represents for it the very model of *kenosis*, of self-effacement (Phil. 2:7–8)? Does it not profess to continue the work of a Shepherd who lays down his life for his sheep? Does it not acknowledge, and have we not heard it acknowledge in Asia in BISA V (p. 59), its gospel duty to risk everything for the growth of God's Kingdom?

The easiest part of the answer is that it is nothing new for churches to fail to live up to their ideals, and that a certain gap between promise and performance is a permanent part of the human condition. But that is only to single out the element of *moral* failure in the churches' predicament. That element is indeed important, but it cannot be fairly assessed except in conjunction with those other elements that are not directly attributable to failure of will.

The easiest of these other elements to acknowledge is the element of second nature. It is a fact that the habits of centuries are not changed overnight. Even if we were to suppose that the hands of the church leaders can be untied from compromising entanglements, and that the resolution to do so is genuine and unqualified, who is to say how much time would realistically need to be allowed for the transition?

Some social changes do not take root in less than a century; few do so in less than a generation. Will it yet be written of the Catholic Church after Vatican II, as it has been written of China after 1949, that "never has so great a change been brought about in so short a time among so numerous a people"?[38] If it is to prove true (and clearly a formidable case can already be made on that side of the argument), we can be sure that it will not be more than an *overall* truth, balancing many advances against many retreats and relapses, in the one case as in the other.

In one sense, of course, all social structure, being ultimately of human invention, being by definition a humanmade part of the human environment, falls ultimately into the category of second nature as opposed to what is natural *tout court*. Yet an irreducible distinction remains between elements of the humanmade environment that people could have made otherwise and elements that they could not.

We cannot alter the fact that social institutions, regardless of any original purpose for their creation, inevitably sink roots in the existing social order, establishing multiple ties of interdependence with it and thus acquiring a stake in its survival, merely because they need some kind of order and because this is the one (and *ex hypothesi* the only one) available to them. Reduced to its most elementary terms, the logic of this is the logic of the saying, Nature abhors a vacuum.

On the one hand, then, a minimum of compromising entanglement follows inevitably from the fact that churches have a social existence and cannot be churches without having a social existence. On the other hand, and in virtue of the same fact, churches are not dispensed from a real share of responsibility, if not for the past of the existing social order (though sometimes there is question of that too), at least for its future.

Once the consensus has been reached among globally representative Christians that the existing world order needs changing, that a change at least to the extent of reducing notorious inequalities is a moral imperative, and that a duty to work for such a change is integral to the task of the Church in the world, then the stage is set for a historic shift in the social role of the Church within the limits of properly historical possibilities.

Whether this implies the possibility or the prospect of a post-Constantinian Church is a matter of definition. In any case, such a church could not be conceived along the lines of pre-Constantinian Christianity.

There can never be again, even if there ever was before, a Christianity capable of facing the world with entirely clean hands, or with hands that are entirely untied.

It is not merely that what is done cannot be undone. It is also that what is now pervasively and intricately interwoven with the fabric of world society cannot be made to behave as if it were not. In the measure that Christianity retains leverage in the world, in that measure it must accept the constraints of its leverage. Even if due regard for the powers that be were not written into the Christian mandate, it would be futile to wax indignant over the fact that it conditions, channels, and in some degree actually limits the possible Christian response to the cry of the people.

Hence, in a situation where priority has shifted to the latter concern, the first condition for effective response is a lucid recognition of what can and what cannot be done—just as energy saved from beating one's head against a wall is energy available for getting around that wall.

What can be done depends most fundamentally on the extent to which a new society is actually in the making. For those who are sure, for example, that some kind of socialism is the real wave of the future, it is ultimately only a matter of waiting for the churches to be carried along with it. The movement of revolution will in due course turn the powers that be into the powers that were; and the same gravitational force that once drew the churches back to the old status quo will just as effectively draw them forward to the new one.

We can see the process at work in this way in regimes where socialism is already the ruling ideology. In the Soviet Union, China, and Eastern Europe apart from Poland, even the hostility of the ruling ideology to religion does not suffice to nullify the rule by which power gravitates toward power and by which Christian contestation of the existing political power tends to come less from the ecclesiastical centers of power than from the ecclesiastical peripheries.[39]

If this mechanism were the only one by which the social role of the Church could be changed, it would be ultimately self-defeating, since that role would remain essentially the same Constantinian role, continuing to give priority to its relations with the powerful over its relations with the powerless.

But in fact there is no proximate prospect of such a purely Macchiavellian resolution of the problem. Even if we could foresee a global future in a recognizably socialist mold, we should have no hope of making that perception widely enough shared among church leaders in Asia today to seem firmer ground to them than the ground they now stand on. It could not be expected in Asia, and it seems no more feasible in the world as a whole: church leaders will never be the first to give up preferring a devil they know to a devil they don't know. But in any case we do not know the shape of the future; and all we have felt confident in predicting about it is that it will not fit, except remotely, any blueprint already known to us.

What we have, then, is a mechanism that is more effective for detaching the churches from their current moorings than for attaching them to any other available ones. Its effect is to strike at the present social roots of ecclesiastical security without supplying any comparably secure alternative. Like Abraham four millennia ago, churches today are being put in a situation where they are less sure of what they must move toward than of what they must move away from.

This could be called providential by those who believe in providence. In any case, it seems to be the more precise truth about the apparent shift in the global orientation of the churches toward social change. A double movement of history, operating interactively on the churches from within and from without, has sufficiently loosened their ties with the prevailing world order of the late twentieth century to enable them, for perhaps the first time in centuries, to consider fundamental options between structural stability and structural change without being subject to a humanly insuperable bias in favor of the former.

Thus is the world Church brought to a state of relative freedom of option within the limits of more or less normal sociological and historical causality.

It would not be possible to assign a weight to each of the individual influences that have combined to offer the churches a stake in some new world order sufficient to offset their stake in the existing one. Perhaps the crucial factor within Christianity is its demographic shift from the First World to the Third—a shift to which Asian Christianity makes its own modest contribution.

A demographic shift in itself would not be decisive without a corresponding redistribution of power. That has been certainly slower to follow—but not so slow within ecclesiastical institutions, bound as they are to ultimate egalitarianism, as within military, economic, and political ones. By the 1970s the Christian demographic shift was already widely perceived as irreversible.[40] Short of a successful effort of undisguised imperialism—already out of the question in Protestant and Orthodox churches, and already ceasing to be thinkable even within Roman Catholicism—it is only a matter of time till the overall center of gravity in the Christian world will shift from North to South.

It could be argued that it is only when the world Church is thus suspended between two world orders—becoming uprooted from one without yet being firmly rooted in the other—that the church institution is even relatively free to make a genuine preferential option for the poor. If it could all be brought about by mechanisms of self-interest, if it were merely a matter of switching sides from yesterday's masters to tomorrow's, there would be no more altruism embodied in church structures than in any others, and no more to be hoped for from them by the poor of the future than by those of the past. The saving grace comes from the fact that, while mechanisms of self-interest cannot be wished out of existence, they can come to operate in ways that neutralize each other, and to some extent can even be manipulated in such a way as to serve a wider interest.

A first condition for effective response to the cry of the people is a lucid recognition of what can and what cannot be done. Here again, energy saved is energy available.

Social structures, after all, are no more than stable patterns of human behavior, reciprocally related to the creation and operation of human values. There is nothing to prevent human actors inside and outside the church institution from deliberately changing the thrust of their own contribution to its functioning. There is also nothing to prevent them, within limits already indicated, from deliberately setting in train the processes that could eventually change the structures themselves through the mediation of changed values, or change the values themselves through the mediation of changed structures.

We say, human actors inside and *outside* the church institution. It cannot be too often recalled that, as a matter of empirical observation, history is not moved forward by religion exclusively, and furthermore that, as a matter of reminders needed and periodically received by religious believers, if religion is God's right hand in the world it is not his only one. Given the principle of the thing, one can find in history in the Christian era any number of reenactments of the biblical scenario of salvation, in which Yahweh had to show that he was nobody's property by finding his uses for Pharaohs and Cyruses as well as for the faithful from Moses through Ezra.

The lesson has clearly been needed as much by Christians as by Jews. Church leaders can normally be relied on to uphold basic Christian ideals of love and justice at levels of abstraction where the individual and especially the institutional cost of implementing them has not yet been counted. By the same token, it is sociologically unrealistic to rely on them, unaided, to continue undeviatingly to uphold these ideals once they are caught in the inevitable conflict between the ideals and the narrower interests of the institution for which they are immediately responsible. That is precisely why they need the contribution, or contradiction, of the ecclesial avant-garde, which has no such stake in the narrower interests of the institution; and that also is why (since the ecclesial avant-garde either lacks institutional leverage in the measure of its radicalism or lacks radicalism in the measure of its leverage) both rearguard and vanguard in the world Church need the pressure of the forces of change in the world as a whole.

We have seen some of the main ways in which this works out in practice nowadays.

For their Pharaoh, provoking them to their Exodus from complicity with power, the churches have had the North-South imbalance in general and the national security regimes in particular. For their Cyrus, cutting short their Exile from evangelical single-mindedness, they have had Marxism in its revolutionary mode, and more generally all secular ideologies of change up to the point at which they become ideologies in power and agencies of consolidation. Within the fold of the faithful the same law of creative repression applies. The vanguard of change has been built up by the same mechanism inside the churches as in the world as a whole. It emerges as a reaction to top-heavy institutionalization, to the convergence and collision of ecclesiastical with political power, and to the ecclesiastical forms of domination of the South by the North.

For those committed to assisting and channeling this impetus for change from within the church institution, the key insight needed remains the insight about power: the fact that power gravitates towards power, and that there is basically no exception to this rule even in the extreme case, even in the case of ecclesiastical power in a system dominated by antiecclesiastical power. The change-oriented ecclesiastical strategist who has firmly grasped this fact is left with only one strategy that can produce the desired results. That strategy will be one of systematically resisting, subverting, and as far as possible reversing the ecclesiastical concentration of power.

What are the chances of any general adoption of such a strategy? Here again we must recall the prime necessity of a lucid recognition of what can and what cannot be done.

What cannot be done short of a social miracle is to arrive at a prevailing pattern in which people invested with effective responsibility for the church institution give effective priority to interests beyond that institution—above all where there is question of subverting power in the institution in the name of those ulterior interests.

"Subversive" individuals near the center, yes: the papacy of John XXIII would seem to have been a case of that kind. A regular pattern of "subversion" from the center, no: for every subversive in a high church post, there will be any number of restorers and consolidators.

A pious wish to look beyond the institution, often enough yes: the immediate successor of John XXIII evinced that wish most poignantly. Effective priority for interests beyond the institution, not really ever as a regular pattern: the system has its built-in ways of ensuring that subordination of its interests does not become a habit.

It must be stressed that this hard reality has nothing essentially to do with bad will or bad faith on the part of persons. There will always be climbers and opportunists, and every institution will always have its share of them, a share determined by the extent to which the interests of the institution and of the opportunists coincide. But there will also always be quite enough people sincerely convinced that loyalty to the institution is the only true guarantee of all legitimate ulterior interests; and the system will similarly seek to filter their access to the levers of power precisely in the measure that they put the system first. It would simply not be a system if it did not.

So much for what cannot be done. There should be no cause for discouragement for those mindful of what can be done.

Between, on the one hand, a social miracle of church change by which a social institution would act as if it were not one, and, on the other, a social mechanism of change that would be entirely and unproductively consequent on a change in the world order itself, there are all the possibilities inherent in the following facts: the fact that the Church, like all social institutions, has a vanguard as well as a rearguard; the fact that it is open to being acted upon at points of leverage intermediate between its center and its fringes; the fact that it is now passing through a period in which it is not rooted as strongly as it would normally be in a particular global order; and the fact that the forces of resistance to change can make and are making their own contribution to change through counterproductive efforts to maintain the hitherto prevailing power relations in the world and in the Church.

In the larger perspective of church history, examples of the operation of the last-mentioned mechanism may be found in the Orthodox schism, the Reformation, the French Revolution, and, as already instanced repeatedly, the rise of Marxism. A movement that may be in a narrower sense a break away from the Church, or an external assault on the Church, can have a larger historical meaning as a revolution within the Church, giving more or less abnormal new outlets to values and energies within the Church when more or less normal outlets for them have been blocked.

This is a point that can sometimes be appreciated better from outside the Church than from within it. A generation before Vatican II, which reaffirmed the priority of the Church as a community of the faithful over the Church as a clerical organization, Gramsci took that very principle as a premise for his argument that the decline of church leadership from its position as "organic intellectual" of the "historical bloc" of Christendom was in direct relation to its loss of roots among the masses of the people.

Within this larger sense of the world Church (an entity existing partly in reality and partly in aspiration), it is not to be expected that any of these major historical actors will withdraw from the stage in any immediately foreseeable future. Some authentic gospel values will continue to find more fertile soil in the secular revolutions than in the clerical organization. Some others will continue to flourish more freely in the soil of the schisms and the heresies than in the soil of the parent church.

It goes without saying that in all these cases—the secular revolutions, the ecclesiastical breakaways, the mother church itself—these authentic gospel values will remain intentionally or unintentionally mixed with values that are quite incompatible with the gospel. But that is only to say, as the gospel parable itself says, that the wheat must remain mixed with the weeds till the harvest of the kingdom. Disconcerting though it may be, this model of the ways in which the gospel gets preached turns out to be in some sense the historical norm.

This model also provides a certain basis for gauging the extent to which the Church can be expected to shift its weight in the balance between the powers that be and the cry of the people.

In every historical epoch, secular revolutionaries play a vanguard role in relation to the mass of believers. In the present epoch, their leverage in the direction of developing a Church of the people is being exercised more strongly and felt more effectively than has been the case for centuries. In Asia, in the name of indigenization and contextualization, the ears of the churches are being opened as never before to the cry of the people as uttered through a unique multiplicity of voices—among which nationalism (and regional transnationalism), Marxism in its Asian modes, Islam, Buddhism, and Hinduism are only the loudest.

Similarly, in every epoch since the Reformation, Protestantism as a whole has played a vanguard role in relation to Catholicism as a whole. In the present one, the rise of ecumenism has meant the decline of resistance to that influence. On the social front this pattern is reproduced in Asia, where the frontierspeople of the CCA have blazed many trails in the name of power for the powerless that were later to be entered upon with the more measured tread of the FABC.

In the epoch opened by Vatican II and by Medellín, the members of the Catholic avant-garde have become a force within Catholicism that has little real precedent since the rise of the clerical church. Their extra leverage comes from the acknowledgement by Vatican II that the Church is the people; from the acknowledgement by Third World church leaders that the people are massively the poor; and, in the case of Asia, from the acknowledgement by the bishops there that a Church of the people in Asia cannot be other than a Church of the poor and of the young. These acknowledgements may remain only verbal at the level of the officebearers; but these latter can neither entirely disavow them nor entirely disavow those within the Church who insist on recalling them and on drawing consequences from them for action at the level of vanguard and rearguard alike.

All of these vanguards have the weaknesses of their strengths. In the measure that they are intensely in touch with their times they risk a loss of perspective on other times. In the measure that they apply all their force to the immediate barrier to be breached they risk finding themselves off balance when and if they break through.

Such are the problems inherent in being the vanguard of a vanguard. It is precisely the loyal followers of a radical (be it Marx or Luther) who are more liable to be frozen in conservatism when their leader is frozen in death. More generally, it is the special risk of an entity like the WCC (as compared with the Vatican), precisely in the measure of its greater openness to the currents of the world around it, that while on the one hand it is freed for costlier militancy against, for example, racism in Africa, on the other hand it is bound to relative silence about repression in the lands where Orthodoxy lives under communism.

The problems of the Catholic social vanguard have much of this in common with the other Christian and the other social vanguards. In addition, the Catholic vanguard has a problem with the Catholic power structure that is entirely its own. To be a change-oriented ecclesiastical strategist; to be

convinced of our earlier conclusion that only one strategy can possibly produce the results being sought; to be accordingly committed to this strategy
(that is, committed to reversing the ecclesiastical concentration of power)—
to be all this within the Catholic Church is to live contradiction at a level
that has no real parallel outside, except perhaps in the case of a humanist
Marxist in a Stalinist party.

That parallel is not without interest. To take one of the milder and simpler illustrations, Communist parties have had their Garaudys, and Catholic universities have had their Girardis; but as long as the model of manage-
ment was Stalinist in the one and papalist in the other, the end of the road
for the persistent dissenter was inevitably expulsion.[41]

And the parallel does not end there. Stalinism was never the only model
for the Party: Eurocommunism has professed to find a place for difference
and dialogue; but it has done so too recently to have had its profession properly put to the test; so the question remains whether there is a future for
Eurocommunism. Similarly, papalism was never the only model for the
Catholic Church: in its extreme form it is only the model of the latest-but-
one of more than twenty general councils. Is there a future for the older
collegial or conciliar model, somewhat timidly reaffirmed by Vatican II?
Because of the timidity and the ambivalence of the reaffirmation, and because of the powerful forces at work to minimize its significance, the future
of difference, dialogue, decentralization, and multipolarity is as humanly
uncertain for the critical tradition within Roman Catholicism as it is for the
antitotalitarian heirs of Marx and Lenin.

We have used the term *Roman Catholicism* in these pages whenever it has
seemed needed to avoid ambiguity. On occasion we have put the "Roman"
in quotation marks in acknowledgement of the paradox the juxtaposition
implies. Roman Catholicism is in fact a term used mainly by Christians who
claim to belong to the Catholic Church mentioned in the Apostles' Creed
without belonging to the Catholic Church that has its headquarters in
Rome. They typically see themselves as non-Roman Catholics; that is,
Catholics without the Roman connection.

In another sense, some Catholics who maintain the Roman connection
also prefer to see themselves as non-Roman Catholics. Insofar as the "Roman" is a contradiction of the "Catholic" (a contradiction not implied in
the mere fact of communion with the church leader claiming succession
from Saint Peter), they are clear that it is the "Catholic" that must be maintained and the "Roman" that must go.

But can the Catholicity in Roman Catholicism ever really prevail over the
Romanness? That is the crucial question for anyone who has ever posed the
more general question of whether the weight of "the Church" in the scales
of society can ever really lie more on the side of change than on that of conservatism or inertia. Because the majority of all Christians are in communion with Rome, and the majority of other Christians are fragmented to a
point where their potential for radical social leverage is too far from the

ideal in the direction of dispersion, the social role of Christianity as a whole, in the world as a whole, depends most crucially on how far Catholicism can overcome its own historic handicap of paralyzing monolithism.

There is room for a wide range of judgment on what is the optimum intermediate point between the extremes. There is less room for doubt that the point of departure before Vatican II was too far from the ideal, in theory and practice, in the direction of centralization. There is also less room for doubt that the point of departure two decades after the opening of Vatican II, if less far from the ideal in theory, was still too far in practice. Not very many would be willing to put it as bluntly as it was put in the "feedback" of the South Korean BISA delegates: *The present Church structure cannot be poor.* But they, like the small boy who spoke indiscreetly of the emperor's lack of clothes, were in fact only bringing the discussion back to the real world.

This is not the place to judge any particular pontificate, especially if it is only a few years old and is destined to outlive the early 1980s. A single pope can be at best a key individual in a line of hundreds of popes, and one of several key factors in the evolution of church and papacy at a particular historical moment. As with all successors of Peter, and for that matter with Peter himself, there must inevitably be a wide gap between ideals and realizations—even in the case of John Paul II. It is the conclusion of these pages that the gap will have been less wide in his case in the measure that his social message contrives to be not merely proclaimed to the world outside the church institution, but also embodied within it.

This may be brought about more effectively with his active cooperation, or more effectively against his active resistance. It is always possible that this is one of the historic cases where the rise of a Church of the people is at a stage where it is more liable to be killed by kindness than by repression. It seems even probable that this is a case where it must be counterproductive to try to contain a Church of South and North within a framework devised for a part of the North, and to contain a Church on the threshold of its third millennium within a framework more adapted to an earlier millennium.

We have seen how it can happen in various local contexts that attempts to dam the undammable can become the most far-reaching forces of change. We may now be seeing how the same thing can happen on the scale of nearly a thousand million Catholics. For why should it not be so, if they and their leader are equally in the hands of that "shrewd Spirit" who, as none other than Karl Marx once remarked, "continually manifests himself in all these contradictions"?[42]

If in fact far-reaching forces in Catholicism are now being built up by being dammed up, and if that is only another manifestation of the "shrewd Spirit," then Pope John Paul II will deserve the thanks of posterity not only for his many positive contributions, but even more for being the instrument of a providence beyond anything he has ever personally planned, and even contrary to some things he has personally wanted. In this matter it seems that it comes to the same thing, whether we read history in the light of Marx or of Jesus. Either way we must conclude that all who have served that Spirit have done so ultimately on the Spirit's terms and not on their own. So it has been with confirmers of the faithful in the line of the shock-treated Peter. So it has been with servants of Yahweh in the pattern of the good pagan Cyrus. So it has been also with would-be-atheist servants of humanity in the manner of Marx.

CONCLUSION: THE OUTLOOK

It is now over three millennia since a minor movement of people across a neck of land between the world's two largest continents gave rise to a memory called the Exodus, and to a hope in a God who said: "I have heard the cry of my people."

It is now almost two millennia since that tradition of memory and hope underwent its greatest single historical transformation, when some of its distant heirs at the same Eurasian crossroads, where it had till then been clinging to its first foothold, heard the same God commanding them: "Go out to the whole world."

It is now a century and a third since a still more distant heir of that tradition reaffirmed a central strand of it with a force that jolted all of it and all of the world of which it had by then become part and parcel.

What Karl Marx in effect set out to do was to bury the ancient memory and reformulate the ancient hope. What he achieved was to contribute to giving a new lease on life to both. At any rate, that was a part of his achievement, and one that may yet prove to have been the most far-reaching part: to contribute to the reawakening of the original resources of social conscience among those who claim to belong to the tradition of Moses and Jesus. Certainly such a reawakening began to be noticeable in the second century of Marxism and the twentieth of Christianity, at a time when one out of every three people on earth was a Christian and when one out of every two Christians lived in a part of the world that had reason to feel a need for a Moses or a Marx.

Contemplating a part of that part of the world, the same Marx posed the question that confronts not only this study but also every possible study of the human future in what remains of its present millennium: "Can mankind fulfill its destiny without a fundamental revolution in the social state of Asia?"[1]

The Asian part of the story of the rematching of Marx and Moses, which we have called Asian Christian social protest, emerged from its prehistory in the mid-1960s—a very recent date in the timescale we have been considering. The present lines are being written at a point in time just halfway between then and the end of the millennium. Having looked that far back, are we in any better position to look that far forward? What is the outlook for the phenomenon in its second couple of decades, given the record of its first?

160

This is not the place to attempt to steal from the future any secrets that properly belong to it. However, since tomorrow began yesterday, something of tomorrow must be available for inspection in what is already yesterday.

Statistical data and trends are one example. What we have in this domain is nothing compared with what we would need to have to make reliable predictions. But for what they are worth the data have been assembled and organized on an unprecedented scale in the *World Christian Encyclopedia* of 1982. Rounding these data, we find we have to do with an Asian Christian population that will have grown from 20 million in 1900 through 100 million in 1970 to a quarter of a billion in 2000; all this in a total Asian population that will have grown from one billion in 1900 through two billion in 1970 to something on the order of 3.7 billion in 2000.

We have some assurance that this picture will not change drastically in the space of a few decades: first, because of the relative inertia of major demographic trends over short time spans; second, because of the inertia of trends in the processing of demographic data. (A new Christian data-collecting enterprise on the scale of the *World Christian Encyclopedia* is unlikely to be repeated within this century.) What the picture most significantly shows is a Christian percentage of the Asian population that will have grown from 2 percent in 1900 through 5 percent in 1970 to something approaching 7 percent in 2000. In other words, it shows a trend in the direction of liberating Asian Christian social protest from the minority complex that has hitherto been the main inhibiting influence on its development.

So far as it goes, this trend is verified not only regionally but also locally. In India and Indonesia, the locus of the two national Christian populations where an easing of the Christian minority complex would be most significant for Christianity as a whole in nonsocialist Asia, the outlook is for an increase in the Christian percentage from 3.5 percent and 9.4 percent respectively in 1970 to 4.7 percent and 13.3 percent in 2000. In South Korea, host of the fourth largest Asian national Christian population after the Philippines, India, and Indonesia, even much lower estimates of that population than those of the *World Christian Encyclopedia* would agree in putting it already past the point where a minority complex would be a major factor in inhibiting its self-expression.

What else would be a major inhibiting influence on the future development of Asian Christian social protest? Obviously, it would be checked at its root by any attenuation of its raison d'être—that is, by any easing of the conditions that gave rise to the need for it. What, then, is the outlook for any such easing in the middle or late 1980s, or in the 1990s?

Most observers in the early 1980s have seen none. On the contrary, with the First and the Second World at this time in the depth of the worst recession in half a century, the outlook for the Third World can only be that things will have to get worse before they get better.

Or could it perhaps be said that, while this might be true on a global scale, it is not precisely applicable to Asia? Certainly the trend of World Bank reports of this period is to locate the most stubborn development failures in Africa and the greatest development breakthroughs in East and Southeast Asia. These breakthroughs are even leading some to envisage the twenty-first century as the century of the Pacific.

This may well be the real long-term outlook. Looking at the big picture, we have already ventured to say that in Asia we have to do with a continental area which, more than any other single one in the closing decades of the twentieth century, makes a plausible center of gravity for the world's affairs.

However, the local and short-term outlook is something else. The facts of the development record of revolutionary China are still clouded in confusion and controversy. The South Asian development outlook has not been notably transformed since Myrdal compiled his dismal dossier on it in *Asian Drama* in the 1960s. The brighter picture in the rest of East Asia and in Southeast Asia is brighter mainly by the criteria of capitalist macroeconomics, characteristically insensitive to greater or lesser measures of built-in maldistribution. In the context of the Philippines, "galloping pauperization" was how seventeen bishops defined its "net effect" at the end of 1981.[2] In the case of the "little Japans" of Taiwan, Hong Kong, South Korea, and Singapore, it has been argued that insofar as they have flourished as "export platforms," they have done so largely because they were a lucky size at a lucky time in the development of the world market. The conclusion of one such argument about them has been to this effect: "Miracles, maybe; models, surely not."[3] In any case, not models of the kind of just, participatory, and sustainable society for which Christian social protest pleads.

Inhibited, therefore, in the short term, not at all by any overall easing of the objective grounds for Christian commitment to fundamental social change in Asia, and less than hitherto by the Christian minority complex that is distinctive to the Asian situation, does it follow that social protest is assured of looming at least as large in the Asian churches in the next decades as in the last?

There is a further possible inhibiting factor to be considered: the factor inherent in the internal autonomy of the churches as organizations and as communities. Could they recoil from their present social commitment, either because of exhaustion or debilitation in a too unequal trial of strength whether globally or locally, or because of internal reassessment of priorities along more traditional lines?

Within certain limits (mainstream Christianity cannot unsay what it has said in the 1960s and 1970s), such a recoil is clearly an open possibility both globally and locally. In the short history of Christian social protest in contemporary Asia we have already seen that any linear model of progressive social involvement of the churches does not fit the facts. In the somewhat longer experience of Latin America it is still more evident that the progress is at best of the two steps forward, one step backward kind. At the global level, we have had occasion to touch on the practical implications of attempts at the top to turn back the clock, or at least step on the brake. At the Asian level, any undue euphoria about the revolutionary potential of the churches would be sobered in 1982 by the convulsions at the main point of convergence in Asia of Christian and Marxist social struggle—the Mindanao-Sulu Pastoral Conference.

The ultimate lessons of these convulsions have yet to be discerned. As far as 1982 is concerned, they culminated in a formal act of dissociation by the Mindanao-Sulu bishops from the Board and the Secretariat of that Conference, though without dissolving these bodies, which then proceeded on their own to schedule the 1983 meeting of the Conference, inviting the bishops as guests.

These events assured two things, duly articulated in comment from both sides: that this most participatory and dynamic of Asian Catholic churches was now openly "a divided church"; and that the fifth triennial conference of 1983 would represent "an MSPC radically different from the last four." It is clear that the immediate cause of rupture was the alleged excessive intimacy of the Secretariat with the left, the Marxist third force, and specifically with the commitment to armed revolutionary struggle of the National Democratic Front and such component movements as the Communist Party of the Philippines and Christians for National Liberation. But there was no agreement even among the bishops that options regarding the third force were the ultimate issue. The ultimate issue was more persuasively identified by one of the bishops as "a symbolic shift in the understanding of church" (from "hierarchical church" to "people's church"). There were two questions about this "people's church": did it really represent the people, and did it leave any place for the bishops?[4]

Thus, at a high price in pain and bitterness, the Catholics of Mindanao-Sulu, with some participation from Protestants and Muslims, provided themselves and Christian Asia with an occasion for a first thorough exploration in words and deeds of the implications of Vatican II's Church of the people and the Asian bishops' Church of the poor. From the outset their own best contributions were rich in passion and intelligence on both sides. If in the process they seem even to themselves to be sunk in a mess and a scandal, that is only because they dared to bring into the open confusions and contradictions that could not remain forever buried under pious rhetoric. Whether they are destined to handle their particular crisis well or badly, the Christian world cannot but learn something from their experience.

The Christian world (again more particularly the Catholic world) also stood to learn something from another Asian Christian confrontation of the early 1980s. In Mindanao, as in Central America and in varying degrees in every part of the world, it was seeing how sharp are the birth pangs of a

Church of all the people. In China, to a greater extent than in any other country, it was seeing what a long way it still remained from being a Church of all the peoples.

The issue in China came into sharp focus in 1981 in connection with the Catholic see of Canton. Moves that had at first looked like a shared effort in bridge-building between the see of Rome and the government-recognized Catholic spokespersons in China broke off abruptly with the bridge in ruins and the two shores seemingly farther apart than ever.

The issue was far from being pure and clear. From one point of view, already adverted to in these pages in references to positions taken by Chinese Christian spokespersons, it reflected a bona fide problem for the parent see and for Christians abroad generally, one that was not so different at bottom from that of Mindanao: how to be really in communion with the Christian, with the Catholic people in China; how to know who really speaks for them in a still relatively closed and manipulative political system. From another point of view it reflected a question that would remain even if there were no particular difficulty from the side of the political system: how much more give will there need to be in the worldwide system of Catholicism before it is worthy to aspire to be a Church of all the people and of all the peoples?

By its own previous standards the Vatican could fairly claim to have been exceptionally and thanklessly tactful and sensitive in its latest China moves. By the test of how far it would still have to go before it could make room for the great separate stream of Chinese experience, the Chinese Catholic critics of the Vatican (not all of them inside the People's Republic) could also plausibly argue that the Canton fiasco was not exclusively due to ecclesiastical shortsightedness on one side.[5]

No one could rightfully wish on Mindanao, China, or Rome the fierce internecine quarrels here in question. These quarrels have added new wounds to old scars; there will be that much more healing to be done in the end. Yet the fact remains that the ends they all seek—a Church of all the people and of all the peoples—are not the sorts of ends that are likely to be gained at any lesser price.

Agnostic common sense would forbid any such easy expectations. A Christian set of values would forbid them still more categorically. If the Mindanao turmoil marks even a step on the way to a Church that can find a fairer place for all its members and ministries, that will have been a priceless contribution, not only to the Church but also to its prospects of service to society everywhere. If the rude rebuff received by the Vatican in the Canton affair is better calculated than any easier medicine to bring home to all concerned the full scale of the challenge of third-millennium Catholicity, it will have been medicine worth swallowing for the sake of the Catholic and Christian and human reconciliation the whole world of the third millennium will need.

With these "ifs" we must conclude. Of the three factors we have singled out as significant for the future of Asian Christian social protest—demographic progress toward outgrowing the Asian Christian minority complex; continuation of a critical imbalance in the sharing of the world's and Asia's goods; and continuation in practice as well as theory of the shift of some of the weight of the churches in the scales of society from the side of the haves to that of the have-nots—the first two are better assured in the short term.

As for the third, in the long term, and as far as true believers are concerned, it ought to be the best-assured of all. In the meantime, and given the limits of what can be honestly concluded from mere empirical evidence, it must be recognized as the factor most at the mercy of human freedom and fickleness, and therefore most subject to fits and starts and twists and turns. As to how exactly, especially in the very shortest term, the "shrewd Spirit" referred to by Marx can still be "manifesting himself in all these contradictions," that is a subject on which the pronouncements of real believers in such a Spirit should not be over prompt or over precise.

APPENDIX 1
KEY WORLD EVENTS: 1945–1969

1945	Aug	World War II ends; United Nations Charter signed
1946		War resumed in Asia as Mao in China and Ho in Vietnam bid for power
1945–55		East Europe passes under Communist governments, COMECON, Warsaw Pact
1947–49		West Europe underwritten by Marshall Plan and North Atlantic Treaty
1945–75		Colonial empires replaced by independent nations in Asia and Africa
1948	May	State of Israel proclaimed; at war with Arabs in 1948, 1956, 1967, 1973, 1982
1948	Aug	World Council of Churches inaugurated in Amsterdam; Orthodox join in 1961
1949	Sep	USSR: first Soviet atomic bomb test ends U.S.A.-weapons monopoly
1949	Oct	China: Mao proclaims People's Republic of China; Chiang Kai-shek holds Taiwan
1950–53		Korea: Korean War hardens Cold War lines of division; partition of Korea resumed
1954	Aug	Vietnam: Geneva Conference ends French Vietnam presence; partition and 1956 election plan
1955	Apr	Afro-Asian identity affirmed in Bandung Conference of 28 nations
1956	Feb	USSR: Khrushchev launches de-Stalinization in Soviet 20th Party Conference
1956	Oct	USSR: limit of Soviet liberalization marked in crushing of Hungarian revolt
1958		Launching of Common Market in Europe, of Great Leap Forward in China
1960	Aug	China: Sino-Soviet split revealed in withdrawal of Soviet technicians
1961	May	West: Castro makes Cuba first Marxist state in hemisphere; isolated by U.S.
1962	Oct	Sino-Indian War; Cuban missiles crisis; Vatican II begins RC renewal

1963	Jul	U.S.-U.K.-USSR test ban treaty begins series of super-power détente accords
1964	Aug	Vietnam: Gulf of Tonkin Resolution mandates U.S. combat commitment
1965	Nov	China: Wu Han polemics begin Great Proletarian Cultural Revolution
1968	Aug	Czechoslovakia: Warsaw Pact troops oust Dubcek regime
1968		New social concern affirmed by churches in Beirut, Uppsala, Medellín
1969	Jul	U.S. Vietnam troop withdrawals begin; Apollo 11 lands first people on moon

APPENDIX 2
KEY WORLD AND ASIAN EVENTS:
1970–1982

1970	Jan	Nigeria: Biafra surrender ends costliest African secession effort
	Sep	Chile: Allende election creates second Marxist state in Western hemisphere
	Dec	Last of three Asian visits by Pope Paul (W. Asia 1964, Bombay 1964, E. Asia 1970)
1971	Sep	China: "heir apparent" Lin Piao disappears; later linked with anti-Mao plot
	Oct	China: UN seat switched by vote from Taipei to Peking
	Dec	Bangladesh: new nation emerges from Indo-Pakistan war
1972	Feb	China: Nixon visit launches move towards U.S.-P.R.C. relations
	Apr	UNCTAD III in Santiago: forum for North-South confrontation
	May	SALT I accords limiting strategic arms signed between U.S. and USSR
	Sep	Philippines: Marcos proclaims martial law
	Oct	S. Korea: Park proclaims martial law
1973	Jan	Vietnam ceasefire under Paris accords ends U.S. troop presence
	Jul	Afghanistan: Daud overthrows monarchy and proclaims first Afghan republic
	Sep	Chile: coup replaces Allende with Pinochet; freedoms suspended
	Oct	Thailand: Thanom military regime overthrown; three years of democracy follow
	Oct	Fourth Arab-Israeli war leaves Israel front briefly at widest limit
1974	Jan	Quadrupling of OPEC oil prices takes effect; disarray for rich and poor economies

	Apr	Portugal: coup begins democratization and dismantling of colonies
	Jul	Greece: junta collapses in Greek-Turk confrontation over Cyprus
	Aug	U.S.: Nixon resigns presidency in climax of Watergate disclosures
1975	Apr	Resistance to revolution collapses in Cambodia and South Vietnam (and, by December, in Laos).
	Apr	Lebanon civil war ends Christian-Muslim entente; Syrian intervention in 1976
	Jun	India: Gandhi proclaims emergency; freedoms suspended for 20 months
	Aug	35 nations sign Helsinki accords on European security and cooperation
	Nov	Bangladesh: Ziaur takes power after coups topple Mujib and Ahmed; slain in 1981
	Nov	Spain: death of Franco begins democratization under King Juan Carlos
1976	Jan	China: death of Chou followed by eclipse of Deng; Hua made premier
	May	UNCTAD IV in Nairobi staves off failure of North-South dialogue
	Jul	Vietnam reunification proclaimed; East Timor annexation by Indonesia legalized
	Sep	China: death of Mao foreshadows fall of "gang of four"; Hua made party chairman
	Oct	Thailand: coup restores military rule under Thanin
1977	Mar	India: election ends Emergency, reversing 2/3 majority of Congress Party
	Jul	Pakistan: coup replaces Bhutto with Zia after disputed election
	Jul	Sri Lanka: election replaces Bandaranaike with Jayewardene, setting new rightist trend
	Jul	China: Deng reinstated as premier; takes charge increasingly
	Nov	Mid-East: visit to Jerusalem by Sadat of Egypt begins major new peace initiative
	Dec	Cambodia breaks with Vietnam over border conflict
1978	Apr	Afghanistan: coup replaces Daud with Taraki in pro-Soviet shift
	Jun	Vietnam joins COMECON; last Chinese aid stopped
	Aug	China and Japan sign peace treaty rejecting "hegemony"
	Oct	John Paul II, first Polish pope, elected after deaths of Paul VI and John Paul I

1979	Jan	U.S.-P.R.C. relations; U.S.-R.O.C. official break; Deng Xiaoping on U.S. tour
	Jan	Cambodia invasion by Vietnam replaces Pol Pot by Heng Samrin
	Feb	In CELAM III at Puebla, Latin American bishops reaffirm activist Medellín line
	Feb	Khomeini replaces Shah in Iran and leads way to Islamic republic
	Feb	China invades Vietnam in "defensive counterattack," then withdraws
	Mar	Egyptian-Israeli Camp David treaty signed by Sadat, Begin, Carter
	Jun	UNCTAD V in Manila fails to bring accord on structural change
	Jul	Nicaragua: leftist revolution ends Somoza regime
	Oct	South Korea: Park slain; limited liberalization cut short after new coup in Dec by Chun
	Dec	NATO ministers approve 1983 deployment of new theater nuclear force to reduce "imbalance"
	Dec	Afghanistan: Soviet troops intervene, replacing Amin with Karmal and provoking internal war
1980	Jan	Zimbabwe: after 7 years of guerilla war, election transfers power to black leader Mugabe
	Sep	Poland: Kania replaces Gierek as First Secretary as Solidarity movement grows from Gdansk
	Sep	Turkey: military rule resumed as Evren takes power from Demirel in coup
	Sep	Iraq invades Iran in the name of nationalism and Islamic orthodoxy
	Nov	U.S.: sweeping electoral shift brings right-wing control of Senate under Reagan
1981	Jun	France: electoral revolution brings left control of Assembly under Mitterrand
	Oct	Europe: groundswell of protest against nuclear arms brings 1 million onto streets
	Dec	Poland: under Jaruzelski, martial law imposed, Solidarity leaders arrested
1982	Apr	Argentine-U.K. S. Atlantic war begins over Falklands/Malvinas; U.K. control restored by June
	Jun	In two mid-East wars, Israel invades Lebanon, Iran pushes back Iraq
	Jun	Second of two UN disarmament conferences ends indecisively despite new peak of public concern
	Sep	China: 12th Party Congress brings qualified reinforcement of post-Mao, pro-Deng trend

Oct   Spain: electoral revolution brings Socialists to power
          under González

Nov   USSR: on death of Brezhnev, Andropov becomes Party
          General Secretary

APPENDIX 3
OTHER EVENTS RELEVANT TO ASIAN CHRISTIAN SOCIAL PROTEST: 1965–1982

1965	Aug	Hong Kong: Priests' Institute for Social Action (in Asia) formed
1966	Jul	Geneva: WCC Conference on Church and Society hears "theology of revolution"
1967		Vatican: Justice and Peace Commission formed; *Populorum Progressio* encyclical issued
1968	Feb	S. Korea: first stand for poor by RC Church wins in Kang Hoa YCW case
	Apr	Beirut Ecumenical Conference on Development: first RC-WCC global joint effort
	Jul	Uppsala: WCC 4th Assembly: rich-poor gap called "crucial point of decision"
	Sep	Medellín: CELAM II calls Latin American Church to solidarity with poor
1970	Aug	Christian protest acts by youth leaders in S. Vietnam, by Kim Chi Ha in S. Korea
	Nov	Manila: Asian bishops plan FABC, promise "Church of poor and young"
1971	Jan	Madras: Indian RC students (AICUF) aim for "radically new society"
	Sep	Bangalore: Asian student chaplains opt for more radical political role
	Oct	Rome: Synod of Bishops finds justice work "integral to" evangelization
	Nov	S. Korea: joint pastoral after Wonju affair denounces social injustice
1972	Apr	Chile: first group of Christians for Socialism formed
	Aug	S. Vietnam: Catholics for Peace indict church privilege and silence
	Sep	Philippines: church protest muted as Marcos proclaims martial law

	Oct	S. Korea: church protest muted as Park proclaims martial law
1973	Jan	Bangkok: end of WCC World Conference on Salvation Today
	Jan	S. Vietnam: chaplains sentenced for use of 1971 Synod Justice statement
	May	S. Korea: Theological Declaration of Korean Christians against Park regime
	Jun	Singapore: Christian Conference of Asia 5th Assembly
	Aug	Bangalore: Asian Seminar on Religion and Development (successor meeting in Baguio in 1975)
1974	Jan	Jogjakarta: 41 priests protest public corruption and repression
	Apr	Taipei: 1st FABC Assembly finds search for justice "integral to" Gospel
	May	Colombo: Towards World Community meeting of five world faiths
	Jun	Philippines: WCC leaders and a CCA leader arrested
	Jun	S. Vietnam: 301 priests denounce corruption; campaign against abuses grows
	Jul	S. Korea: between arrests, Bishop Tji makes Declaration of Conscience
	Oct	Rome: Synod of Bishops on evangelization
1975	Apr	S. Korea: NCC leaders arrested for embezzlement; convicted in Sep;
		Vietnam: Hue and Saigon archbishops call Catholics to cooperate with new regime
	Jun	India: church protest muted as Gandhi proclaims Emergency
	Dec	Nairobi: WCC 5th Assembly calls for "evangelism *and* social action"
1976	Mar	Singapore: 15 priests denounce government sterilization policy
	May	Hong Kong: Asian joint meeting of Christian students (WSCF and IMCS)
	Aug	Indonesia: Sawito affair; manifesto of Catholic students
	Aug	S. Korea: top Christian leaders again among dissidents sentenced
	Oct	Philippines: referendum-plebiscite brings out church divisions
	Dec	Philippines: 4 church media suppressed; 70 church personnel arrested
1977	Jan	Philippines: bishops unite in pastoral critical of government

	Feb	FABC-OHD Asian seminar reviews bishops' social program (BISAs 1-3)
	Apr	Vietnam: Hue archbishop protests repression of Buddhists and Catholics
	Jun	CCA 6th Assembly calls for "continued priority on human rights"
	Aug	Taiwan: Presbyterian Declaration on Human Rights
1978	Jan	Indonesia: student leaders arrested in new protest and reaction
	Apr	S. Korea: bishops unite in support of Dong-Il workers, YCW, URM
	Jun	Hong Kong: confrontation in RC Church over Golden Jubilee School case
	Nov	Calcutta: FABC 2nd Assembly reaffirms 1974 Assembly, but focuses on prayer
1979	Jan	Sri Lanka: Third World Theologians, in 1st Asian meeting, for a "liberating" Asian theology
	Feb	Puebla: John Paul II and CELAM III give mixed signals on social action
	May	Baguio: BISA V marks East-West rift among Asian bishops on social action
	Nov	S. Korea: post-Park regime renews crackdown on Christian activists
	Dec	Taiwan: Human Rights Day events lead to 1980 jailing of Presbyterian general secretary Kao
1980	Mar	San Salvador: Archbishop Romero slain at Mass, catalyzing Christian protest in w. hemisphere
	May	S. Korea: Christian and other protest muffled after bloody crushing of Kwangju uprising
	Jun	Spectrum of Christian social attitudes reflected in Asia in three world mission congresses 1979–80
1981	Feb	Philippines: mixed signals again from John Paul II on social action during Asian visit
	May	Bangalore: CCA 7th Assembly: Living in Christ with People; bishop proposes local socialism
	Jun	China: furor over pope's naming of Canton archbishop dramatizes issue of local church autonomy
	Sep	John Paul II, in encyclical *Laborem Exercens*, reaffirms priority of labor over capital
	Oct	John Paul II intervenes in Jesuit Order to assert authority and brake radicalism
1982	Mar	Philippines: Mindanao-Sulu bishops "dissociate" from their Pastoral Conference Secretariat
	Mar	S. Korea: Pusan arson sequel reopens Church-State confrontation; priest jailed

Jul   Philippines: Cardinal Sin seen as calling for Marcos
            resignation
Aug   S. Korea: Justice and Peace Commission joins call for
            Chun resignation
Sep   Philippines: new wave of pressures on Church, leading
            to united episcopal protest Feb. 1983
Nov   Sri Lanka: arrests of Jaffna clergy in Tamil-Sinhala
            conflict
Nov   West: national defence policies challenged in draft state-
            ments prepared for U.S. Catholics and Church of
            England.

APPENDIX 4
ASIAN NATIONAL AND
NATIONAL CHRISTIAN
POPULATIONS
CIRCA 1980

	Pop.: (◊◊◊)	Christns.: (♦♦♦)	Millions	10	20	30	40	50
China	890	1.8						
India	694	27.1						
Indonesia	155	17.5						
Japan	118	3.5						
Bangladesh	85	0.4						
Pakistan	83	1.5						
Soviet Asia	59	14.4						
Philippines	52	49.2						
Vietnam	49	3.6						

Country			
Thailand	49	.5	◆◇◇
Turkey	45	.2	◇◇◇
Iran	40	.3	◇◇
South Korea	37	11.4	◆◆◆◆◆◆◆◆◆◆◆◇◇◇◇◇◇◇◇◇◇◇◇◇◇◇◇◇◇◇◇◇◇◇◇◇◇
Burma	35	2.0	◆◆◇◇◇◇◇◇◇◇◇◇◇◇◇◇◇◇◇◇◇◇◇◇◇◇◇◇◇◇◇◇◇◇◇
Afghanistan	22	0.0	◇◇◇◇◇◇◇◇◇◇◇◇◇◇◇◇◇◇◇◇◇◇
North Korea	18	0.2	◇◇◇◇◇◇◇◇◇◇◇◇◇◇◇◇◇◇
Taiwan	17	1.3	◆◇◇◇◇◇◇◇◇◇◇◇◇◇◇◇◇
Sri Lanka	15	1.3	◆◇◇◇◇◇◇◇◇◇◇◇◇◇◇
Malaysia	14	0.9	◆◇◇◇◇◇◇◇◇◇◇◇◇◇
Nepal	14	0.0	◇◇◇◇◇◇◇◇◇◇◇◇◇◇
Iraq	13	0.5	◆◇◇◇◇◇◇◇◇◇◇◇◇
Saudi Arabia	11	0.1	◇◇◇◇◇◇◇◇◇◇◇
Syria	9	0.8	◆◇◇◇◇◇◇◇◇
Kampuchea	9	0.1	◇◇◇◇◇◇◇◇◇
Yemen Arab R.	8	0.0	◇◇◇◇◇◇◇◇
Hong Kong & Macao	5	0.8	◆◇◇◇◇
Laos	4	0.1	◇◇◇◇
Lebanon	3	2.0	◆◆◇
Israel	3	0.1	◇◇◇
Gulf States	2	0.1	◇◇
Jordan	2	0.1	◇◇
Singapore	2	0.2	◇◇
Yemen P.R.	2	0.0	◇◇
Mongolian P.R.	2	0.0	◇◇
Bhutan	1	0.0	◇

APPENDIX 5
DISTRIBUTION OF ROMAN CATHOLICS AND OTHER CHRISTIANS CIRCA 1980

(♦ = 1 million R.C.; ◊ = 1 million O.C.)

	R.C.	O.C.	Millions	10	20	30	40
Asia Total	69.5	72.9	♦♦♦				
			♦♦♦♦♦♦♦♦♦♦♦♦♦♦♦♦♦♦♦♦♦♦♦♦♦♦♦♦◊◊◊◊◊◊◊◊◊◊				
			◊◊◊◊◊◊◊◊◊◊◊◊◊◊◊◊◊◊◊◊◊◊◊◊◊◊◊◊◊◊◊◊◊◊◊				
			◊◊◊◊◊◊◊◊◊◊◊◊◊◊◊◊◊◊◊◊◊◊◊◊◊				
Philippines	41.6	7.6	♦♦♦				
			♦♦◊◊◊◊◊◊◊				
India	11.8	15.3	♦♦♦♦♦♦♦♦♦♦♦♦◊◊◊◊◊◊◊◊◊◊◊◊◊◊◊				
Indonesia	4.3	13.1	♦♦♦♦◊◊◊◊◊◊◊◊◊◊◊◊◊				
Soviet Asia	0.0	14.4	◊◊◊◊◊◊◊◊◊◊◊◊◊◊				
South Korea	1.1	10.3	♦◊◊◊◊◊◊◊◊◊◊				
Vietnam	3.4	0.2	♦♦♦◊				
Japan	0.4	3.1	◊◊◊◊				
Lebanon	1.5	0.5	♦◊				
Burma	0.4	1.6	◊◊				
China	1.1	0.7	♦◊				
Pakistan	0.5	1.0	♦◊				
Sri Lanka	1.1	0.2	♦				
Taiwan	0.4	0.9	◊				
Malaysia	0.5	0.4					
Syria	0.2	0.6					
Hong Kong & Macao	0.3	0.5					
Iraq	0.3	0.2					
Thailand	0.2	0.3					
Bangladesh	0.2	0.2					
Iran	0.0	0.3					

Note 1: Figures rounded to nearest 100,000

Note 2: R.C. figures represent "affiliated" in *WCE*

Singapore	0.1	0.1
North Korea	0.0	0.2
Turkey	0.0	0.2
Jordan	0.0	0.1
Saudi Arabia	0.0	0.1
Gulf States	0.0	0.1
Israel	0.0	0.1
Laos	0.0	0.1

APPENDIX 6
RELATIVE
INSTITUTIONALIZATION
OF CATHOLICISM IN
ASIAN NATIONS

13 Asian Territories in Order of Catholic Population (♦ = .5 million)

1. Philippines ♦♦
♦♦♦♦♦♦♦♦♦♦♦♦♦♦♦♦♦♦♦♦♦♦♦♦♦♦♦♦♦♦♦

2. India ♦♦♦♦♦♦♦♦♦♦♦♦♦♦♦♦♦♦♦♦♦

3. Indonesia ♦♦♦♦♦♦♦♦

4. China (1949) ♦♦♦♦♦♦

5. Vietnam ♦♦♦♦♦♦

6. Korea ♦♦

7. Sri Lanka ♦♦

8. Pakistan ♦

9. Japan ♦

10. Burma ♦

11. Malaysia ♦

12. Taiwan ♦

13. Hong Kong ♦

13 Asian Territories in Order of Catholic Pastoral Personnel (♦ = 1,000)

1. India ♦♦
♦♦♦♦♦♦

2. Philippines ♦♦♦♦♦♦♦♦♦♦♦♦♦♦♦♦

3. Japan ♦♦♦♦♦♦♦♦♦

180

4. Indonesia   ◆◆◆◆◆◆◆

5. South Korea ◆◆◆◆◆

6. Sri Lanka   ◆◆◆

7. Taiwan   ◆◆

8. Thailand   ◆◆

9. Hong Kong ◆

10. Malaysia   ◆

11. Burma   ◆

12. Pakistan   ◆

13. Bangladesh ◆

14 Asian Territories in Order of No. of Pastoral Personnel per 1,000 Catholics (◆◆ = 1)

1. Japan   ◆◆

2. Thailand   ◆◆◆◆◆◆◆◆◆◆◆◆◆◆◆◆◆◆

3. India   ◆◆◆◆◆◆◆◆◆◆◆

4. Taiwan   ◆◆◆◆◆◆◆◆◆◆◆

5. South Korea ◆◆◆◆◆◆◆◆

6. Hong Kong ◆◆◆◆◆◆◆◆

7. Singapore   ◆◆◆◆◆◆◆◆

8. Bangladesh ◆◆◆◆◆◆

9. Sri Lanka   ◆◆◆◆◆◆

10. Burma   ◆◆◆◆◆

11. Malaysia   ◆◆◆◆◆

12. Pakistan   ◆◆◆◆

13. Indonesia   ◆◆◆

14. Philippines ◆

SOURCES FOR APPENDIXES 4, 5, 6. For comparability of data all figures except those for Appendix 7 have been cited from the *World Christian Encyclopedia*, though its data will undoubtedly need revision eventually in one particular or another. It will take at least another couple of decades to make a balanced overall assessment of this prodigious compilation, but as a whole it is already set to be a benchmark of global Christian statistics for the rest of this century. Some of the more important glosses that need to be made right away are the following:

1. Preliminary reports on the July 1982 census of China announced a figure of 1,008 million for the total PRC population. This would mean that the *WCE* figure for mid-1980 is too low by about 120 million. This would make a significant difference in percentages and other comparisons at the Asian level.

2. The *WCE* figure for Christians in China in 1980 (1.8 million) might have seemed optimistic in that year, but would be considered too low by 1982. By then, even usually sober sources spoke in terms of up to 10 million Christians in the People's Republic, and one formidably equipped evangelical monitoring center claimed up to 50 million. Any revision on that scale would of course transform the related Asian figures for Christian statistics even more than the general Asian population picture would be transformed by the (still provisional) Chinese census figures.

3. Final results of the February 1981 census of India reported a population of 685 million. This implies a *WCE* overcount for mid-1980 of at least 25 million.

4. The *WCE* figure for Christians in India (27 million) is higher by a good 10 million, and for Christians in S. Korea (11 million) is higher by a good 5 million, than the figures conventionally received. The *WCE* figure for the total Christian population of Asia in the old geographical sense (in UN terms, East Asia plus South Asia plus Soviet Asia) is higher by 25 million than the figure previously arrived at as the best supported for the purposes of this study. Some of the reasons for this upward revision are elucidated in the *WCE* section on methodology.

5. In the case of Soviet Asia, (*a*) general population figures have been taken from early 1980s editions of *Asia Yearbook* of *FEER*, (*b*) figures for Christians are compiled from *WCE* breakdowns for Asian jurisdiction of the Orthodox Church, with some extrapolations for other denominations.

6. In text and appendixes, percentage calculations are made on the basis of WCE figures for 1980: 4,374 million for the world population, 2,750 million (a compiled figure) for the Asian population, 1,433 million for Christians in the world, and 142 million for Christians in Asia.

7. For Appendix 6 the *WCE* figures would not claim to be as up-to-date or as precisely related to a single year as those available from the early 1980s editions of *Annuario Pontificio* (Vatican), *l'Asie en chiffres* (Paris), or the *Catholic Almanac* (Huntington, Indiana).

8. See also, in list of sources below, *Bilan du Monde*, Hoke, Secretaria Status, *World Christianity*.

APPENDIX 7
THE NOTION OF
TRANSNATIONAL RELATIONS

The "transnational dimension" has been a recurring theme in these pages. In academic writing on international relations this phenomenon is generally considered to have been neglected in the past, and to have been coming into its own only during the 1970s, the same decade that saw the rise of Asian Christian social protest.

The mental block that excluded transnational thinking was the literal understanding of international relations as meaning essentially relations between nation states. Since their rise around the fifteenth century, and especially since their consolidation around the eighteenth, nation states have dominated the field of relations within the human community to the point of making the latter look, in the analogy of Wolfers, like a billiard table on which states are the billiard balls. It has taken a vast twentieth-century proliferation of nongovernmental movements and organizations crossing state boundaries to make the billiard table image fade in favor of a cobweb image more applicable to the world of today, and for that matter to world history as a whole.

Theory is still slow to catch up with this reality. Superpower strategic thinking, NATO-style analyses of power relations, help to keep the state-centric stereotypes alive. Even in the study of international relations as an academic discipline the stereotypes die hard. As recently as 1964, a survey of the role of theory in international relations distinguished phases and emphases—the diplomatic history phase, the current events emphasis, the phase of emphasis on law and organization, and the then most recent trend of realism in regard to power politics—without at all adverting to any need for a shift of emphasis from international to transnational thinking. Even as recently as 1970, Keohane and Nye could still note that "a state-centric view of world affairs prevails."[1] Though their assault on this way of thinking was described in 1973 as "path-breaking," a further assault was found needed by Mansbach and others in 1976.[2]

The debate is not over, but it has not left the field unchanged. In 1968 it was already observed in *The International Encyclopedia of the Social Sciences* that "the tendency to reify nations is diminishing."[3] In 1973 Huntingdon claimed that "today man's capacities are outrunning the nation-state system."[4] In 1976 Mansbach et al. spoke of "the growing irrelevance of the state-centric model."[5] In 1977 Berman and Johnson described "international society" as becoming "increasingly a transnational society."[6]

We have been examining the rise of Asian Christian social protest in the context of this rise of "transnational society." We have seen something of how it contributes to diminishing the tendency to "reify nations." We have had a chance to observe the extent to which it shows, in one geographic area of one transnational enterprise, that "man's capacity for organization is outrunning the nation-state system."

Huntingdon, the author of the latter contention, explicitly adverts to the Marxian analogy—"as capitalist forces outran feudal relations." In doing so he is touching on another limitation needing to be transcended in thinking about international relations. For all the cross-fertilization that has taken place in that thinking, it might as well be described as two monologues, one in the East and one in the West. Hence the importance of "including Marx as a 'silent partner' . . . in the unspoken East-West dialogue," all the while bearing in mind that "it is with the non-silent partners that the last word rests."[7]

At bottom, anything answering the description of a "transnational paradigm" is no more than the recognition that governments and government agencies, while remaining the most formidable figures on the international stage, by no means have that stage to themselves. The mere advertence to that fact is a "paradigm shift" of some importance by itself. Consciously or unconsciously, we are all dependent on paradigms, and it is precisely those "practical men, who believe themselves to be quite exempt from any intellectual influences," that are usually "unconscious captives of paradigms created by 'some academic scribbler of a few years back.' "[8]

In the case of the "path-breaking" paradigm of Keohane and Nye, it is claimed that "the state-centric paradigm covers only four of the thirty-six possible types of politically important interactions across state boundaries that are identified by the world politics paradigm."[9] What this is in effect saying is that the number of "possible types of politically important interactions across state boundaries" equals the square of the number of significant actors that can be distinguished by the test of relative freedom from state control. Since every actor can potentially impinge on every other, this makes for a much more "complex conglomerate model" than the state-centric one.

In this unlimited multiplicity of interstate and transnational relations, those relations for which the churches are responsible are actually among the oldest. Churches have always been transnational actors, precisely in the measure that they have remained true to their universalist aspirations, refusing to be reduced to subunits of states. As far as that goes, what has been happening in Asian churches has ample precedent in Christian history, and there is a novelty only in the degree to which it has been happening. The more important novelty lies in the extent to which Christian transnationalism is now resisting its cooption by the prevailing power structure in transnational society.

---

1. Harrison, pp. 3ff.
2. Keohane and Nye, p. 9.
3. IESS, vol. 8 (1968), p. 66.
4. Huntingdon, p. 368.
5. Mansbach, chapter 2.
6. Berman and Johnson, p. 263.
7. Kubalkova and Cruikshank, pp. xii, xv, xvi.
8. Keohane and Nye, pp. 379ff.
9. Ibid., pp. 381ff.

NOTES

Introduction: The Problem

1. From the "Message" of the First Asian Bishops' Conference, held in Manila in November 1970. Text in *Teaching All Nations*, 1971, no. 1:21.

2. From the report from the section "Justice and Service" in the Sixth Assembly of the CCA (Penang, 1977). Text in *CCA News* (1977): 108.

3. From the "Final Statement of the First Asian Theologians' Conference" sponsored by the EATWOT (Wennappuwa, 1979). Text in Virginia Fabella, ed. *Asia's Struggle for Full Humanity*, p. 158, and *Document Reprint Service*, 1979, no. 4:8.

4. See Appendix 7 on the notion *transnational*.

Chapter 1: The Global Background

1. The first recorded slave war took place in Sicily in 138–32 B.C. Even here the information is what one would expect from victors recalling the vanquished.

2. The variety of "historical routes from the pre-industrial to the modern world" is put in unusually broad perspective by Barrington Moore, *Social Origins of Dictatorship and Democracy*.

3. Jean-Jacques Rousseau, *Discours sur l'origine et les fondements de l'inégalité parmi les hommes*, p. 66.

4. Karl Marx and Friedrich Engels, *Manifesto of the Communist Party*, pp. 79, 120f.

5. On the power of the people, notice the Chinese Constitution of 1982 ("All power belongs to the people"); the Indian Constitution of 1950 ("The people of India solemnly resolve . . ."); the Soviet Constitution of 1977 ("All power is vested in the people"); and the American Constitution of 1787 ("We the people of the United States . . ."). These purport to speak for the four largest national populations, including about half the world's people. Such is the theory. For one view of the reality see Peter Berger, *Pyramids of Sacrifice*.

6. Almost half the world's population, including China, India–Pakistan, and Indonesia, achieved or recovered full political self-determination in the decade 1946–55 alone.

7. See text, p. 124, for the best-accepted estimate of the inequality in the 1970s.

8. The denunciation was explicit and repeated in Robert McNamara's presidency of the World Bank during the 1970s. During the Clausen presidency (from 1980) a change of tone was widely noticed, but see the *International Herald Tribune*, April 17–18, 1982, for renewed emphasis on the Bank's critical role vis-à-vis its dominant member, the United States.

9. *The Economist,* 19 August 1978, pp. 64–66.

10. The financial elite of the North found their most-noticed forum of the 1970s in the Trilateral Commission, with members from the United States, Western Europe, and Japan. The Commission showed itself on the one hand to be no friend of unrestricted democracy, and on the other hand to be not entirely comfortable as the bedfellow of the cruder military regimes.

11. See, for example, two books originally published in German in the same year (1968): Joachim Kahl, *The Misery of Christianity,* and Viteslav Gardavsky, *God Is Not Yet Dead.*

12. In fact, despite Gal. 3:28 and Col. 3:11, "Christian" justifications of slavery still appeared as late as the nineteenth century.

13. For the nuances implied in that "more or less," see Robert M. Grant, *Early Christianity and Society.*

14. For the "original fervor," see Acts 2:44–46, 4:32–37. For the texts of Gratian, and for the Church as a landlord, see R. H. Tawney, *Religion and the Rise of Capitalism,* pp. 45, 69ff.

15. Where Gratian sees no place for profits from trading, and where Saint Thomas sees a place only for the wages of the trader's labor, Saint Antonino finds room for other sources of value besides labor and materials (Tawney, pp. 47, 48, 53).

16. It was not altogether facetious on Tawney's part to write (p. 48): "The true descendant of the doctrines of Aquinas is the labor theory of value. The last of the Schoolmen was Karl Marx."

17. To see how far this "rereading" can go, consult José Porfirio Miranda, *Marx and the Bible* and *Marx against the Marxists.*

18. Max Weber, *The Protestant Ethic and the Spirit of Capitalism,* p. 183.

19. For documentation on Medellín and after, see IDOC International, *The Church at the Crossroads.*

20. Walter M. Abbott, ed., *The Documents of Vatican II,* pp. 199f.

21. Joseph Gremillion, ed., *The Gospel of Peace and Justice,* p. 514.

22. "Although it is not yet widely recognized, the military establishments and the Catholic Church are also among today's forces for social and political change in the other American republics. This is a new role for them. For since the arrival of the *conquistadores* more than 400 years ago, the history of the military and the Catholic Church, working hand in hand with the landowners to provide 'stability,' has been a legend in the Americas" (*Keesing's Contemporary Archives* [1969]: 23714). Rockefeller's bracketing of the military with the Church as a force for social change was presumably influenced by the case of the left-wing military regime and program that took over Peru in 1968. A decade later it could safely be said that these words of 1969 had proved more broadly prophetic about the Church than about the military. The full text of *The Rockefeller Report on the Americas* with an introduction by Tad Szulc of the *New York Times* was published by Quadrangle Books (Chicago, 1969).

23. Tawney, p. 280.

Chapter 2: The Asian Background

1. Transcending Eurocentricity is still unfinished business for historians, with isolated exceptions like Arnold Toynbee, and for historical atlases, with no real exception before *The Times Atlas of World History.*

2. It has been noted in connection with the original limits-to-growth thesis (see Donella Meadows, et al., *The Limits to Growth*) that "geographic limitations have not played an important role in any of the collapse models described" (H.S.D. Cole, et al., *Thinking about the Future,* p. 25). It is also argued (pp. 119–22) that a "dual-world model" (i.e., one that takes account of the developed/underdeveloped division) would give very different results at least in the medium term. In short, even if some basic validity is attributed to the limits thesis, Asia can be seen as the last continent for which it is relevant. For a chart of energy consumption in 35 countries, see H.S.D. Cole, et al., *Thinking about the Future,* p. 93.

3. Among the continents, only Europe has a larger proportion of arable land than Asia, but only Asia-outside-the-Soviet Union has less than half its land under cultivation, pasture, and forest combined (*Oxford Economic Atlas of the World,* p. 6).

4. Gunnar Myrdal adverts to the parallel at the outset of *Asian Drama* (vol. 1, p. x), as well as in its subtitle, *An Inquiry into the Poverty of Nations.* Note that the "Asian drama" of which he speaks is more precisely a drama of South and Southeast Asia.

5. For whatever can be said in favor of the thesis that the rich are still the best hope of the poor, *The Economist* may be as good a continuing source as can be found.

6. On the current economic reality of Asia, the range of difference in interpretation and emphasis even among specialists was reflected in editions of the 1970s in the leading yearbooks for Asia, *The Far Eastern Economic Review Yearbook* and Europa's *The Far East and Australasia.*

7. Note the titles of two basic books, each concerned with one of the main periods in question: Laurence E. Browne, *The Eclipse of Christianity in Asia* and K. M. Panikkar, *Asia and Western Dominance.*

8. See note on sources for Appendixes 4, 5, 6.

Chapter 3: The Colonial Antecedents

1. For detailed estimates of the Christian percentage of Asian ethnic groups, see Donald Hoke, ed., *The Church in Asia,* pp. 693–97, and David B. Barrett, ed., *World Christian Encyclopedia,* p. 10. Vietnam is an exception in that Catholics there belong to the majority ethnic group rather than to the minorities.

2. The rural percentage of Christians emerges as less than 30 percent of the population in the scattered areas where large-scale statistics exist on this point. See William Biernatzki, et al., *Korean Catholicism in the 1970s,* p. 174, for Catholics in Korea; Francis Xavier Bell, *The Catholic Church in Thailand,* vol. 7, p. 4, for Catholics in Thailand; François Houtart, *Religion and Ideology in Sri Lanka,* p. 369, for Christians in Sri Lanka. For the larger picture see Barrett.

3. Such at least is the thesis of Palmer. See especially Spencer Palmer, *Korea and Christianity,* p. 110, note 11, for religious affiliation of Korean political leaders during 1952–62: Protestant 32.5 percent, Confucian 17.5 percent, Buddhist 13.3 percent, Catholic 8.5 percent.

4. CELAM (Consejo Episcopal Latinoamericano) was founded in Rio de Janeiro in 1955.

5. Karl Marx, *Kritik des Hegelschen Staatsrechts,* cited in T. B. Bottomore and M. Rubel, eds., *Karl Marx,* pp. 41f.

6. See François Houtart, *Religion et modes de production précapitalistes.*

7. Ibid., p. 135 and chapter 7.

8. See Jerrold Schecter, *The New Face of Buddha.*

9. See Holmes Welch, *The Buddhist Revival in China* and *Buddhism under Mao.*

10. Maxime Rodinson, *Islam and Capitalism,* p. 218.

11. Ibid., p. 157.

12. Cited in Kosuke Koyama, *Waterbuffalo Theology,* p. 47.

13. Parig Digan, "Friars on Trial," pp. 47, 48, 32, citing Emma Helen Blair and James A. Robertson, eds., *The Philippine Islands, 1493-1898,* vol. 52, pp. 259-61, 236-39.

14. See Ivan Illich, *Deschooling Society* and *Limits to Medicine.*

15. David Moberg, *The Great Reversal,* esp. p. 30.

16. Spencer Palmer, *Korea and Christianity,* esp. p. 95.

17. Robert J. Miller, ed., *Religious Ferment in Asia,* pp. 22-36.

18. Donald W. Treadgold, *The West in Russia and China,* vol. 2, chapter 2.

19. Ibid., chapter 3.

20. I. Scheiner, *Christian Converts and Social Protest in Meiji Japan,* p. 8; Parig Digan, "Christian Socialism in Japan," p. 445.

21. G. O. Totten, *The Social Democratic Movement in Prewar Japan,* p. 120.

Chapter 4: The Post-Colonial Setting

1. *Informations catholiques internationales,* 1 Oct. 1962; *Bilan du Monde* 1:31.

2. Floyd Anderson, ed., *Council Daybook,* vol. 1, p. 24.

3. For most countries (France would be an exception) the theme "church and society" found an important place in religious information only after the opening of Vatican II.

4. Harry Haas, *Informations catholiques internationales,* 15 July 1961; reflections of a chaplain to Asian youth.

5. D. S. Amalorpavadass, *Informations catholiques internationales,* 1 Dec. 1964, citing an Indian Protestant bishop.

6. Joseph Vadakkan, *A Priest's Encounter with Revolution,* p. 89; *Informations catholiques internationales,* 15 Nov. 1961, Aug. 1965.

7. This formulation appears in a SELA information leaflet.

8. Banished from the Philippines for his social involvement in the 1940s, Hogan became in 1961 the first executive secretary of SELA. Silenced by his bishop in 1965, Vadakkan was unilaterally restored to good standing in 1977.

9. PISA is given 2 column inches in *Informations catholiques internationales,* 15 Sept. 1965.

10. The author was one of this first set.

11. Events in outline in *Informations catholiques internationales*: 15 Sep. 1965; 15 Feb., 1 Mar., 1 Apr., 15 Apr., 1 May, 15 May 1968; Aug., 1 Nov. 1969; 1 Apr., 1 Sep., 1 Nov., 1 Dec., 15 Dec. 1970. Text of message and resolutions of Asian bishops in *Teaching All Nations,* 1971, no. 1:15-31.

12. *FABC Papers* 13:24, note 10.

13. Joseph Gremillion, *The Gospel of Peace and Justice,* p. 597.

14. Federation of Asian Bishops' Conferences, *His Gospel to Our Peoples,* vol. 3, pp. 160-66. The speech is given in Latin and English, the latter being notably weaker. We have followed the original Latin.

15. *Informations catholiques internationales* (Nov. 1977):49.

16. *Document Reprint Service* (Aug. 1980):11.

17. Kim to author, Dec. 1979, personal testimony.

18. Federation of Asian Bishops' Conferences, *Evangelization in Modern Day Asia,* p. 35; *His Gospel,* vol. 2, p. 341; *FABC Papers* 13:25.

19. Federation of Asian Bishops' Conferences, *Evangelization,* p. 24; *His Gospel,* vol. 2, p. 334.

20. *FABC Papers* 13:18.

21. Against the background of such criticism, the final statement of 1978 is at pains to stress the continuity of the topics of 1970, 1974, and 1978. Ibid., p. 13.

22. W. Roetenberg, "The Asian Bishops' Office for Human Development," *Sunday Examiner,* 3 March 1972; "The Challenge of the Office for Human Development," *Impact,* Oct. and Nov. 1972. The quote is from p. 352 in the October issue.

23. Parig Digan, "Asia Journey," 1980, p. 11.

24. *Info on Human Development,* Aug. 1976.

25. Ibid., Jan. 1977, March 1977.

26. Ibid., June 1979.

27. Catholic Bishops' Conference of India, *Report of the General Meeting,* pp. 30, 31.

28. Digan, "Asia Journey," 1980, p. 11.

29. *Christian Conference of Asia: Sixth Assembly,* p. 39.

30. Ibid., pp. 70, 68. A resolution to raise 25 percent of the administrative budget "from the region" (p. 11) would require "at least double" its "present contribution" (p. 68). In fact, according to the minutes of the 1981 Assembly, "churches in Asia were only contributing 8.24 percent of the administrative budget of the CCA" (*CCA: Seventh Assembly,* p. 7).

31. T. K. Thomas, ed., *Testimony amid Asian Suffering,* pp. 41f.

32. *CCA News,* 15 Aug. 1974.

33. Ibid. (Jan. 1980): 10; (July 1980): 3, 8.

34. *Keesing's Contemporary Archives* (1968): 23012.

35. *Informations catholiques internationales* (1 Jan. 1976): 6; *CCA News,* Dec. 1975.

36. *CCA News,* 15 Jan. 1973.

37. Ibid., 15 June 1973.

38. Ibid., 15 Oct. 1974.

39. Ibid. (Dec. 1975): 2.

40. Ibid., p. 9.

41. Ibid., p. 3.

42. Federation of Asian Bishops' Conferences, *His Gospel,* vol. 2, p. 269.

43. *CCA News,* Feb. 1976, editorial.

44. Ibid., Jan. 1976, editorial.

45. See Yap Kim Hao, ed., *Asian Theological Reflections on Suffering and Hope.*

46. *Christian Conference of Asia: Sixth Assembly,* p. 37.

47. Ibid., pp. 29, 31, 39, 29.

48. Ibid., pp. 17, 9, 11, 116, 108.

49. Ibid., p. 116. More on this later.

50. *CCA News* (Nov. 1977): 1.

Chapter 5: The Transnational Avant-Garde

1. Gunnar Myrdal, *Asian Drama,* vol. 2, p. 796.

2. Ibid., p. 798.

3. Cited by Ho Kwon Ping, "Bad News for Asia's Poor," *Far Eastern Economic Review,* 15 Sep. 1978. Reprinted in *Info on Human Development,* Oct. 1978.

4. *Christian Conference of Asia: Sixth Assembly,* pp. 83, 79.

5. See Y. Kim, "Christian Koinonia in the Struggle and Aspirations of the People of Korea," in Yap Kim Hao, ed., *Asian Theological Reflections,* pp. 37–48, esp. pp. 39 and 46. See also John C. England, ed., *Living Theology in Asia,* pp. 25–31.

6. Parig Digan, "Asia Journey," 1979, p. 9.

7. See, for example, M. M. Thomas, *Revolution in India and Christian Humanism,* esp. p. 12.

8. Digan, "Asia Journey," 1980, p. 25; Mil Roekaerts, *Christians and the Emergency in India,* p. 30.

9. Yap, p. 77; Saral K. Chatterji, ed., *The Meaning of the Indian Experience,* pp. 79f.

10. Letter from the General Secretary of the NCCI to the CCA and the WCC, in M. M. Thomas, ed., *Christians and the Emergency,* pp. 39–40.

11. See Chapter 7, note 30.

12. WSCF-IMCS, *The Struggle for Self-Reliance in Asia Today,* p. 20.

13. Ibid., p. 65.

14. Ibid., p. 4.

15. Ibid., pp. 21, 24, 100, 122, 123, 6.

16. On communism see positions taken by BISA IV (*Info on Human Development* [Mar. 1978]: 5), and by the CCA (*CCA: Sixth Assembly,* p. 96).

17. WSCF-IMCS, pp. 20ff.; Digan, "Asia Journey," 1979, p. 13.

18. Parig Digan, *Indonesia,* pp. 18–19.

19. WSCF-IMCS, p. 86.

20. Digan, "Asia Journey," 1979, p. 14; "Asia Journey," 1980, p. 4.

21. Digan, "Asia Journey," 1980, pp. 5, 14, 24.

22. *Info on Human Development* (Nov. 1980): 10.

23. Ibid., 1 Jan. 1975, 1 Aug. 1975; ACFOD *Constitution,* p. 1.

24. *Document Reprint Service* 79/04: 3, 6, 7, 8; Virginia Fabella, ed., *Asia's Struggle for a Full Humanity.*

25. *Info on Human Development (IHD)* (Jan. 1980): 7–8.

26. *Informations catholiques internationales* (Apr. 1980): 36–38. For New Delhi sequel see *ICI* (Oct. 1981): 21–23.

27. Digan, "Asia Journey," 1980, pp. 5–6. The ideas were expressed to the author by de la Torre in an interview in prison in 1980. The formulation is the author's own.

28. Parig Digan and Jonas Johnson, eds., *Christianity and the New China,* vol. 2, pp. 94–101; Edicio de la Torre, ed., *Pintíg; IHD* (June 1980): 20–22, and supplement (*OHD Papers* 5).

29. *IHD* (Jan. 1981): 13.

30. John C. England, "Kim Chi Ha and the Poetry of Christian Dissent," p. 137.

31. Digan, "Asia Journey," 1980, pp. 10f.

Chapter 6: The Underlying Local Contexts

1. *LWF-IL*, Mar. 1981, no. 32:4.
2. Parig Digan, *The Christian China-watchers,* pp. 47–49.
3. Digan, "Christian Socialism in Japan," p. 452.
4. Digan, "Asia Journey," 1980, p. 14.
5. Ibid., p. 14f.
6. That is, if one accepts official figures and those current among Christian Filipinos. Moro spokespersons, however, claim a Muslim population of 5.5 million in the southern Philippine islands, which would make them over 10 percent of the population of the archipelago and a majority in what they regard as their national Bangsa Moro territory. See Permanent Peoples' Tribunal, *Philippines: Repression and Resistance,* p. 271.
7. In Sri Lanka an insurrection of radical youth was suppressed in 1971, but parliamentary radicalism was not silenced. Among Christians in Sri Lanka, an Anglican bishop and a Catholic bishop have been among Asia's few self-proclaimed socialist church leaders. The country has provided more than its Asian share of radical Christian intellectuals. Thailand, for its part, provided the OHD with its second head, Bishop Bunleuen, and with a notable national social action office, the Catholic Council of Thailand for Development. Both have had to bear the lash of anticommunism; and this unseated a secretary of the Church of Christ in Thailand, who had also headed a Coordinating Group for Religion in Society. In Singapore there has been only isolated grassroots criticism of the Lee Kuan Yew government, notably in connection with the sterilization controversy of 1976, while the official Catholic Church compromised its position to save its schools. For the main confrontation experience in Hong Kong (in 1978) see Chapter 7, note 30.
8. For a summary see *Far Eastern Economic Review Asia Yearbook*, 1977, p. 184.
9. For one gauge of the state of Catholic-Communist dialogue in Vietnam at the end of the 1970s, see *Echange France Asie*, Dossier 72, Feb. 1982, both for a secret Party document it publishes on how to deal with the Catholic Church, and for the interpretation by its Paris clerical editors. On both sides it is clear how little five years of a "new" relationship could do to overcome a century of mortal enmity between Communist and Catholic worldviews.
10. The Presbyterian position, the root cause of its General Secretary's incarceration, was spelled out in a *Statement* (1971), an *Appeal* (1975), and a *Declaration on Human Rights* (1977) urging measures to make Taiwan "a new and independent country."
11. The South African comparison was made to the author in an interview of Dec. 1979. Digan, *Asia Journey*, 1979, pp. 12–13.
12. T. K. Thomas, ed., *Christianity in Asia*, pp. 91–93.
13. Digan, "Asia Journey," 1980, p. 10.
14. See p. 39.
15. Quoted in *National Catholic Reporter* (20 March 1981): 14.
16. Saral K. Chatterji, ed., *The Meaning of the Indian Experience*, p. 84.
17. For analysis along "mode of production" lines, see any of the works of François Houtart.

18. See esp. Association of Major Religious Superiors, *Ichthys*.

19. Robert Youngblood, "Structural Imperialism and the Catholic Bishops' Conference of the Philippines," pp. 21–22.

20. *Far Eastern Economic Review* (21 Aug. 1981): 17–24.

21. Jaime Cardinal Sin, *Exhortation against Violence*, p. 5.

22. See Felix Casalmo, *The Vision of a New Society*.

23. Permanent Peoples' Tribunal, p. 274.

24. Digan, "Asia Journey", 1980, pp. 5, 9.

25. Ibid., pp. 2–9.

26. The question of communist infiltration and manipulation has periodically convulsed church bodies in sensitive positions, such as the NASSA and the MSPC. The 1982 convulsions of the MSPC are touched on in the Conclusion of this study.

27. Youngblood, esp. pp. 2, 14, 18.

28. Revealing in this connection are the minutes (available from AMRS) of a meeting on 10 May 1975 between members of AMRS and the nuncio.

Chapter 7: An Overall Transnational Perspective

1. Joseph Gremillion, ed., *The Gospel of Peace and Justice*, p. 388; *Keesing's Contemporary Archives* (KCA) (1976): 27563.

2. Karl Marx and Friedrich Engels, *Manifesto of the Communist Party*, 1848, pp. 82, 83, 85.

3. Ibid. p. 92.

4. Ibid., p. 42.

5. This favored theme of Robert McNamara in his World Bank period (1968–80) had not really waited till then for authoritative capitalist recognition. *The Economist* (17 Oct. 1981, p. 18) quoted it from Adam Smith himself.

6. *KCA* (1974): 26548.

7. On Cancún see *KCA* (1982): 31360.

8. Willy Brandt, et al., *North-South*, p. 7.

9. Barrington Moore, Jr., *Social Origins of Dictatorship and Democracy*, pp. 111–155.

10. John Kenneth Galbraith, *The Affluent Society*, p. 86.

11. Marx and Engels, p. 27. The quotation is taken from A.J.P. Taylor's introduction to this edition of the *Manifesto*.

12. C. Wright Mills, *The Marxists*, p. 129.

13. The Solzhenitsyn remark on ideology is taken from *The Gulag Archipelago* (Glasgow: Collins/Fontana, 1974), p. 174.

14. See Chapter 1, note 18.

15. Mills, pp. 45, 101.

16. Ibid., pp. 97, 102.

17. Galbraith, p. 22.

18. Robert O. Keohane and Joseph S. Nye, Jr., *Transnational Relations and World Politics*, p. 376.

19. On Leo XIII's preaching of class resignation in the very act of accepting democracy, see Pierre Delooz, *Participation in the Catholic Church*, p. 4, note 3.

20. Stuart Schram, ed., *The Political Thought of Mao Tse-tung*, p. 373.

21. Hoare and Smith, eds., *Selections from the "Prison Notebooks" of Antonio*

Gramsci, pp. 219–223; Hugues Portelli, ed., *Gramsci et la question religeuse,* pp. 189–90.

22. See works by Houtart cited in Bibliography.

23. Keohane and Nye, p. 388.

24. For one illustration see Kirchhoff's "Corporate Missionary" ("Those who believe in capitalism must fight back") side by side with ICL Research Team's *The Human Cost of Bananas.* Both statements appeared in 1979. The banana survey includes "Castle & Cooke in Mindanao"; Kirchhoff spoke as president of the same multinational, which derives half its revenues from the Third World. According to Kirchhoff, "Castle & Cooke is a stabilizing force in our host countries, contributing to their political and economic well-being." According to the Mindanao survey, "If this study were to make one recommendation, it would be that the Government allow the banana industry to die a peaceful death." According to 1975 figures (*Info on Human Development [IHD]* [Sep. 1980]: 22), the banana industry as a whole in the Philippines could have raised wages to nine times their current amount, and still have made a profit.

25. Keohane and Nye, pp. 388f.

26. See Chapter 4, note 7.

27. Edward Norman, *Christianity in the Southern Hemisphere,* p. 196.

28. Penny Lernoux, *Cry of the People,* especially Part Three.

29. A range of views on this are represented in Digan, "Asia Journey," 1980, pp. 2–9.

30. On the Singapore sterilization controversy see *Informations catholiques internationales* (ICI) (Apr. 1976): 53, and Digan, "Asia Journey," 1980, p. 11. For a most extensive dossier on the Precious Blood Golden Jubilee School affair, see IMCS Asia, "The Golden Jubilee School Issue." More recently, a small storm has centered on one of the kind of Hong Hong monitoring centers we have discussed. For a brief account see "Asia Monitor Centre: In the eye of the storm," *South China Morning Post* (Hong Kong), 28 Feb. 1982.

31. R. H. Tawney, *Religion and the Rise of Capitalism,* p. 280; John R. Orens, *Politics and the Kingdom,* p. 13.

32. *Far Eastern Economic Review,* 10 July 1981, p. 13.

33. Ibid., 21 Aug. 1981, p. 22.

34. In a letter of 4 Sep. 1981 from Cardinal Sin of Manila to the president of the U.S. Conference of Catholic Bishops, the cardinal wrote: "Our youth no longer see America in a liberating role but as one who arms our soldiers to kill their fellow Filipinos." *IHD* (Oct. 1981): 2. As for the rise of anti-Americanism in South Korea, as usual it was a topic in local documentation long before getting recognition in international media. See however a 1982 assessment by a former director of the Office of Korean Affairs of the U.S. State Department: "Since the burning of the American Cultural Center in Pusan on March 18, the United States is confronted with anti-Americanism unparalleled in the 100 years since it opened diplomatic relations with Korea." Donald L. Ranard, *International Herald Tribune,* 8 May 1982, p. 4. Ranard traces the change to the same betrayal of freedom charged by Cardinal Sin, whose allegation he quotes.

35. See Ron O'Grady, *Bread and Freedom,* for an attempt to make the necessary distinctions.

36. *Ichthys* (May 1981): 33–35. Widely reprinted in other media.

37. See Jean Remy, et al., *Produire ou reproduire?*, esp. pp. 90–92 and 368.

38. Alain Peyrefitte, *Quand la Chine s'éveillera . . .* , p. 299.

39. Lutheran World Federation (LWF), *Theological Reflection on the Encounter of the Church with Marxism*, p. 17. For the record within the Warsaw Pact countries, see Erich Weingartner, *Church within Socialism*. More generally, see also LWF, *The Encounter of the Church with Movements of Social Change*. In China and Vietnam the pattern is still taking shape, but inevitably the power situation sorts out and gives public monopoly to those voices that, for whatever reason, speak within the limits of what the powers that be judge to be permissible.

40. See, for example, *International Review of Mission* (Geneva), Jan. 1970; *Le Monde*, 21 April 1973.

41. For the main facts of the expulsions, see *Keesing's Contemporary Archives* (1970): 24053 in the case of Garaudy, and, in the case of Girardi, see *ICI* (Nov. 1969): 15, (Nov. 1973): 28f., (Dec. 1973): 31.

42. José Porfirio Miranda, *Marx against the Marxists*, p. 281.

Conclusion: The Outlook

1. *New York Daily Tribune*, 25 June 1853. Cited in Gunnar Myrdal, *Asian Drama*, vol. 3, p. 1852.

2. Francisco Claver, "A Pastoral of Total Faith-Commitment," p. 2.

3. André Gunder Frank, "Asia's Exclusive Models," pp. 22f.

4. See Mindanao-Sulu Pastoral Conference; Claver; *Far Eastern Economic Review* (10 Sep. 1982): 31–32.

5. See "Vatican and China."

BIBLIOGRAPHY

For an unfinished story, especially when it is at the same time a subversive story and a story scattered over the homelands of half the human race, there can be no definitive sources. In the case of Asian Christian social protest the difficulty of finding and evaluating the facts is even greater than that of assembling and dealing with data about Asia in general.

This only increases the importance of the storyteller's spelling out where he got the story. Wherever we cannot baldly say, Such and such is so, it is all the more necessary to say, Our suggestion that such and such is so is based on such and such evidence. This will be of some help to contemporary readers who are as ignorant as ourselves about the future but at least live in the same world as ourselves with our contemporary sources. It should also be of help to any future readers, who will not need our sources to know what happened next in the story but may find it significant to compare the documentary scene as it is found reflected here and as it will be then.

On ground that is all too often marshy and misty, it is wise to make the most of any beaten tracks that are available. Hence, fugitive or ephemeral documentation is used here only where there is no better authenticated substitute for it, and then only with as much caution and cautioning as the case seems to require; and wherever data or testimonies have found their way into more permanent, more widely trusted, and more generally accessible records, these are cited by preference.

To trace the phenomenon under study, it would by no means suffice to consult the files of a secular serial collection of global scope such as *Keesing's Contemporary Archives*, or of a secular serial collection of Asian-Australian scope such as the *Far Eastern Economic Review*, or of any similar collection in the field of Christian information such as *Informations catholiques internationales* or *Vida Nueva* from the Western Christian heartlands and *The Sunday Examiner* or *CCA News* from Asia itself. Precisely in the measure that these sources are relatively mainstream, they risk failing to reflect the fresh currents and the undercurrents that are the stuff of which movements of social protest and social change are made. Yet in the measure that they do reflect these newer phenomena, they also provide certification that these latter have definitively arrived.

The fact remains that the phenomena discussed here are in large measure still in the category of undercurrents, for which there is no documentation that is not itself more or less fugitive and at least threatened with being ephemeral. It would scarcely be fair to the inquiring reader merely to give chapter and verse for these sources as if the mere fact of citing them sufficed to establish whatever point is to be documented. Some effort must therefore be made to introduce these sources, occasionally situating them as to time, place, and tendency insofar as that is compatible with the need to be brief and wary of overfacile categorizations.

A still more fundamental fact must be allowed for: namely, that the author is not an all-seeing eye or a mechanical monitor but himself one of the several billion people involved in these affairs. As it happens, he is a Christian, and not an Asian, but one who has been immersed in Asian affairs for about three decades, in part as an observer seeking to understand and explain, in part as an actor on the scene. For many of the nuances in this book's treatment of the facts and the interpretations of Asian Christian social ferment, no particular source can be cited because none has been decisive. In the final analysis its judgments repose on an overall experiential "feel" for the situation, which, with all its limitations, draws on a more complex web of oral and written sources than could be itemized here.

The following list of sources is far from exhaustive. The first purpose of the list is to simplify references in the notes. A further purpose is to provide a more representative reading list (more representative, that is, essentially for the *transnational* dimension of Asian Christian social protest) than would emerge automatically from the notes. In the case of most of the sources cited in the notes, the connection is marginal to that source or to this study or to both. Where a source is judged to be of particular importance for an understanding of the subject, even if it happens not to have been cited on any particular point, this list provides a place where it may find recognition. Readers whose only concern is a very selective reading list may ignore all items, whether cited in notes or not, except those printed in bold type.

With one or two exceptions, no sources will be cited from any non-Western language. This is not such a limitation as it might seem at first sight. If the focus of this study were on grass-roots local experiences, there would be much primary material in local Asian languages. Since its focus is instead on the continental dimension and context of Asian Christian social protest, there is in fact no Asian language that would be less inadequate than English as a primary vehicle of overall perspective.

Abbott, Walter M., ed. *The Documents of Vatican II*. New York: America Press, 1966.

Alinsky, Saul. *Rules for Radicals: A Practical Primer for Realistic Radicals*. New York: Random House, 1971. One of the acknowledged influences among the Asian avant-garde.

Anderson, Floyd, ed. *Council Daybook: Vatican II*. 3 vols. Washington, D.C.: National Catholic Welfare Conference, 1965-66.

Anderson, Gerald, ed. *Christ and Crisis in Southeast Asia*. New York: Friendship Press, 1968.

———. *Asian Voices in Christian Theology*. Maryknoll, N.Y.: Orbis Books, 1976.

Asian Conference on Religion and Peace. *Peace through Religion*. Tokyo: ACRP, 1977.

Asian Meeting of Religious (AMOR). Manila: Asian Service Center for Women Religious, 1971–80. A loose-leaf file on AMOR and on five AMOR meetings.

L'Asie en Chiffres 1982. Paris: Echange France-Asie, 1982.

Association of Major Religious Superiors (AMRS). *Ichthys*, formerly *Signs of the Times*. Manila: AMRS, 1975–. Principal parts of a major mimeographed collection of independent documentation on the New Society in the Philippines, mainly exposing abuses of power. More extensive and representative in coverage and circulation than any other would-be voice of the voiceless.

Balasuriya, Tissa, ed. *Asian Bishops and Social Justice: A New Orientation?* Colombo: Centre for Society and Religion, 1976. Forty-eighth issue of a series called *Quest*, including also *Jesus Christ and Human Liberation* and *Eucharist and Human Liberation* (Maryknoll, NY: 1979), from one of the more radical of the Catholic clergy in the Asian avant-garde.

Barnet, Richard J., and Ronald E. Müller. *Global Reach: The Power of the Multinational Corporations*. London: Jonathan Cape, 1975, and New York: Simon and Schuster, 1974.

Barrett, David B., ed. *World Christian Encyclopedia: A Comparative Study of Churches and Religions in the Modern World: AD 1900-2000*. Nairobi: Oxford University Press, 1982. See note on sources for Appendixes 4–6.

Bell, Francis Xavier. *The Catholic Church in Thailand: A Socio-Religious Survey: 1972-74*. 8 vols. Bangkok: National Catholic Survey Office, 1974.

Berger, Peter. *Pyramids of Sacrifice: Political Ethics and Social Change*. Harmondsworth (England): Penguin, 1977.

Berman, Maureen R., and Joseph E. Johnson, eds. *Unofficial Diplomats*. New York: Columbia University Press, 1977. A collection on nonstate actors in international relations.

Bibliography of Asian Studies. Ann Arbor, Mich.: Association for Asian Studies, annual. The most inclusive current bibliography: some thousands of items annually.

Biernatzki, William, et al. *Korean Catholicism in the 1970s*. Maryknoll, N.Y.: Orbis Books, 1975.

Bilan du Monde 1964: Encyclopédie catholique du monde chrétien. 2 vols. Lille: Casterman, 1963.

Blair, Emma Helen, and James A. Robertson, eds. *The Philippine Islands, 1493-1898*. 55 vols. Cleveland: Clark, 1903–09.

Bottomore, T. B., and M. Rubel, eds. *Karl Marx: Selected Writings in Sociology and Social Philosophy*. Harmondsworth (England): Penguin, 1963.

Brandt, Willy, et al. *North-South: A Programme for Survival: Report of the Independent Commission on International Development Issues*. London: Pan, 1980.

Browne, Laurence E. *The Eclipse of Christianity in Asia from the Time of Muhammed till the Fourteenth Century*. Cambridge: Cambridge University Press, 1913.

Buhlmann, Walbert. *The Coming of the Third Church: An Analysis of the Present and Future of the Church*. Slough (England): St. Paul, and Maryknoll, N.Y.: Orbis, 1976.

Camara, Helder. *Spiral of Violence*. London: Sheed & Ward, 1971. Another influential voice and influential concept in Third World protest.

Casalmo, Felix [pseud.]. ***The Vision of a New Society***. **Manila: n. p., 1980.** A meticulous documentary analysis of the martial law regime, of its self-justification, and of a hundred or so episcopal reactions during its first seven years.

Catholic Bishops' Conference of India (CBCI). *Report of the General Meeting . . . 1979*. Ranchi: CBCI, 1979.

Centre Tricontinental (CETRI). *Movements de libération et luttes populaires en Asie du Sud, du sud-Est, et de L'Est*. Louvain-la-Neuve: CETRI, 1979.

Chatterji, Saral K., ed. ***The Meaning of the Indian Experience: The Emergency***. **Bangalore: Christian Institute for the Study of Religion and Society, 1978.**

Chenu, Marie-Dominique. *La "Doctrine Sociale" de l'Eglise comme idéologie*. Paris: Cerf, 1979.

Christian Concern for People's Struggle: National Convention. Delhi: Delhi Forum for CCPS, 1978.

CCA News. **Singapore: Christian Conference of Asia, monthly.**

Christian Conference of Asia: Sixth Assembly. Singapore: CCA, 1977.

Christian Conference of Asia: Seventh Assembly. Bangalore: CCA, 1981.

Christians for National Liberation (CNL). "Program of the Christians for National Liberation." Issued after CNL second national congress in late 1981. Distributed by Komité ng Sambayanang Pilipino (KSP), Utrecht (Holland).

Claver, Francisco. "Prophecy or Accommodation: Dilemma for a Discerning Church." *The Month* (London), March 1980. An Asian bishop's defense of the prophetic stance.

———. "The Empty Tomb of Kibawe." *Ichthys*, May 1981. An Asian bishop's articulation of nonviolent resistance.

———. "A Pastoral of Total Faith-Commitment." Report of a meeting of seventeen Philippine bishops held in September 1981. Malaybalay (Philippines), Nov. 1981.

Cole, H. S. D., et al. *Thinking about the Future: A Critique of "The Limits to Growth."* London: Sussex University Press, 1973.

Crozier, Michel, and Erhard Friedberg. *L'Acteur et le Système: les contraintes de l'action collective.* Paris: Seuil, 1977. Sociological considerations highly relevant to the problem of corporate Christian social protest.

Currie, Robert F. *The Church: Credible Sign of Peoples' Liberation?: Socio-political and Theological Analysis of a Church Movement in Bihar, India.* Mangalore: Centre for Human Concern, 1978. The same problem in one concrete instance.

de la Torre, Edicio, ed. *Pintíg: Sa Malamig na Bakal (Life Pulse in Cold Steel: Poems and Letters from Philippine Prisons).* Hong Kong: Resource Centre for Philippine Concerns, 1979.

Delooz, Pierre. *Participation in the Catholic Church.* Brussels: Pro Mundi Vita, 1981.

Desrochers, John. *The Social Teaching of the Church.* Bangalore: John Desrochers, 1982. Uniquely inclusive survey of papal teachings, other major Catholic documents, World Council of Churches statements, FABC and CCA and Indian church statements.

Digan, Parig. "Friars on Trial: A Study of the Philippine Friar Memorial of 1898." M.A. dissertation, Catholic University of America, 1956.

———— "Christian Socialism in Japan." *Japan Missionary Bulletin.* (August 1971): 443–52.

————. *Indonesia.* Brussels: Pro Mundi Vita, 1977.

————. *The Christian China-watchers: A Post-Mao Perspective.* Brussels: Pro Mundi Vita, 1978.

————. "Asia Journey." An unpublished diary covering eight Asia journeys from 1972 through 1980.

————, ed. *South Korea under Emergency Rule.* Brussels: Pro Mundi Vita, 1975.

————, and Jonas Johnson, eds. *Christianity and the New China.* South Pasadena, Calif.: Ecclesia Publications, 1976.

Doherty, John F. *A Preliminary Study of Interlocking Directorates among Financial, Commercial, Manufacturing and Service Enterprises in the Philippines.* Manila: n.p., 1979.

Document Reprint Serivce **(DRS). Hong Kong: International Movement of Catholic Students Asia. (IMCS).** About 20 issues yearly since 1977.

Eagleson, John, and Philip Scharper, eds. *The Radical Bible.* Maryknoll, N.Y.: Orbis Books, 1972. A glimpse of the resources available in the Bible to Christian radicals.

Echange France-Asie. Paris: Missions Etrangères. Monthly monographs documenting Asian affairs.

The Economist. London. Sophisticated weekly digest and analysis of world events from a professedly right-of-center standpoint, such as might be expected from a periodical claiming that its readership controls half the Gross World Product.

Elwood, Douglas J., ed. *What Asian Christians Are Thinking: A Theological Source Book*. Quezon City: New Day Publishers, 1976.

Emergency Christian Conference on Korean Problems, ed. *Documents on the Struggle for Democracy in Korea*. Tokyo: Shinkyo Shuppansha, 1975.

England, John C. "Kim Chi Ha and the Poetry of Christian Dissent." *Ching Feng* (Hong Kong) 3 (1978): 126–51.

———. *Living Theology in Asia*. London: SCM Press, 1981, and Maryknoll, N.Y.: Orbis Books, 1982.

Evangelization in Modern Day Asia. See Federation of Asian Bishops' Conferences.

FABC Papers. Hong Kong: Federation of Asian Bishops' Conferences, occasional. Selected reprints.

Fabella, Virginia, ed. *Asia's Struggle for Full Humanity: Towards a Relevant Theology: Papers from the Asian Theological Conference, Jan. 7–20, 1979, Wennappuwa, Sri Lanka*. Maryknoll, N.Y.: Orbis Books, 1980.

The Far East and Australasia. 12th ed. 2 vols. London: Europa, 1982.

Far Eastern Economic Review. **Hong Kong, weekly.** Since 1968, the leading source of weekly news and analysis with Asia-wide (and Australasia-wide) coverage.

Far Eastern Economic Review Yearbook. Hong Kong: *FEER*, annual.

Federation of Asian Bishops' Conferences. *Evangelization in Modern Day Asia: The First Plenary Assembly* **(of the FABC). Hong Kong: FABC, 1974.**

Federation of Asian Bishops' Conferences. *His Gospel to Our Peoples . . .: Texts, Documents and Other Papers from the FABC in connection with the Third General Synod of Bishops 1974*. **3 vols. Quezon City: Bea Institute, 1975.**

FERES (International Federation of Institutes for Social and Socio-Religious Research). *Religion and Development in Asia: A Sociological Approach with Christian Reflection*. Baguio: FERES, 1975. Report of the Baguio FERES Seminar, or Second Asia Seminar. The previous one was held in Bangalore in 1973.

Fierro, Alfredo. *El Evangelio Beligerante*. Estella (Navarra): Ed. Verbo Divino, 1974. *The Militant Gospel: An Analysis of Contemporary Political Theologies*. Maryknoll, N.Y.: Orbis Books, 1977.

Foreman, Charles W., ed. *Christianity in the Non-Western World*. Englewood Cliffs, N.J.: Prentice-Hall, 1967.

Frank, Andre Gunder. "Asia's Exclusive Models." *Far Eastern Economic Review*, 25 June 1982.

Freire, Paulo. *Pedagogy of the Oppressed*. New York: Herder, 1970; Penguin, 1972. Another of the key books fuelling Third World Christian social protest.

Galbraith, John Kenneth. *The Affluent Society*. Harmondsworth (England): Pelican, 1970.

Gardavsky, Viteslav. *God Is Not Yet Dead*. Harmondsworth (England): Penguin, 1973.

Gheerbrant, Alain. *L'Eglise rebelle d'Amérique Latine*. Paris: Seuil, 1969. *The Rebel Church in Latin America*. Harmondsworth (England): Penguin, 1974.

Grant, Robert M. *Early Christianity and Society: Seven Studies*. New York: Harper & Row, 1977.

Gremillion, Joseph, ed. *The Gospel of Peace and Justice: Catholic Social Teaching since Pope John*. Maryknoll, N.Y.: Orbis Books, 1976. Text and background of twenty-two documents produced between 1961 and 1975.

Gutiérrez, Gustavo. *Teología de la liberación: Perspectivas*. Lima: CEP, 1971. *A Theology of Liberation: History, Politics, and Salvation*. Maryknoll, N.Y.: Orbis Books, 1973. Also among the seminal books of Third World Christian social protest.

Haas, Harry, and Nguyen Bao Cong. *Vietnam: the Other Conflict*. London: Sheed & Ward, 1971. Rare in its time as reflecting a break with a solid front of Catholic anticommunism in the Republic of Vietnam.

Hanson, Eric O. *Catholic Politics in China and Korea*. Maryknoll, N.Y.: Orbis Books, 1980. Ranges over the colonial and the contemporary experience, and over Vietnam, Taiwan, China and Korea.

Harrison, Horace V., ed. *The Role of Theory in International Relations*. Princeton: Van Nostrand, 1964.

Hayter, Teresa. *Aid as Imperialism*. Harmondsworth (England): Penguin, 1971. World Bank, IMF, and AID "imperialism" as diagnosed by a former World Bank employee.

His Gospel to Our Peoples . . . See Federation of Asian Bishops' Conferences.

Hoare, Quintin, and G. N. Smith, eds. *Selections from the "Prison Notebooks" of Antonio Gramsci*. London: Lawrence & Wishart, 1971.

Hoke, Donald, ed. *The Church in Asia*. Chicago: Moody Press, 1975. A country-by-country compendium of data.

Holland, Joe, and Peter Henriot. *Social Analysis: Linking Faith and Justice*. Washington, D.C.: Center of Concern, 1980; rev. and enl. ed. published with Orbis Books, 1983. Proposed as a radical Christian perspective beyond conventional capitalist and Marxist models.

Houtart, François. *Religion and Ideology in Sri Lanka*. Bangalore: TPI, 1974. Proposed as a particular Marxist perspective on Ceylonese society before, during, and after its colonial phases.

———. *The Non-Socialist Societies of South and East Asia after the Vietnam War*. Louvain: n.p., 1976. Conclusion, p. 31: no alternative to "the socialist model."

———. "Christianity and Socialism." *Document Reprint Service* 8/80. A 1978 talk to clergy and religious in Ho Chi Minh City.

———. *Religion et modes de production précapitalistes*. Brussels: Editions de l'Université de Bruxelles, 1980.

————, and G. Lemercinier. *Church and Development in Kerala.* Bangalore: Theological Publications of India, 1979. Argument: the pattern institutionalizes underdevelopment.

Huntingdon, Samuel. "Transnational Organizations and World Politics." *World Politics* 25 (1973): 333–68.

Ichthys. See Association of Major Religious Superiors.

ICL Research Team. *The Human Cost of Bananas.* Manila: n.p., 1979. Field research in the Philippine banana industry.

IDOC International. *The Church at the Crossroads: Christians in Latin America from Medellín to Puebla: 1968–78.* Rome: IDOC, 1978.

Illich, Ivan. *Deschooling Society.* Harmondsworth (England): Penguin, 1973. Another name and notion, along with those of Gutiérrez, Camara, Freire, Alinsky, and later Oscar Romero, often echoed among Asian Christian radicals. See also same author's *Limits to Medicine,* Penguin, 1977.

Impact. Manila. "A monthly Asian magazine for Human Development."

Info on Human Development (IHD). **Manila: Office for Human Development, monthly.**

Informations catholiques internationales **(ICI). Paris, fortnightly and later monthly.** Among the less inadequate Western Sources on Asian Christian events.

International Commission of Jurists. *The Decline of Democracy in the Philippines: A Report of Missions by W. J. Butler, J. P. Humphrey, and G. E. Bisson.* Geneva: ICJ, 1977.

International Movement of Catholic Students (IMCS). See *Document Reprint Service* (DRS).

IMCS Asia. "The Golden Jubilee School Issue: A Struggle against Oppression in Hong Kong." Hong Kong: IMCS Asia, 1978.

IMCS Asian Team. "The Catholic Students Movement in Asia Today—An Overview." Hong Kong: IMCS Asia, 1980.

"International Relations." *International Encyclopedia of the Social Sciences,* vol. 8. London: Macmillan, 1968.

Jedin, Hubert, et al. *Atlas zur Kirchengeschichte: Die Christlichen Kirchen in Geschichte und Gegenwart.* Freiburg: Herder, 1970.

John XXIII. See Gremillion.

John Paul II. *Laborem Exercens.* 1981. Encyclical on labor.

Kahl, Joachim. *The Misery of Christianity: A Plea for a Humanity without God.* Harmondsworth (England): Pelican, 1971.

Keesing's Contemporary Archives: Record of World Events. **London: Longman, weekly 1931–82, monthly 1983–.**

Keohane, Robert O., and Joseph S. Nye, Jr. *Transnational Relations and World Politics.* Cambridge, Mass.: Harvard University Press, 1970.

Kim, Stephen Cardinal. "The Church for the Asia of Today." In *Evangelization in Modern Day Asia.* Hong Kong: Federation of Asian Bishops' Conferences, 1974. Address to the 1974 Synod of Bishops.

Kirchhoff, D. J. "Those Who Believe in Capitalism Must Fight Back."
   Barron's National Business and Financial Weekly, 19 February 1979.
Korea Communiqué. **Tokyo: Japan Emergency Christian Conference on
   Korean Problems, quarterly or oftener.**
Koyama, Kosuke. *Waterbuffalo Theology.* Maryknoll, N.Y.: Orbis Books,
   1974.
Kubalkova, V., and A. A. Cruickshank. *Marxism-Leninism and the Theory
   of International Relations.* London: Routledge, 1980.
Latourette, Kenneth Scott. *A History of the Expansion of Christianity.* 7
   vols. New York: Harper & Row, 1937–45.
———. *Christianity in a Revolutionary Age.* 5 vols. New York: Harper &
   Row, 1962.
Lernoux, Penny. *Cry of the People: The Struggle for Human Rights in
   Latin America—the Catholic Church in Conflict with U.S. Policy.* Har-
   mondsworth (England) and New York: Penguin, 1982.
Ling, Trevor. *Buddha, Marx, and God: Some Aspects of Religion in the
   Modern World.* London: Macmillan, 1966.
Lutheran World Federation (LWF). *The Encounter of the Church with
   Movements of Social Change in Various Cultural Contexts (with Special
   Reference to Marxism).* Geneva: LWF, 1977.
———. *Theological Reflection on the Encounter of the Church with Marx-
   ism in Various Cultural Contexts.* Geneva: LWF, 1977. Final summing-
   up of an international three-conference process.
LWF Marxism and China Study Information Letter. Geneva: LWF, occa-
   sional. Cited as LWF-IL.
Manikam, Rajah B., ed. *Christianity and the Asian Revolution.* New York:
   Friendship Press, 1954.
Mansbach, R. W., et al. *The Web of World Politics: Non-State Actors in
   the Global System.* Englewood Cliffs, N.J.: Prentice-Hall, 1976.
Mannheim, Karl. *Ideology and Utopie.* London: Kegan Paul, 1936. In part
   from *Ideologie und Utopie.* Bonn: Cohen, 1926. Valuable on "the lan-
   guage of protest."
**Marx, Karl, and Friedrich Engels. *Manifesto of the Communist Party.*
   Harmondsworth (England): Penguin, 1967.** Produced essentially by
   Marx alone in Brussels in 1847–48. Translation of 1888.
Meadows, Donella, et al. *The Limits to Growth: A Report for the Club of
   Rome's Project on the Predicament of Mankind.* New York: New
   American Library, 1972.
Miller, Robert J., ed. *Religious Ferment in Asia.* Lawrence, Kans.: Kansas
   University Press, 1974.
Mills, C. Wright. *The Marxists.* Harmondsworth (England): Penguin,
   1963. Analyses and documents.
Mindanao-Sulu Pastoral Conference (MSPC). "Meeting of the Mindanao-
   Sulu Bishops with the MSPC Board and the Secretariate." Davao, Phi-
   lippines: MSPC Office, March 1982.

————. "Minutes of the MSPC Expanded Board Meeting." Cagayan de
Oro City, April 1982.

————. "The Real Issue in the MSPC." Letters of Bishops Claver,
Quevedo, and Capalla, May–July 1982.

Miranda, José Porfirio. *Marx y la Biblia*. Salamanca: Sígueme, 1971. *Marx
and the Bible: A Critique of the Philosophy of Oppression*. Maryknoll,
N.Y.: Orbis Books, 1974; London: SCM Press, 1977. An informed if
unconventional view.

————. *El cristianismo de Marx*. 1978. *Marx against the Marxists: the
Christian Humanism of Karl Marx*. Maryknoll, N.Y.: Orbis Books,
1980; London: SCM Press, 1980. See comment above.

Mische, Gerald, and Patricia Mische. *Towards a Human World Order:
Beyond the National Security Straitjacket*. New York: Paulist Press,
1977.

Moberg, David. *The Great Reversal: Evangelism versus Social Concern*.
London: Scripture Union, 1972.

Le Monde. Among Western dailies with pretensions to global news coverage, *Le Monde* (Paris) is often a likelier source of gleanings on Asian
Christian social protest than *The New York Times, The Times* of London, and *The International Herald Tribune*.

Moore, Jr., Barrington. *Social Origins of Dictatorship and Democracy:
Lord and Peasant in the Making of the Modern World*. Harmondsworth
(England): Penguin, 1967.

Myrdal, Gunnar. *Asian Drama: An Inquiry into the Poverty of Nations*.
3 vols. New York: Pantheon, 1968.

Norman, Edward. *Christianity in the Southern Hemisphere: the Churches
in Latin America and South Africa*. London: Oxford University Press,
1981. A conservative perspective.

Office for Human Development (OHD). "The Church in Asia after
the BISAs: An Exploratory-Assessment Study on BISA Bishop-
participants." Manila: OHD, 1981. Results of a 1980 questionnaire.
N. B. p. 50: "The data on hand do not warrant the conclusion that a
significant change in emphasis has taken place."

O'Grady, Ron. *Bread and Freedom: Understanding and Acting on Human
Rights*. Geneva: World Council of Churches, 1979. By a CCA (Christian
Conference of Asia) officer.

Orens, John R. *Politics and the Kingdom: The Legacy of the Anglican Left*.
London: Jubilee Group, 1979.

Oxford Economic Atlas of the World. 4th ed. London: Oxford University
Press, 1972.

Palmer, Spencer. *Korea and Christianity: The Problem of Identification
with Tradition*. Seoul: Hollym, 1967.

Panikkar, K. M. *Asia and Western Dominance*. London: Allen, 1959.

Paul VI, Pope. See Gremillion.

Pieris, Aloysius. "Non-Christian Religions in Third World Theology." In Virginia Fabella, M.M., and Sergio Torres, eds. *Irruption of the Third World*, 113–39. Maryknoll, N.Y.: Orbis Books, 1983. Presented at the Fifth EATWOT Conference in New Delhi in 1981, after a similar presentation at the Fourth Conference in Wennappuwa; a phase in Pieris's attempt to articulate a sort of unified field theory of Oriental religious thought and liberation theology.

Permanent Peoples' Tribunal. *Philippines: Repression and Resistance: Permanent Peoples' Tribunal on the Philippines*. London: Komite ng Sambayanang Pilipino, 1981. Record of a session held in Antwerp in 1980.

Petit, Clyde E. *The Experts*. Secaucus, N.J.: Lyle Stuart, 1975. A sobering collection of quotes, dedicated to "those who fell on all sides in Indochina because of The Experts."

Peyrefitte, Alain. *Quand la Chine s'éveillera*. . . . Paris: Fayard, 1973.

Portelli, Hugues, ed. *Gramsci et la question religeuse*. Paris: Editions Anthropos, 1974. Quotes with presentation.

Religion and Society. Bangalore: Centre for the Study of Religion and Society, quarterly.

Remy, Jean, et al. *Produire ou reproduire?: Une sociologie de la vie quotidienne*. Brussels: Editions Vie Ouvrière, 1978.

Rodinson, Maxime. *Islam and Capitalism*. Harmondsworth (England), Penguin, 1974.

Roekaerts, Mil. *Christians and the Emergency in India*. Brussels: Pro Mundi Vita, 1980.

————. *Church and State in the Philippines: An Assessment of the Domestic Impact of the Visit of Pope John Paul II to the Philippines*. Brussels: Pro Mundi Vita, 1981. Latest of three reviews by Pro Mundi Vita of the Philippine New Society.

————, et al. *Economic Patterns and Social Justice in Non-Socialist Countries of Asia*. Brussels: Pro Mundi Vita, 1979.

Rousseau, Jean-Jacques. *Discours sur l'origine et les fondements de l'inégalité parmi les hommes* (1755). Paris: Classiques Garnier, 1962.

Salazar, Ralph, and Sophie Bodegon, eds. *"Of Joys and Hopes, of Griefs and Anxieties": 15 Years of NASSA: 1966–81*. Manila: National Secretariat of Social Action, 1981.

Schecter, Jerrold. *The New Face of Buddha: Buddhism and Political Power in Southeast Asia*. Tokyo: Weatherhill Press, 1967.

Scheiner, I. *Christian Converts and Social Protest in Meiji Japan*. Berkeley: University of California Press, 1970.

Schram, Stuart, ed. *The Political Thought of Mao Tse-tung*. Harmondsworth (England): Penguin, 1969. Documents with background.

Schumacher, E. F. *Small Is Beautiful: Economics as if People Mattered*. New York: Harper & Row, 1973.

Secretaria Status. *Annuarium Statisticum Ecclesiae*. Vatican Press, annual from 1969.

Smith, Adam. *An Inquiry into the Nature and Causes of the Wealth of Nations* (1776). 2 vols. London: Everyman, 1910.

Smith, Bardwell. *Religion and Social Conflict in South Asia*. Leiden (Netherlands): Brill, 1976.

Sin, Jaime Cardinal. *Exhortation against Violence: A Joint Pastoral Letter of the Philippine Hierarchy*. Manila, 1979.

Solidaridad II. Hong Kong: Resource Centre for Philippine Concerns, 5 or 6 issues per year. One of the more finished productions documenting opposition to the Marcos regime.

Spencer, Robert F., ed. *Religion and Change in Contemporary Asia*. Minneapolis: University of Minnesota Press, 1971.

Sunday Examiner. Hong Kong, weekly. A Catholic newspaper of local and global religious news.

Tawney, R. H. *Religion and the Rise of Capitalism: A Historical Study*. 2nd ed. Harmondsworth (England): Penguin, 1938.

Teaching All Nations. Manila: East Asian Pastoral Institute, quarterly. Renamed *East Asian Pastoral Review* in the 1980s.

Thomas, M. M. *Revolution in India and Christian Humanism*. New Delhi: Forum for Christian Concern for People's Struggle, 1978.

———. *Christians and the Emergency: Some Documents. Religion and Society* (1977).

Thomas, T. K., ed. *Testimony amid Asian Suffering*. Singapore: Christian Conference of Asia, 1977. From the Sixth CCA Assembly.

———, ed. *Christianity in Asia: North-east Asia*. Singapore: Christian Conference of Asia, 1979.

The Times Atlas of World History. London: Times Books, 1978. Less detailed than, for example, *Westermanns Grosser Atlas zur Weltgeschichte*, but marking an advance in global balance and perspective.

Totten, G. O. *The Social Democratic Movement in Prewar Japan*. New Haven, Conn.: Yale U. Press, 1966.

Treadgold, Donald W. *The West in Russia and China: Religious and Secular Thought in Modern Times*. 2 vols. Cambridge: Cambridge University Press, 1973.

Vadakkan, Joseph. *A Priest's Encounter with Revolution: An Autobiography*. Madras: Christian Literature Society, 1974.

"Vatican and China." *Yi (China Message)*, April–June 1982. Special issue of a review edited by a Chinese priest and a Catholic group in Hong Kong. Documentation and analysis of the Canton See controversy.

Voices from the Third World. Manila: Ecumenical Association of Third World Theologians, semiannual.

Ward, Barbara. *The Angry Seventies: The Second Development Decade: A Call to the Church*. Rome: Pontifical Justice and Peace Commission, 1970.

————, and René Dubos. *Only One Earth: The Care and Maintenance of a Small Planet*. Harmondsworth (England): Penguin, 1972. Produced for the UN Environment Conference of 1972.

Weber, Henri. *Nicaragua: La révolution Sandiniste*. Paris: Maspero, 1981. An interim report, cautiously positive, after the first eighteen months of this would-be Christian revolution.

Weber, Max. *Die Protestantische Ethik und der Geist das Kapitalismus*. 1904, reprinted 1920. *The Protestant Ethic and the Spirit of Capitalism*. London: Unwin, 1930, reprint of 1971.

Weingartner, Erich, ed. *Church within Socialism: Church and State in East European Socialist Republics*. Rome: IDOC, 1976.

Welch, Holmes. *The Buddhist Revival in China*. Cambridge, Mass.: Harvard University Press, 1968.

————. *Buddhism under Mao*. Cambridge, Mass.: Harvard University Press, 1972.

World Bank (International Bank for Reconstruction and Development). *World Development Report*. Annual from 1978.

World Christianity: Area Studies on the Status of Christianity. 3 Asia vols. (Middle East, Eastern Asia, South Asia). Monrovia, Calif.: Missions Advanced Research and Communication Center (MARC), 1979.

WCC Task Force for Human Rights in Korea. *Report on the Situation of Human Rights in the Republic of Korea 1978*. Geneva: World Council of Churches, 1978.

World Council of Churches. *Uppsala to Nairobi 1968-1975: Report of the Central Committee to the Fifth Assembly*. Geneva: WCC, 1975.

World Student Christian Federation; International Movement of Catholic Students, Asia Region. *The Struggle for Self-Reliance in Asia Today: Pan Asian Assembly*. Bangkok: WSCF & IMCS Asia, 1976.

Yap Kim Hao, ed. *Asian Theological Reflections on Suffering and Hope*. Singapore: Christian Conference of Asia, 1977.

Youngblood, Robert. "Structural Imperialism and the Catholic Bishops' Conference of the Philippines." Report of a 1979 survey by a visiting research fellow at the University of the Philippines. Unpublished, 1980.

INDEX

210